Minister
to the
Cherokees

Minister to the Cherokees

A Civil War Autobiography

James Anderson Slover

Edited by
Barbara Cloud

University of Nebraska Press
Lincoln and London

© 2001 by the University of Nebraska Press
All rights reserved
Manufactured in the United States of America

∞

Library of Congress Cataloging-in-Publication Data
Slover, James Anderson, 1824–1913.
Minister to the Cherokees: a Civil War autobiography / James Anderson Slover; edited by Barbara Cloud.
p. cm.
Includes bibliographical references and index.
ISBN 0-8032-4283-2 (cl. : alk. paper)
1. Slover, James Anderson, 1824–1913. 2. Baptists—United States—Clergy—Biography. I. Cloud, Barbara Lee. II. Title.
BX6495.S525 A3 2001
286'.1'092—dc21
[B]   00-066668

Frontispiece: James Anderson Slover, about 1900

*To my parents, Nina K. Hicks
and the late Virgil R. Hicks*

CONTENTS

Acknowledgments   xv

Introduction   xix

1   1
James Anderson Slover—His Parentage—Birth—Events and incidents of the first ten years of his eventful life.

2   13
Death of Grandfather Slover—Birth of his youngest brother—At the old Mill again with his brother Isaac—Marriage of his sister Katherine—A cousin from Illinois visits his father's family—Harvesting wheat—Mowing hay and taking care of it—His Mother makes nurse of him—His Father's family moves three times in three years—Marriage of his sister Sallie—He is hired out to work—His school facilities during his boyhood.

3   17
His religious experience—Conversion—He unites with Dumplin Creek Baptist Church—Has a narrow escape for his life January twelfth 1843—His brother Abraham gets married—The winter fever or Typhoid Pneumonia—His first trip down the Tennessee River on a flat boat—Incidents of his return trip—His brother John gets married—Visits his people in Jefferson County with his sister Elizabeth—Is employed by Randals brothers for six months—Mexican War and why he did not volunteer—In school again.

4   25
His call to the Ministry—Enters Black Oak Grove Seminary near Mossy Creek in Jefferson County, East Tennessee, early in March 1847—Is captured by a young lady, a farmer's

daughter—Courtship by letter after leaving the Seminary—His prospects frustrated by the young lady's father—Seeks the heart and hand of another and is married January the seventeenth 1850—Teaches school—Is present at execution of a Negro man in Dandridge—Concludes to go West to Arkansas with his friend Samuel Cook—The building of a flat boat for emigration—Some of the incidents while making the long trip by water—Detained at Van Buren on account of sickness—Reaches Washington County in October—Again in the school room with the "Toothpickers" so-called—Is ordained to the field work of the Gospel Ministry in June 1853—Revivals of that year—Is called to the Pastorate of Missionary Chapel Church—Again in the school room—Teaches his last school in 1856.

5   38

His first school in Arkansas—The character of this school—School closes with little credit to teacher and less to the Patrons—A new field sought—Teaches a summer term of five months and cultivates a small farm—The new location—Finds a Baptist church—His wife is baptized—Buys a young black mare as a saddle animal for his wife—The mare threw her Mistress—Also her sister—Smart "Ellicks" and Wiseacres—Locates near Elm Spring on forty acres of Government land—Enters the same under the graduation law—Again in the school room—His first child is born—Changes his church relationship—Is ordained to the full work of the Ministry—A protracted meeting is held—Good results—Is met, at Mount Zion Association, by a delegation from Missionary Chapel Church—Becomes its pastor—Compelled to teach school again—Secures a good school near Evansville—His second child is born there—Returns to his little farm in January 1856—Teaches his last school in that year—Incidents at Latties schoolhouse.

6   47

He accepts an appointment from the Southern Baptist Convention through the Domestic and Indian Mission Board located at Marion, Alabama, to preach to the Cherokee

Indians—His visit to the Chief for an interview in regard to locating in the nation—Moves to Tahlequah—Begins operations as a Missionary—Cold snap in April—Russel Holman, Corresponding Secretary, visits the field—The Missionary is interrogated as to his plan of operations, touching the vexed question of Slavery—His answer is well received—A girl baby comes to his home to stay—His first year's labor closes—Indians give him a name—Incredulity of the Natives.

7   51

Encouraging prospects—Travels and preaches—Makes a trip to Fayetteville, Arks.—Takes sick—Narrow escape from drowning—Dwelling house built—A Cherokee Lawyer interprets His sermons—Family increased by one—Churches organized—Association formed—A Judge interprets for him—Incidents—The Civil War begins—Actual hostilities or first gun is fired April the tenth 1861—He is employed as Chaplain for the first Cherokee Regiment under Col. Stand Watie, Confederate Mounted Volunteers, serves eight months—Cherokee Nation secedes in the fall of 1861—Terms &c &c—He concludes to abandon the field.

8   65

The Union Troops under Gen. Blunt on Cherokee Territory—Stand Watie's headquarters burned and his staff made prisoners—Gen. Blunt's letter to Chief Ross—Ross's ingenious answer—Mutiny of the Treaty Regiment—In company with his brother preacher E. L. Compere, the Missionary visits Chief Ross for information—Temporarily abandons his field—Three hundred Union soldiers make a raid on Tahlequah wanting the Missionary and seventeen other men—He stops outside of Indian Territory with Deacon J. W. Greer's family—His anxiety and mental trouble—His hazardous trip to Tahlequah and final abandonment of the Mission.

9   94

Another Skedaddling necessary—Preparations for a move to Texas—Has charge of an old preacher and family—Rainy weather—A breakdown in the mountains—Missionary fills *the old preacher's wagon wheel at night—Stops at Richmond near Red River—Learns of the death of two brothers in Cherokee County, Texas—The Civil War closes—Is made acquainted with Mrs. Josephine M. Rodgers, a Rebel soldier's widow—Whom he afterward marries.*

10   98
The Missionary and widow's courtship and engagement—His visit with the Domestic and Indian Mission Board—Southern Baptist Convention in Alabama—His sickness in Marion, Alabama—Returns by Crystal Springs, Mississippi—Archibald Fitzgerald and what his brother Aaron said of his copper—Sees the Rev. E. L. Compere and wife—Chances for courtship while making this visit—Is appointed Domestic Missionary by the Board—And finally reaches home in November and finds his affianced suffering from a fall from a horse—They get married in February 1866.

11   105
His labor as Missionary of the Southern Baptist Convention ceases—Is appointed to the Office of County Clerk of Little River County—Elected Justice of the Peace in 1868 in Little River County—A serious time in Rocky Comfort on the day he finishes his duties as Clerk—Little River County under martial law—Loses his horse and saddle—Militia soldiers in Richmond—Makes a trip to Washington County preparatory to crossing the Plains to California—Emigrates to California—A whole year on the road—One summer near Visalia—Locates on Tule River in Tulare County.

12   121
The Preacher locates a Preemption on the Tule River—Joins the Baptist church in Visalia—Is appointed by the American Baptist Home Mission Society to preach in Visalia and vicinity—His first attempt at farming in California—Dry season—Irrigating wheat—Crop short—Stage stand and Post Office at his residence—Another new comer in his family—His daughter Fannie narrowly escapes being burned to death—He is elected School Trustee and clerk of the Board—Is elected to the Office of Justice of the Peace—

Another severe attack of erysipelas—The Doctor's bill—His daughter Rachel Jane marries Hugh W. Riggs—The last babe is born and dies—Borrows money at two per cent per month to pay for land—Gets United States Patent for the Preemption—Attends a South Methodist protracted meeting for six weeks—The Grange—Mutual Aid Society of Los Angeles, California.

13 125
With his farming in Tulare County, California, a failure—Two years in three total failures—Mortgage increases—The fifth crop is very cheap—No fence law passed for Tulare—His last year in California—Makes a desperate effort to make a good crop—Contemplates a move to Jackson County, Oregon—Mortgage foreclosed on his farm—Land redeemed by his two sons and son-in-law—He moves to Oregon in September 1881—Incidents of his trip.

14 130
He emigrates to Oregon—Preparations for the trip—The move and incidents of travel—Is unloaded at the residence of his friend, G. F. Pennebaker—Soon locates in a rented house belonging to Wm. Erbe of Ashland, Jackson County, Oregon—The terms rather hard—Makes the best crop perhaps ever made on the farm—Gains the confidence of the Oregonians around him—Nine months on the Erbe farm—Buys hotel property in Jacksonville, Oregon—Moves and takes charge of the hotel—Changes places in the same town—Daughter marries A. F. Eddy—His son James A. goes into the employ of Dr. Roberson to learn the drug business—Has a cash sale—Moves to Roseburg—Nine months in the Hotel business there—The business there—The business closes on him—Attempts another cash sale—Emigrates south of Grants Pass.

15 138
Homestead—His first improvised cabin—Builds a house ten by twelve feet as a homestead residence—Erects a good dwelling house, wood and poultry house—Clears and

fences several acres of land—Plants an orchard—Miners desire to prospect for gold quartz—Harbin's placer—The Miners' contest—Homesteader loses forty acres of his Homestead—He submits his final proof—Riley Morrison enters a protest—He conceives a plan to build a house for New Hope Baptist church—Building erected under the supervision of a building committee—Dedication of the new church house—Incidents.

16 146
His move from his Homestead—Works on Deacon Glass' house—Is sick with pneumonia—Telephones to Ashland for medicine—All winter in Ashland—Holds a protracted meeting with New Hope church in May 1899—Again prostrated with pneumonia—Daughter Mrs. Eddy goes to San Francisco to attend the Baptist anniversaries—Three years labor on his son-in-law's Ashland farm—Homestead trouble renewed—Surveying had to be done before Patent could issue—Personal interview with the Commissioner, Binger Herman, at Medford—Homestead trouble ended after the lapse of 14 years.

17 149
A long desire gratified—Visits relatives and preaches in Tulare County, California—Receives fifty dollars from his (New Hope) church—Notifies his daughter at Ashland, Ore., to go east to the Southern Baptist Convention—Preparations for the long journey—Sends letter to Manly J. Breaker, D.D., *to meet him at train in St. Louis—Visits old-time friend at Farmington, San Joaquin County, California—four weeks in Stockton—Boards the train the second day of May at eleven* P.M. *for St. Louis—Reaches the city one day behind time—All night in City—Boards the train at eight* A.M. *Wednesday the 7th for Asheville,* N.C.—*Two and a half days at Convention—Left Asheville for East Tennessee—A week with friends at Mossy Creek—Reaches his sister's at Sandy Ridge on May 19th—Many places of his boyhood days visited in Jefferson and Sevier counties—On the 8th day of August leaves his sister Katherine via Mossy Creek, Cleveland, Chattanooga,*

Tenn., and Bridgeport, Ala., for Elmyra, Mo., arriving on the 12th of Sept.—On the 15th celebrates his 78th birthday there—Visits relatives in St. Joseph, Clinton and other places in Missouri—On the 23rd of October boards the Santa Fe train for his brother, Thomas Slover's, at Henderson, Okla.—Spends four months with relatives in Oklahoma and Indian Territory—March the 12th boarded the Santa Fe train at Purcell, Indian Territory, for Visalia, Calif.—Incidents of the journey—Visits in Visalia, Calif.—March the 27th boards the Southern Pacific train for home in Ashland, Ore.

18   159
He takes charge of rented garden—A trip to Grants Pass and his (New Hope) Church in Sam's Valley—A cart for conveyance—The cart and horse for sale—A sudden attack of cholera morbus while en route for home—The kindness of a good brother and wife—Reaches home safely—Has grippe—Weeds grow all the same—Berries to take to packing house—He is notified that a purchaser for his Homestead is ready to conclude the deal—They meet at the Real Estate office of Dan Richards in Gold Hill—Visit to Homestead—A deed is made and four hundred dollars received as the consideration—Then the Preacher boarded the train for Grants Pass to meet with the Rogue River Association—Returns to Ashland—Places his money in First National Bank of Ashland, Ore.—Stores wood for the winter—The family moves to another house—Pleasant winter passes—Three hundred dollars invested in the Story Cotton Company of Philadelphia, Pa.

19   163
He leaves Ashland, Ore., for San Francisco, Calif.—Work for Book and Bible House—Also for Royal Manufacturing Company, Detroit, Mich.—In April 1905, he goes to Tulare County to spend the summer with daughter and granddaughter—He preaches to Woodville church and baptizes two—Then accompanies his daughter to Sanger, the town of her residence and church membership under Pastor Williams—A move to Rosedale, Kern County—Attends

Baptist Association at Orosa—Death of daughter and funeral services conducted by her Pastor, Rev. Williams—Interment in Tulare Cemetery—He with granddaughter returns to her home at Woodville—The Preacher sorely afflicted with an ingrown toenail and boils—Two weeks rusticating at the Deer Creek Hot Springs—His return to Porterville—Thence to Woodville—In the latter part of October he makes his way to Dinuba and Fresno to visit grandchildren and acquaintances—And thence to San Francisco, his home.

20   168
Change of houses—The new residence—The Preacher again killing time with Brazil silverware—Granddaughter Edna Riggs' letter relative to her marriage—The great Earthquake and fire of San Francisco, April 18th, 1906—Works six days for Uncle Sam on refugee camps—Another visit with grandchildren—Visits one week in Visalia—The marriage of granddaughter Edna and Elbert S. Hicks at San Diego—He remains there until the third day of September—Meets his niece in Los Angeles, whom he never had seen—Arrives in Tulare City at ten A.M. Sept. 4th and is taken to his granddaughter's, Mrs. J. W. LaMarsna, at Woodville—A carpenter's job—Death of Carrie Jenks at San Diego—In March 1907 begins canvassing for Royal Manufacturing Co.—His equipage and success—Changed localities—At Dinuba with his granddaughter, Edna Hicks—Begins canvassing July 6th—Edna Hicks' first child—Starts for San Francisco about the 20th of November—Parlier and Fresno City and whom he meets at those places—Leaves Fresno City in the night of 29th of November for San Francisco—Arrives there in forenoon of 30th.

Notes   173

Selected Bibliography   197

Index   205

ACKNOWLEDGMENTS

Editing the autobiography of James Anderson Slover has been a fascinating intellectual exercise that grew out of a labor of love. My father had, on occasion, shown me the account book in which his great-grandfather had written his autobiography. One Christmas, desperate for a gift for my father and knowing that he wanted to be able to give copies of the memoir to relatives, I offered to "desktop publish" it. Although I am a historian, I am only mildly interested in family genealogy, and I did not really expect to find in Slover's autobiography any particular attraction. But as I proceeded with this "gift," I found myself increasingly caught up in the story.

A university professor for the past twenty-odd years, I have concentrated my historical research on the American West and, because I specialize in journalism history, on the frontier press.[1] In my study of the western press I have been intrigued by the thousands upon thousands of people, journalists or not, who packed up everything they owned and hauled it across prairies, snowy mountain passes, deserts, rivers, and oceans in search of a better life. Never mind the difficult conditions and the mortality rate along the trail. Never mind that word trickled back that conditions in the promised land did not live up to their promise. The people kept coming. James Anderson Slover was one of those people.

The rigors of the Oregon Trail are well documented and familiar to historians of the West, but I, at least, had never read anything quite like Slover's account of flatboating down rivers from Tennessee to Arkansas, "skedaddling" from the Union army in Indian Territory, and working his way up the West Coast to Oregon, preaching the Gospel as he went. It is a story worth a wider audience than a few relatives.

As one who sometimes cannot remember what she had for breakfast, I wondered on first reading how much the story was embellished or modified thanks to Slover's advanced age when he wrote. Hindsight, nostalgia, and selective perception color memories and, thus, memoirs. I have endeavored to verify as much of his account as possible from other sources, and his version holds up well. The text generally reflects a man with a keen memory as well as considerable facility with language, even though he had little formal schooling.

It is unlikely, judging from the fact that the manuscript copy is largely free from scratched-out words, that he sat down and wrote the memoir from start to finish in one draft. Fortunately for the editor, someone, presumably a relative, typed a copy of the handwritten memoir sometime in the 1930s or 1940s. I worked primarily from that typescript, although I kept the original at my side for verification.

Slover undoubtedly consulted more than his memory. There is no suggestion that he had kept a diary upon which he could draw, but he obviously did some research for his volume. He credits a textbook for the background on the Civil War that he includes in his manuscript; I have omitted much of this from the published version because it is conventional material. It appears that he either kept a great deal of material from his various church assignments (not too likely given the rigors of his travels) or had access to sources such as the *Proceedings of the Southern Baptist Convention* that he could consult for details. Still, most of the autobiography clearly comes from his remembrances.

As any memoir will, the autobiography raises as many questions as it answers. Slover says relatively little about his family, except to record births, deaths, and marriages. Only on a few occasions does he hint at what his wives (he married twice) and children (he had five by each wife) endured at his side. He disappoints us by saying too little about some experiences, such as the San Francisco earthquake. I suspect he saw little reason to detail happenings or discuss people that were within the ken of the children for whom he wrote. When he was compiling the memoir, the earthquake would have been fresh in people's minds; there was no need to recount its tragic events. Similarly, his second wife would have been known to his audience. But his first wife had been dead some forty years, and he might have given her a greater role in his narrative.

Whatever its shortcomings, Slover's autobiography provides an additional dimension to the historical events in which he participated. As the first Southern Baptist missionary to the Cherokees—and this during the Civil War—Slover was caught up in one of the most intense dramas of his century. As part of the stream of pioneers moving westward, he played a small role in changing the face of the nation. I am grateful to my father, Virgil Riggs Hicks, who was Slover's great-grandson, for preserving the memoir and giving me permission to make it available to the public. I regret that he did not live to see it in print.

In editing the memoir I have approached Slover's prose with a gentle hand, punctuating and making minor modifications where needed for clarity, but generally retaining his language, structure, spelling, and style in order to preserve the flavor of his expression. Thus the format Slover used of providing an outline at the beginning of each chapter, a common feature of histories of that period, has been retained. I have also sought to assist the reader by providing information about key players, places, and events, and have included sources where additional information is available. Where I have merely saved the reader a trip to the dictionary or atlas, I have not provided a source.

Documenting Slover's eighty-nine years and thousands of miles of travels took me into many fields, and I appreciate the work of those who have researched the history of the Southern Baptists, the Cherokees, land law, the Civil War, local events, and other topics with which Slover's life intersected. I am indebted to the Document Delivery staff at the University of Nevada, Las Vegas, Libraries who obtained material from afar, the Southern Baptist Historical Library and Archives in Nashville, the Southern Oregon Historical Society in Medford, the Sequoia Genealogical Society in Tulare County, California, colleague Willard Rollings of the UNLV Department of History, UNLV's Hank Greenspun School of Communication for a travel grant, and the many people who have put nineteenth-century records on the World Wide Web. Encouragement from the University of Nebraska Press; my mother, Nina Hicks; and my husband, Stan, kept me working on this for the several years it took to pull the pieces together.

INTRODUCTION

The sky was bleak gray and the air like ice when James Anderson Slover rode into Indian Territory in 1857. With each step his horse broke through the crusted snow. Looking back fifty years later, Slover called that January trip "disagreeable," but at the time the thirty-three-year-old farmer-preacher likely worried little about the frigid terrain. This journey meant that he had employment and could provide a regular income for his family: he was on his way to establish himself as the first Southern Baptist missionary to the Cherokee Nation. Four years later, however, when the Cherokees were forced to take sides in the American Civil War, the stable life Slover had sought disappeared in the gunfire of brothers shooting at brothers.

In the memoir that follows, Slover remembers his years with the Cherokees, years of intrigue, drama, and fear occasioned by the conflict that split the Cherokees as much as it divided Americans. Slover also details other high points of his long life, which spans both much of a century and much of the continental United States. He was born in Tennessee in 1824, a dozen years before fellow Tennessean Davy Crockett met Santa Ana at the Alamo. He died in California in 1913, seven years after helping build shelters for people made homeless in the great San Francisco earthquake of 1906. The years in between are filled with mostly commonplace activities, but through Slover's narrative the reader glimpses the lives of ordinary people who are sometimes called upon to do extraordinary things.[1]

We have Slover's story because at the age of eighty-three he responded to encouragement from his son and namesake, James Anderson Slover Jr., to write his life story. Slover filled 277 pages of an eight-by-thirteen-inch account book, which cost $1.25. He wrote of his personal adventures, as well as about wedding customs, smart-aleck pupils, spectacular meteor showers, and other aspects of life in the nineteenth century. The memoir provides a vivid picture of what it was like to migrate via the great rivers of the continent, to "skedaddle" and hide from Union troops and pro-North Indians during the Civil War, and to repeatedly carve a new life for oneself and one's family.

Slover lays the groundwork for his eventual career as a Southern Baptist preacher by describing his early life in eastern Tennessee. He was obviously close to his mother, certainly closer than to his father. She was a devout Methodist; his father was not at all religious. It was Slover's willingness to accommodate his mother's keen desire to attend a Methodist revival meeting that forced him to delay his own attendance at a camp meeting, thus putting him in the arms of the Baptists.

The Tennessee of Slover's young manhood reveled in the revivalism that had spread into the state in the early 1800s. Presbyterians are credited with introducing the camp meeting, originally an outdoor gathering with one or more preachers haranguing crowds who camped on the site, sometimes for weeks, but Baptists and other denominations embraced the concept eagerly.[2] Although by the 1840s the Baptists had generally moved their meetings indoors, the one Slover attended apparently fit the original format of an extended stay in the forest.

The Baptists were particularly successful in frontier states like Tennessee because their organizational structure emphasized democracy and autonomy, giving frontiersmen an opportunity to participate actively in their own salvation.[3] And indeed they did participate. Members of the Dumplin Creek Baptist Church, the local congregation Slover joined after his conversion, took seriously their responsibility to keep one another on a straight and narrow path. Minutes show that they met regularly to conduct the business of the church, which included chastising and sometimes expelling members who failed to conform to standards of conduct.[4] Individual churches also had full responsibility for the selection and payment of their preachers. Sometimes, too, individual churches sponsored missionaries, although support was more likely to come from the regional associations of churches that were formed.

Slover did not immediately become a preacher or missionary after finding religion, but when he later took to the pulpit he resembled the majority of his ministerial brethren who had little formal education and whose primary means of support was farming. As historian William Warren Sweet has noted about the Baptists, "It was a devoted and self-sacrificing ministry, but with an extremely limited outlook."[5]

Slover's formal education began at the age of eight and consisted of a series of short stints in the classroom. His first exposure to school totaled eight days, ending after the teacher spent the afternoon at a local tavern. He attended subscription schools; these were created prior to the establishment of public school systems by parents who banded together to raise enough money or other resources to support a teacher for short periods, generally between times of peak farming activity. Altogether Slover may have attended enough of these subscription schools for two or three months at a time to compile the equivalent of about two years of education. He was eager to learn, studying on his own, and in his memoir he boasts of being better educated than many of his teachers. After his conversion to the Baptist faith, he had a more extended period of education—five months—which earned him a certificate to teach, and he taught a succession of subscription schools, first in Tennessee and later in Arkansas.

Slover never discusses the reasons for his decision to leave his birthplace in the rolling green hills of Tennessee, just east of Knoxville, or for his eventual move to the West Coast, except to note that relatives had preceded him. However, the timing of the first move places it as part of a larger exodus from Tennessee in the 1850s. Poor farmers—most of them tenants rather than owners of the land they tilled—moved westward as the plantation system took hold in the state and they found it difficult to compete with the large enterprises that had the use of slave labor. Little able to contribute significantly to the economy, tenant farmers were essentially surplus population.[6] Slover recounts the frequent moves his family made in eastern Tennessee as his father rented one farm after another, and the young man clearly hoped for a life less transient than the one he had hitherto experienced.

He wanted a farm of his own, but he had only to observe the shift taking place in eastern Tennessee to realize that he needed to look elsewhere to secure his future. He knew, too, that teaching occasional subscription school would not provide him with an adequate living, especially after he married. Besides, there was nothing to keep him in Tennessee; his mother was dead, his father had remarried, and the paternal ties were weak.[7] Slover's bride, Harriet M. Ingram, and her mother were willing to leave eastern Tennessee, so the decision was made to join other friends and relatives and move to Arkansas. They placed their belongings on a flatboat on the French Broad River near Knoxville, floated into the Tennessee River, through Muscle Shoals and other waters now mostly tamed by the Tennessee Valley Authority, into the Ohio River, then down the Mississippi to the Arkansas, roughly a thousand miles on water.[8]

Arkansas has been called "a child of Tennessee" because so many residents of that state moved there in the migration of the 1850s.[9] But Tennesseans took many of their problems with them. For example, the plantation system that Slover and others sought to escape developed similarly in Arkansas, and the small farmers struggled there as they had at home.[10] As a result, after his move to Arkansas, Slover still had to look for additional avenues to keep bread on his table. He taught school briefly, but he soon found his true vocation in the ministry. It was in Arkansas that Slover received his religious calling, and he led a busy life of teaching, preaching, and farming as his family grew.

By the time Slover had his first preaching assignment, the Baptist Church had split into northern and southern denominations, in large part over slavery issues. In 1845, Baptists who lived in southern slave states took exception to the position of Baptists in the North, who refused to baptize slave owners, and they broke away to form the Southern Baptist Convention.[11] Being, as he often said, a "Southern man," Slover naturally became a *Southern* Baptist.

As a Southern Baptist preacher in Arkansas in the 1850s, Slover made the acquaintance of others of his faith, among them Henry Buckner, the Southern Baptist missionary to the Creek Indians in Indian Territory, what is now eastern Oklahoma.[12] Buckner sympathized with the financial circumstances of his young colleague and offered to recommend him to the Southern Baptist Board of Missions for a missionary post in Indian Territory. Thus in the winter of 1857 Slover moved his family to Tahlequah, the principal town in the Cherokee Nation, located just a few miles from Park Hill, the home of Principal Chief John Ross. The Cherokees, removed to Indian Territory along with the Creeks and Choctaws in 1838 in a forced migration that became known as the Trail of Tears because of the hardships and deaths experienced, welcomed missionaries of several faiths.[13] At least five were actively seeking converts in the Nation prior to Slover's arrival: northern Baptists, Methodist Episcopalians, Presbyterians, Congregationalists, and Moravians.[14] The Cherokees were particularly receptive to the Baptists and Methodists because these missionaries employed Cherokee preachers and held services in various communities around the Cherokee Nation instead of at a single mission site, making it easier for rural families to attend.[15]

Slover's path had undoubtedly crossed that of the Cherokees long before he arrived in Tahlequah. The forested hills of his birthplace were originally Cherokee country; the Tennessee River was formerly the Cherokee River.[16] Slover's grandfather Abraham had a flour mill on Muddy Creek, not far from Dumplin Creek where in 1785 the Cherokees signed a treaty giving up some of their ancient territory to the white men.[17] Slover must have encountered Cherokees in the course of growing up and may have watched as they began their trek along the tragic Trail of Tears to the plains of Indian Territory in the future state of Oklahoma, but there is no hint in his recollections of familiarity with or nostalgia for Cherokee connections.

Nor does Slover seem to have been committed to devoting his life to converting the Cherokees, as a number of his contemporaries had. He was a practical man, and the post Buckner helped him get was certainly an opportunity for him to spread a gospel in which he strongly believed; at least as important, it was a means of survival. Farming in Arkansas barely provided a living for himself and his growing family, and although he supplemented his income by preaching at community churches as much as possible, most of his congregations were as poor as he was and able to contribute only a little to his and his family's well-being. Appointment as missionary meant a secure salary of $500 a year, an income on which he and his wife and children could survive. But four years after he accepted the post, the Cherokee Nation was drawn into the American Civil War, a conflict that exacerbated an existing schism in the tribe and threatened Slover's life.

The division in the Cherokees that so complicated Slover's missionary responsibilities dated to long before the Trail of Tears, but it was both a cause and result of it. As early as 1794, some of the Cherokee people living in and near North Carolina had recognized the threat posed by white incursion into their ancestral home and agreed to sell their land in exchange for land west of the Mississippi River and an annuity. In 1835, another group signed the Treaty of New Echota, which committed all the Cherokees to move to Indian Territory. Still another group was highly critical of the treaty signers, calling the pact a "false" treaty and insisting on the right to remain in traditional Cherokee territory. The factions that resulted became known as the Ridge-Boudinot or Treaty or Removal Party (Major Ridge, his son John, and Elias Boudinot were the leaders of this party) and the Ross or Patriot Party (John Ross, principal chief from 1828 to 1866, was the leader of this group, which sought to remain in their traditional area).[18] Eventually the Cherokees were forced to move, and the difficulties experienced in the westward journey and settling on the new land widened the split between the factions. Bad blood persisted between the Treaty Party and Ross and his followers. In 1839, soon after the move was accomplished, the Ridges and Boudinot were ambushed and killed, probably by members of the Ross faction. By 1860, in addition to differences over the disposal of lands, the two factions disagreed over slavery and whether they should join the North or the South. The Treaty Party favored slavery and the South; Ross and his followers sided with the North.[19]

When the North and the South went to war, the Cherokees initially tried to remain neutral, relying on the United States government in Washington DC to honor its treaty obligations.[20] However, war disrupted the North's ability to meet those obligations. The United States was unable to transfer funds promised for payment for lands or to provide the Cherokee Nation with protection from outside forces such as the Confederate army. Left without this resource, the Cherokees decided they could no longer rely on the North and gave their allegiance to the Confederacy, but it was a halfhearted allegiance.[21] Many Cherokees had little enthusiasm for fighting on the Southern side, and after the Battle of Caving Banks in the Cherokee Nation and the Battle of Pea Ridge in northwestern Arkansas, Confederate Indian soldiers deserted in considerable numbers.[22] As the Union army exhibited strength, Chief Ross turned to the North once again for protection. More fearful of the South than the North, and more sympathetic to the latter's cause, he surrendered to the Union army and became a prisoner of war.[23] He spent most of the rest of his life in Washington DC trying to get the government to deal with his people fairly. Meanwhile, his followers, as well as those of the Treaty Party leaders, were left in Indian Territory to cope with the poverty and devastation of war.[24]

Slavery was, for the Cherokees as for other Americans, only one factor that brought the Indian nation to war, but it was an important one. Although the Cherokees had a long history of slave ownership, they were by no means united on the issue. And as was often the case elsewhere in the South, wealthy landowners, in this case the mixed-bloods who were members of the Treaty Party, supported slavery. Meanwhile, full-bloods who favored abolition had the encouragement of two influential northern Baptist missionaries, Evan and John B. Jones, father and son. The two Joneses worked closely with abolitionists and encouraged the formation of the Keetoowah Society, a secret organization of Cherokees to promote patriotism, ethnic and tribal identity, and loyalty and to counter other secret societies composed of proslavery interests.[25] The Keetoowahs became known as "Pin" Indians because of the pins they wore as a badge, and in their zeal to press their cause, some of the members terrorized the surrounding countryside.[26]

The issue of slavery clearly dominated Slover's years among the Cherokees. When he wrote about it nearly fifty years later, however, he was circumspect in his discussion. In particular, he failed to address candidly the question of his views on slavery or whether he personally owned slaves. In the autobiography he insisted that he was only concerned with the relationship between man and God, not man and man. He claimed he willingly baptized slave, slaveholder, and abolitionist if they placed themselves in God's hands. Indeed, Slover probably did not distinguish between slave and slaver when it came to baptism. Nevertheless, he likely was being disingenuous. It has been suggested that he did own a slave during his Arkansas–Indian Territory years. Northern Baptist missionaries Evan and John Jones complained that Slover bragged about owning a slave and did all he could to support slaveholders and thwart antislavery interests.[27]

Although the Joneses' claim can be attributed to the fact that they apparently sought every opportunity to discredit their Southern Baptist competitor, Slover's background is consistent with slave ownership. The eastern Tennessee of his youth relied less on slaves than did other parts of the state, but slavery was indeed practiced in the region. The second wife of Slover's grandfather Abraham brought slaves with her when she married into the Slover household, and his own wife's family included slave owners.[28] He occasionally refers to African Americans he seems to know well who were probably slaves, perhaps his, before the Civil War. Given his usually strapped financial situation, he is unlikely to have been able to buy a slave, but he may have been given one in appreciation for his preaching or in exchange for other services such as farmwork.

He tries to appear neutral in his memoir, but in describing an encounter with African Americans in California he exhibits racist attitudes. Certainly there is little doubt that Slover the missionary accepted the institution of slavery. Nowhere in the autobiography does he attack slavery, and a Southern Baptist colleague, T. H. Compere, one of several Comperes with whom Slover worked closely, came out publicly and strongly in favor of it. In the *Arkansas Baptist,* Compere complained about abolitionist newspapers being sent to Arkansas. "We regard slavery as scriptural, and moral in its tendency, and by far the best situation in which the African can be placed," he wrote.[29] He advised senders of abolitionist literature to keep their "murderous and diabolical documents" to themselves. Others have noted that when they preached to slaves, Baptist preachers in Arkansas told them to obey their masters, and Chief John Ross repeatedly noted that slavery was legal in the Cherokee Nation and should not be considered an issue.[30] Slover surely would have approved.

Slover's support of slavery put him in the camp of the Treaty Party, then led by Stand Watie, who was the slain Boudinot's brother and John Ridge's cousin.[31] Watie, elected chief by the Confederate Cherokees when Ross left the Nation, had his own secret society, the Knights of the Golden Circle, which mounted a vigilante effort comparable to that of the Pins.[32] Even before the Cherokees decided to link their destiny to the Confederacy, Watie had formed a regiment of volunteers for the Confederate army, ostensibly to protect the Nation but also to strengthen his position against Ross.[33] Later, when the Cherokees joined the Confederacy, Watie's troop was one of two Cherokee regiments established; the second was headed by John Drew and represented Ross's interests.[34] Apparently hoping to ensure some income in these uncertain conditions, Slover served briefly as chaplain to Watie's regiment; he does not explain why he left.[35] His friend E. L. Compere subsequently became chaplain and helped the Confederates get supplies past the Union forces.[36]

Slover's reputation as a "Southern man" put a price on his head as the North came to control Arkansas and Indian Territory. Although the missionary was hardly a threat to the Union forces—he does not seem to have taken up a gun except to hunt game for his table, and even that rarely—at times he feared for his life and was forced to "skedaddle," fleeing the invading forces or the Pin Indians who allied themselves with the North. Slover blamed the northern Baptist Evan Jones for stirring the Pins and other full-bloods against him. "I think Jones and party have learned that it would be dear blood for them to shed mine," he wrote to E. L. Compere in June 1861, about the time Jones left his mission in the Cherokee Nation and went to Kansas, where he spent most of the remainder of the war, returning only for brief visits to meddle in Cherokee politics.[37]

In 1861 the Cherokee Nation was still officially neutral; nevertheless, factions were well formed and prepared to take action against opposing views. The pro-Confederacy forces were strong enough to drive outspoken abolitionists such as Jones from the territory.[38] At the same time, the abolitionists contributed their share to the fear and violence that pervaded the countryside. In his letter to Compere, Slover recounts the death of a Native minister:

> The native minister, an honest inoffensive and pious man, was murdered—called out of his own house at night and shot.[39] He run—they followed and cut his throat. The cause is hard to ascertain and rumors

here, 1st Because he would not leave the Southern Baptist Church and go back to the Northern, of which he once was a member. 2nd Because he had withdraw from a secret organization known here by the term "Pins," he refusing to unite again, 3rd Because of his money of which every body that knew him, knew that he did not have a *red* cent. The first seems to be the most plausible, for another Cherokee minister similar situated (except he is not a *pin*) has been waylayed but escaped. Others have been threatened that if they preached in certain quarters that they would be killed, this is the game they (Jones party) have been playing for the last three years.

In a cautious postscript to his frank letter, Slover showed his continued unease: "If you say anything about the contents of this letter keep my name secret as you know how to keep a secret of a worthy Brother committed to your breast."

After three years of war, Slover gave up attempting to minister to the Cherokees and returned to Arkansas. There survival continued to require skedaddling from bushwhackers, and occasionally from an officially constituted military force.[40] More often, he found himself arguing or pleading to save his horse or mule from the soldiers who scavenged the countryside for food, clothing, horses, and other supplies. Without his horse he would have been unable to get to churches to preach or to town to buy supplies, or to conduct other business that required him to go more than a few miles from home. His service as a preacher and his reputation as a hardworking farmer encouraged others to speak on his behalf, and several times this saved him from the depredations of the soldiers.

Although his descriptions are often vivid, Slover's recollections only hint at the enormous tensions of the time, tensions confirmed in other accounts of the period.[41] This war, like others before and after it, dislocated individuals and disrupted normal social intercourse. The threat of violence was only part of the problem. War disturbed the economic system: debtors could not pay what they owed, creditors had to extend loans to have any hope of getting some return, and merchants attempted to insist on cash payment—all of which meant that poor farmers like Slover had difficulty getting what they needed to plant and harvest their crops.[42] This was, however, a neighborly society, with almost everyone willing to lend a hand to help someone in need, acquaintance or stranger, and offering particular respect for a man of the cloth. As Slover moved around, staying out of reach of enemies, his family benefited from the goodwill of those who sheltered them.

In Arkansas for the first year or two following the conclusion of the fighting, Confederates like Slover were treated relatively well by the victors. Slover ran for minor office in still another attempt for a stable income, and although he narrowly lost the vote, he was subsequently appointed to office by a pro-Union administration. However, economic and social conditions soon deteriorated. Reconstruction Acts passed by Congress beginning in 1867 made things difficult for former Confederates, and tension grew as the Ku Klux Klan, founded in 1865, took root. Violence perpetrated by Klan members became so severe in southern states, including Arkansas, that even the Klan's imperial wizard, former Confederate general Nathan Bedford Forrest, decided members were out of control: this early incarnation of the Klan was disbanded in 1869.[43] Slover does not mention the Ku Klux Klan, and it is doubtful that he had any personal involvement with it because he was not given to terrorism and violence, but it seems likely he was touched by its actions, coming, as he did, from the poorer stratum of society in which the Klan was particularly active.

Discouraged by political, social, and economic conditions, as well as by the weather that interfered with successful farming, Slover once again looked West. Having remarried after the death of his first wife, and with relatives already on the West Coast, Slover was naturally drawn into the stream heading for California. And again, he, his family, and his friends were part of a larger migration.

Thousands of people moved West after the Civil War. The population of western states and territories nearly doubled from 1860 to 1870 as Americans sought to build new lives after the turmoil and destruction of the conflict. Aided by improved transportation and communication, they were attracted by prospects of free land and continuing discoveries of gold and other minerals. Less than a month before the Golden Spike was driven at Promontory, Utah, linking the east and west legs of the first transcontinental railroad, Slover and his migrant companions wheeled their wagons onto the Gila Trail, a southern pathway to California. An old Spanish route through Texas, New Mexico, and Arizona to the Pacific shore, the Gila Trail was followed and improved by the Butterfield Overland Mail, which in the 1850s set up more than two hundred stations along the way.[44] Some eight thousand goldseekers followed the Gila Trail in 1849, but this path generally was less well traveled by migrant companies than more northerly routes such as the Oregon Trail.[45] Travelers tended to avoid southwestern territories because they feared drought and the fierce Apaches, among other hazards. Nevertheless, for migrants from southern states, the Gila Trail not only was more direct, it avoided postwar harassment from northerners. Further, unlike trails through the Sierra Nevada and other mountain ranges to the north, it was passable in winter. Slover's group was large enough that the Apaches did not challenge it, and the migrants passed through the country peacefully.

It would not be fair to say that Slover found California to be the "promised land." As in Tennessee, Arkansas, and the Cherokee Nation, he again had to struggle to provide for himself and his family. At each place he stopped, he lived simply and managed at times to acquire small acreages. He patented a claim of land in Arkansas, bought property in California, and homesteaded in Oregon. Owning land was clearly important to the preacher, and his land transactions were designed for his own use, not as a front for other interests. It was common during this period for speculators to finance migrants in claiming and improving land until the latter could get a patent or homestead. When the settler had title to the property, he or she turned it over to the speculators under whatever financial arrangement had been agreed upon. The speculator was then free to remove the timber or mineral resources the land might hold and develop or resell the property. The financial backers increased their wealth, and the individual fronting for them went away with money in his or her pocket.[46] As desperate as he seemed at times, Slover never seems to have employed that as a way to make money.

Slover's financial naïveté, ignorance, and trust in the integrity of his fellow man combined to ensure that he never advanced much beyond a subsistence level. Sometimes he claimed someone cheated him out of something he was due; at other times weather—drought or flood—destroyed his crop. Everywhere he tried to farm, he was too poor to be competitive with large landowners who could finance improvements that cushioned the effect of bad weather or poor markets. In Tulare County in the Central Valley of California, where Slover settled in the 1870s, irrigation meant the difference between crop success or failure, and having irrigation meant joining one of the ditch improvement districts, an investment Slover claims he could not afford.[47]

California's land policies in the late nineteenth century were clearly biased in favor of large property owners. In the 1860s California had put

8 million acres of public land on the market, land intended for farms of 160 acres. That could have resulted in fifty thousand farms, but only about seven thousand new farms were established. Describing California's land policies, Paul W. Gates says people looking for land to homestead "were badly served while all possible means were used to facilitate the creation of large holdings, notwithstanding all the professions that were being made about withholding public lands for the actual settler."[48] Slover's eventual failure in California apparently was due as much to uncooperative weather as to land policy, but for the preacher, the result was the same as he was again thwarted in his attempt to put down permanent roots.

Slover turned briefly to the Granger Movement, hoping it would lead to economic reform that would benefit small farmers. In 1867 the Patrons of Husbandry, or Grange, was established nationally, and in 1873 it moved into California. Slover was quick to become a member. In organization the Grange had much in common with the Masons, which Slover had joined sometime earlier, perhaps when working with the Cherokees who were active in Masonry.[49] Both the Grange and the Masons were built on notions of brotherhood and secret society, but the Grange also had as its goal the improvement of the lot of the farmer. Reform, however, takes time, and when the Grange failed to effect immediate change, farmers like Slover quickly lost interest.[50] In the flush days of enthusiasm for the movement, Slover accepted the post of Grange master, but as general interest dwindled he turned his attention from activism back to his more immediate need to provide for his wife and children.[51]

Regardless of his financial difficulties, Slover always managed to keep a roof over his family's head and provide for their next meal. If farming would not support his family, he would find other honest means. When his own crops were poor, he hired himself out to more successful farmers. Fortunately, he was not averse to wielding an ax or a hayrake, and he took considerable pride in his prowess as a laborer, especially as he aged. Also, in California, as he had in Arkansas, he turned to public service to supplement his farm income, holding, at various times, positions as postmaster or justice of the peace.

The fever of migration continued after Slover's arrival on the West Coast and well into the last quarter of the century. From 1870 to 1880, western population increased 80 percent, and it grew another 70 percent the following decade. The Pacific Northwest, in particular, benefited from the western movement; Oregon, for example, grew from 174,000 residents in

1880 to 317,000 in 1890.[52] Slover, still searching for a place to put down roots, followed a friend to the Rogue River Valley in southern Oregon to become part of still another pioneer society. Here neither drought nor big agricultural concerns hindered him, but land law that gave precedence to mining claims caused him to lose part of his homestead.[53] Nevertheless, he managed to patent the homestead while also doing missionary work and raising money to build a new church.

And he preached. The itinerant tradition of the Southern Baptists opened doors to him. As he traveled around the Central Valley of California, sometimes to visit friends and relatives, sometimes in search of other employment, discovery that he was a preacher would usually result in an invitation to the pulpit and perhaps a small token of the congregation's appreciation. But West Coast Baptists proved to be no more solvent than those to whom Slover had ministered elsewhere. Despite preaching and missionary appointments in California and later in Oregon, and however much the church did for his soul, Slover, like most other Southern Baptist preachers, continued to rely principally on the farm for his physical well-being.

Having as a young man committed himself to God, Slover remained true to his beliefs throughout his life, taking the opportunity to preach wherever he found it, for pay if possible, but often, apparently, for nothing. In southern Oregon, the Rogue River Association and the Middle Oregon Association of Southern Baptists tried to "sustain him as a missionary" but lacked the funding. "Yet he preaches considerably in destitute places, at his own charges. But being poor, with a family to support, his preaching is much limited."[54]

Slover was a stern theologian, refusing to budge in his opposition to "alien immersion" (baptism by immersion but by other denominations), insisting that an individual could be accepted into a Southern Baptist congregation only if he or she had had a Southern Baptist baptism. Slover never wavered on this issue. Church records from his later years in Oregon remark about his insistence that every member must have a Southern Baptist baptism.[55] Slover says nothing that suggests his preaching style and rarely hints at the content of his sermons, but his success in revival meetings testifies to his persuasiveness and ability to touch souls, and his rigorous affirmation of his faith did not deter converts.

After his second wife died in 1898, Slover, by then seventy-four years old, gave up trying to farm and moved in with his daughter and son-in-law in Grants Pass, Oregon. He continued, however, to earn his own way in the world as best he could, selling silverware door-to-door or doing handyman work around his daughter's house. Eventually he moved with his family to San Francisco, and he was there for the great San Francisco earthquake of 1906. In his eighties, he rolled up his sleeves and went to work building shelters for the homeless. Later that year he reroofed a granddaughter's house and built cupboards and a porch.

Few individuals emerge as personalities in Slover's story, but the narrative gives a sense of people's interdependency during this period. It was a time when a traveler could stop at a farmhouse and be given food and a place to sleep, when life was slower, harder, but perhaps more charitable. However, there were also people ready to take advantage of a trusting soul, and Slover encountered them, too. Many others of his generation could no doubt have told much the same story of human relationships.

The autobiography ends after Thanksgiving in 1907 when Slover returned to his daughter's home in San Francisco after traveling the length of California to be with various relatives. Six years later he died.

In 1861 Slover wrote that he hoped for "a blessed immortality beyond the grave."[56] We cannot know whether he received the kind of immortality he sought, but in recording his life, he has gained immortality of another sort.

Minister to the Cherokees

I

James Anderson Slover—His Parentage—-Birth—Events and incidents of the first ten years of his eventful life.

James Anderson was a Judge of the Circuit Court of the Judicial District of East Tennessee at the time of the birth of James Anderson Slover; his parents called their boy for this judge, hence his name. His grandfather Abraham Slover was one of the two little boys which escaped when their father's family was massacred about the year 1756, in the Colony of Virginia, not a great ways from Wheeling, in West Virginia.[1]

This Slover was from Germany, but how long before the fearful massacre the present generation of Slovers has no means of knowing.[2] According to the best information in the possession of the subject of these pages, the escape of the little boy Abraham was on this wise: He and his older brother John was some two or three hundred yards from the dwelling at play when the massacring party of Indians made the attack upon the family.[3]

After finishing the work of killing and scalping the family indiscriminately, they set fire to the house. Not until the flames were leaping and curling up in the air did the little boys know that anything was wrong at the residence. Each one sought his own hiding place; Abraham, the younger, secreted himself in a small cavern formed by two large spur roots of a large tree, completely hiding his little person from the view of the passing Indians mounted upon Indian ponies. The older boy John, who was eight years old, secreted himself in a small cavern formed by two large spur roots of a large tree, and would occasionally watch the movements of the Indians. Poor John—he had better never looked to see which way the red skins were going to go, for they caught sight of him, raised the "Yell," or whoop, and captured him. Of course he was cautious not to speak of his little brother who was hid not far away.

John was kept by this tribe of Indians until after the Revolutionary war. Then he was either exchanged for some captured Indians, or he was bought from them by the white people.[4] Who became the guardian of the now distressed little Abraham, the writer has no means of knowing. But during Washington's Presidency, John was employed by the Government as a guide in Col. Crawford's expedition on the frontier.[5] He was captured with Col. Crawford, who, by the way, was burned to death the next day after the capture at night, but from some cause Slover was kept for at least fourteen days, when it was decided by the Indian Council to put him to death the next day by burning.[6] Accordingly he was tied, after being stripped naked and painted jet black, to a post or tree with raw-hide cords and the wood placed in a circular position about four feet from the post to which he was tied, and a fire kindled; but before the fire got under way enough to effect anything, there instantly arose a fearful rainstorm, although at the time of applying the torch, there was not a cloud to be seen in the elements.

The Indians, being thus defeated, concluded to keep him over night and burn him the next day. He was confined with the same rawhide cords, to a joist with slack enough for him to lie down and two Indian men placed in the old cabin to guard him. He knew his doom was sealed unless he could get loose and away before daylight. He very easily got one hand loose, but did not let the guards know anything about it; the guards would smoke and then walk around, set down and smoke again, to drive sleep away. Slover finally fell on a plan to get them off to dream land. "By snoring in pretense," in a very short time the guards were snoring in good earnest. The prisoner now loosed the other hand and after knawing and pulling at the cord about his neck to no avail until the night was about gone he found to his happy surprise that the cord around his neck was tied in a bow or slip knot, he was consequently loose and mounted on a pony by the dawn of day and gone, he says. At 11 o'clock A.M. same day, he was seventy-five miles toward the white settlement, and the pony run down so that he had to go on foot.

Knowing that the fiends would follow him, he endeavored to delude them in tracking him. For several days he wandered around making as much distance between himself and the Indians as was possible; on reaching a river which he had to cross—perhaps it was the Muskingum River—at any rate he had to swim it, and as he made the south bank, the Indians yelled at him in hot pursuit, but they did not attempt to cross after him for he was in the white man's country. He lived to be very old, and raised a family in Indiana on the Wabash River.[7]

Abraham, at some time not known to J. A. Slover, emigrated to East Tennessee and raised his family of five boys in Jefferson County and on Muddy Creek, on which stream he had a grist mill, as such mills were called in the days of "Yore." Of these boys John was the youngest, and very early in the Nineteenth Century was married to Rachel Taffe, an amiable young lady from Virginia and one year his junior. She was the daughter of a Revolutionary soldier.[8] Of this union there were twelve children born to them, the first was born in the year 1812 and the twelfth in the year 1835. All of them lived to be men and women, and save one boy, they were all married, before death overtook them.

Our James A. was the eighth child and fifth son, four boys and three girls being his seniors. He was born near the south bank of Muddy Creek west of his Grandfather's mill, in Jefferson County, East Tennessee, and on the fifteenth day of September A.D. 1824. It seems that while he was an infant his father moved his family to, and took charge of, and run the old mill for his father, who was now about seventy-six years old.

Here for the benefit of the rising generation must be a graphic description of the old time grist mill-house and the water power that run it. The mill-houses of those days, with the exception of those erected on large rivers, were usually built of hewn logs; perhaps this one may have been partly of logs and partly of frame work with weather boarding on the sides—no such thing as "Rustic" was thought of then.

Inside and as support of the mill-stones was a huge frame made of four large pieces of hewn timber, placed in bed pieces of the like dimensions, so as to stand perpendicular, and as high as the first floor or ten or twelve feet high. The machinery that run the mill-stone was all in this basement. These four upright pillars were leveled on top and formed a square, thoroughly sway-braced in the basement so as to hold them steady. This was called the frame of the nether millstone, for it was imbedded firmly on the top of this frame, an iron shaft having a "trundlehead" below the bed stone and a support for the upper stone which had a hole directly in the center, about eight inches in diameter. Then above was a square frame made of timbers about three inches square, and around the upper stone was a hoop or band about one foot wide, which was dropped over the upper stone and closely fitting on the floor at equal distances from the stone all around, say about one inch.

A spout or shute carried the meal or whatever was ground in the mill to a large chest in the basement, where it was sacked in the same sacks in which the grain had been brought. Then the miller or man who done the grinding would throw the bag across a horse's back, as often without a blanket as with one, and a man, boy, woman, or girl would mount from the old stile which stood near the door of this basement story, and head for home, perhaps having to ride six or eight miles.

On the last-mentioned frame was constructed the hopper, which was so constructed that it was from three to five feet wide each way at the top, and two or three inches at the bottom, and immediately under this three-inch hole was placed what was called the shoe or feed-box, by which the miller would regulate the grain so as not to allow too much nor too little grain enter at any time.

The machinery which run the upper stone and the botting apparatus [a kind of brake that regulated the flow of grain] were in those days all of wood. Parts known as shaves and cogwheels were artfully constructed with the drive or waterwheel which was located outside of the building with one end of the huge shaft inside the house. The waterwheel was strongly built about twenty-five feet in diameter, with buckets about three or four feet long, and was known as an undershot wheel.[9] Immediately in front of this wheel was a large reservoir called at this particular mill a "forebay." It was about eight or ten feet deep, and on the inside as wide as the length of the buckets on the waterwheel, furnished with an outlet for the water to strike the buckets underneath the wheel, also with a gate to regulate the flow of the water, and a lever reaching inside the house at a convenient spot for the Miller to handle it at will.

This forebay or reservoir was built watertight and at the outlet of a large pond made by an excavation in the hillside that formed a levy with the dirt on the low side. This pond served the purpose of holding a head of water directly above the mill, and was furnished with a wastegate or shute for the protection of the levy.

This pond was connected with what was then called a mill-dam, some distance up the creek, by a mill-race or large ditch constructed on as high ground as was necessary to carry the water from the dam to the pond at the mill. The mill-dam was about one half mile up the creek from the mill, and was constructed by building cribs or pens out of round timbers, about four feet wide, and from eight to ten feet long. Enough of these were built to reach from one bank of the stream to the other, then filled with rocks. These cribs were a little higher than the high banks of the creek. Hewed or sawed timber was imbedded in the bottom of the stream about six feet above these cribs, and the same kind of timbers located immediately on the upper wall of the cribs. Timbers of suitable size were framed into lower and upper square timbers, and this frame was floored with heavy plank. When finished with plank water tight, it stood at about three-quarter pitch or steeper; and when the dam was full of water, it was about twelve feet deep.

He but faintly remembers his Grandmother Slover. One and only one circumstance can he call up, but that is fresh in his mind: there was a small sugar orchard on the old mill farm. This orchard had a goodly number of sugar-trees scattered as nature had grown them, and the trees had been tapped and the water had to be gathered from the troughs and carried to camp for boiling. And as his Grandmother would go to collect the sugar water he would toddle along behind her. He remembers that she looked very old, wrinkled, and stooped forward like a head of wheat as it begins to ripen.

She passed away before her Grandboy Jim was old enough to remember anything about a funeral. His Grandfather, old as he was, got married again to an old maid. She owned a Negro woman with three or four children and one of them fell headlong into the forebay or reservoir and was drowned. After the death of the old man, she took her Negroes and went to live with her own people but did not live long.

Several years before the death of Grandfather Slover, an arrangement was made for his oldest brother (Isaac W.) to go and live with his Grandfather on condition that if Isaac would take care of him until his death he would will him the mill and farm, and so he did. The Grandfather died in May A.D. 1835, being eighty-five years old. About four years after his death Isaac W. was married [December 1838] to an amiable young lady, Elisa Thornton. In August after he had been married in the winter, he died of bilious fever.[10] In October following his death, his widow was delivered of a child, a boy, and of course his mother give him his father's name. So Isaac Wiley Slover still owns the property of his Great Grandfather Slover, or did in the year A.D. 1898.[11]

About the Spring of 1828, the little boy's father (John Slover) left his father's mill and moved down the Muddy Creek about five miles to a farm which once belonged to him, but he lost it, as he used to tell his children, by putting his name on a note of hand with another person, he (Slover) being security, which event happened before J. A. Slover was born.

On this farm the little boy rapidly developed, from three and a half years to eight and a half years old. This farm was just across the creek from the birth place of the youngster, but the dwelling house was more than a quarter of a mile north. He here learned his first lesson about farming, by seeing his father and older brothers plow, plant and gather corn, and make hay on the large meadow that belonged to the farm.

The first plow that he remembers seeing used was then styled and known as a "barshear."[12] Its construction was a two- or two-and-a-half-inch bar with a flat shear [blade] welded on the top, the bar being swauged [shaped] to a point, and the shear varied in length owing to the size of the team. One such as used on this farm, being for two horses, was about twelve inches wide at the heel of the shear where it was supported by a small bar of iron riveted in the bar and the other end welded on the under side of the shear. The bar was about twenty or twenty-two inches long from heel to point.

The stock consisted of handles, beam standard and a wooden mouldboard [or moldboard; it pushes the soil lifted by the blade into a furrow], dressed in shape to turn the dirt. The standard stood perpendicular under the beam, and in an iron socket on the bar at the lower end, and the mouldboard was pinned to this standard with wooden pins. One of the handles was bolted to the heel of the bar, and at a suitable distance up this handle the rear end of the beam was teneted into the handle. The other handle was pinned to the board, angling back so as to make both handles about the same length. There were usually three cross pins between the handles, one at the bottom one where the beam entered and the other near the crook of the handles.

The whole stock was usually made by the farmer, and a country blacksmith would make the irons. There was a similar-made plow invented by a man by the name of Cary.[13] This Cary plow differed from the "barshear." Instead of a flat shear, it was raised to an angle of forty-five degrees or more at the junction of the mouldboard and the shear. These Cary plows were generally made for one horse; but later on they were made strong enough for two.

There was not a tool constructed of wood in whole or in part but what was made by hand on the farm; all the harness except the tug or trace chains were made by hand. Collars were made of corn shucks, hames split from a spur root of whiteoak, plow lines made of rope homemade. Bridle bits were bought or made by the country blacksmith, and leather purchased, then the bridle was made by hand on the farm.

A few rather painful incidents were the misfortune of the boy Jim, while his father resided on this farm, which now was owned by an old merchant, John Fane, who lived in Dandridge, the county seat of Jefferson County.

A windstorm blew down a small mulberry tree about one hundred and fifty yards from the dwelling house. The weather being pleasant, the idea struck the little boy to get an axe and go out and cut the tree up and make firewood of it. Accordingly he found an axe and told his Mother that he was going to trim the limbs off the little mulberry tree. Then away he went to the unfortunate tree and the first limb that he cut off was small and being up from the ground, the sharp axe went through the limb and into the top of one of his feet. This was the first cut he ever had. He instantly dropped the axe and put out for his mother or someone to bind up the unfortunate foot, and that was the last chopping he did for about seven weeks.

About six months after this mishap, his father sent him out early in the morning to the woodpile for some small round sticks of wood, and he was barefooted, with a white frost all over the ground and woodpile, he attempted to chop a small limb of black oak wood for the fireplace, and about the third lick, he struck his foot, and then was laid up again for a month or more. It was not long after this cut foot got well that his father was plowing the garden and planting potatoes with a mare that had a young colt, not more than ten days old, and she was naturally bad tempered. His father unhitched the mare to let her eat grass in the fence corner, and the little boy was sitting on the top of the fence. The bit was slipped out of the mare's mouth, the headstall was around her neck, and the rein was put in the little boy's hand to hold.

Pretty soon the old shuck collar with the hames and chains slid down to the animal's ears. She threw up her head viciously and seized the boy's right arm with her teeth, and pulled him down making a terrible bite at the elbow of the arm; the scar is still there.

It was here on this old farm that his education began, and he attended his first school. His oldest sister Mary taught him his letters in the summer of 1832.[14] And about the time he was eight years old he was sent to school, his first term lasted eight days, or in other words, that was all the time he went that year and he learned to spell in words of two syllables. In that country and at that time children were not thought old enough to go to school under eight years of age; perhaps it was thought they could not stand to study from eight o'clock in the morning until four in the afternoon with only one hour's rest at noon.

A description of school facilities of that age of East Tennessee should here be given, especially in the country. Schoolhouses were usually built of logs and those in the more wealthy localities were hewed logs, but whether hewn or round with the bark on, they were covered with four-foot boards riven from Spanish oak or some other kind that would split straight. Instead of rafters, straight poles were used and called ribs. The gable ends were built up of the same material of the body of the house: that is to say, if round logs were used for the body, the gables were of the same. To hold the boards in place a butting pole was made by splitting a log in the center.[15]

There were two logs called eavebearers; these jutted over the corners a sufficient length to receive the butting pole. The first course of boards were laid on two of these ribs with the lower end butting against the butting pole, then two or three pieces about thirty inches long were placed at each end and in the center—these were called knees—then good sized poles were placed above these knees, called weight poles, every course of boards received a like weight pole and knees until the roof was on.

Very seldom a house had any window and but one door. The cracks were chinked and then daubed with clay, except one and that one was made larger by sawing the log above the crack and the one below half in two, and dressing these two logs to a face, thus making a window the full length of the schoolhouse. A wide board or plank was so constructed that it served all the students which were allowed to write.

The seats were slabs with the bark on them and legs of round sticks driven into an inch-and-a-half hole bored at an angle of forty-five degrees or less; no backs to these seats and twelve or fifteen children would occupy one of these seats owing to the length of the bench, and all spell or read aloud while learning their lessons; no silent school in that land.

The little boy's first teacher's name was William Henderson and the name of the first schoolhouse was Sandy Ridge. He remembers the old house with a huge fireplace, but the weather was quite warm and fire was not needed.

On the fifth day of this short term, the teacher left the school at noon and went to a still-house [tavern] about a half or three quarters of a mile away, and run by a man by the name of Swan. The teacher spent nearly all that afternoon drinking whiskey. The scholars played themselves tired; then as the teacher did not come, one of the large boys played teacher, but this would not go—each girl and boy of any size, and a plenty of them ranging from twelve to eighteen, would not be taught by one of their number and about three o'clock the fun began in Old Tennessee style. They turned over every bench in the house, and played all kinds of jokes on each other—laughed and yelled like Indians.

Finally about four o'clock the large boys barred up the door and waited inside for the schoolmaster, and a few minutes after four o'clock, behold, the teacher came and was about half drunk, but he saw what was up, and did not order the boys to open the door, but calling their attention, dismissed the school until Monday of the next week. Of course this put an end to the fun for that day, and three days of the next week closed the little eight-year-old boy's first school term.

He very well remembers some of his childhood sports. Only one is narrated in these pages, that of holding mimic meetings. A half dozen or more little boys and girls would assemble at a neighbor's house, select a convenient place and arrange seats of the best material at hand. A pulpit or platform was arranged, and one of the small boys requested to play preacher; he would mount the platform and call on someone to lead the singing, after which the preacher would tell the congregation to kneel for prayers, but the prayer was generally silent. Then he would go through the motion of preaching, then some little "Chorus" was started by the little people and all would sing and shake hands after the camp meeting style. In due time they would close, perhaps sing a song as a closing exercise. These children were, for the most part, [those] the mothers took to church with them. Here they imbibed the idea of playing the part of preacher and congregation.[16]

Early in the Spring of 1833 his father and family left the old farm and located on a farm lying on the south side of the French Broad River and owned by an old man by the name of Hugh Martin, and known as the Dorithy farm. It contained a large quantity of river bottom land, and a still larger quantity of upland, conveniently accommodated four families with houses and lands to cultivate.

About this time his oldest sister was married to a man by the name of John Hill.[17]

On this farm he learned the use of a hoe, for the plan of working corn in those days in that country was for a boy with a hoe to follow each plow, replant any hills of corn where there was but one stalk and all places that had failed to produce any stalks at all. Not being inclined to work, the eight-year-old boy would leave his hoe when he thought he had done enough, and go a quarter of a mile or more home, especially when the sun would get hot.

He remembers the hard frost of the twenty-second day of May 1833. The corn was about knee high to a man and as green and thrifty as could be, but on the morning referred to above it was all dead to the ground and as soon as the sun arose, the corn soon turned black and looked like it had been boiled. Some of the tenants on the farm plowed the frozen corn up and planted again, but Slover's father, John, took chances on his making corn and did not disturb the frozen crop, and he was the man that had the big ears of corn while others had tall stalks with little or no corn on them.

During this summer the boy had a narrow escape for life from a fall. The loft over the kitchen was not nailed down, and for some cause or other, two of the twelve-inch planks had been removed which made a two-foot hole just about the center of the loft. The wasps had built many nests on the rafters and sheeting of the house. He told his mother that he would go up in the loft and punch those wasp-nests off. She paid no more attention to what he said, not thinking that he would dare to go up and disturb the stinging things, but he meant it, and soon had a stick sufficiently long to answer his purposes, and up he went to give the intruders battle. It was fine fun as long as they did not come close to his head, so in his glee, he forgot about the hole where the two plank had been removed, and intent on destroying the last of these nests, and as he walked carelessly along, down he went to the lower floor, a distance of about ten feet. His mother happened to be in the kitchen, and she lifted him up to his feet, but he was for a moment senseless. No bones were broken, but this satisfied his war-spirit and he did not disturb the wasps any more.

About the middle of July he was again started to one of the old-field schools which was to last three months. However, it was seldom that a farmer's boy even got the benefit of a full three months school in any one year. It was at this school he got his first and last licking while attending school.

The writing bench was, in this house, in a separate apartment from where the teacher heard the lessons recited. And there a great big boy eighteen years old, with all the other boys and girls that had been writing, was standing before the teacher spelling. About seven or eight small boys quietly slipped into where the writing had been going on and seated themselves on the seat by the writing bench. The big boy above named looked in and saw them (and among them was Jim Slover); he instantly exclaimed, calling the teacher by name. "Mr. Craig, the boys are spoiling pens." The teacher jumped up from his seat and called to the little boys to come out, and as they came he met them at the door with his rod of correction, which was a small switch and each boy got two licks as he passed out at the door.

In November of this year (1833) he saw the great sight of the falling stars.[18] He was but two months past nine years of age, but the commotion in the family together with the fact that the elements were full of what was then called falling stars, so impressed his childish mind that he has never forgotten the fearful sight.

The winter passed without any particular incident happening to the boy except a very singular dream toward the close of winter. The farming tools had been put in order for starting the plow, and one of those large two-horse barshear plows had been brought from the blacksmith shop and left standing in the front yard all night. Then during the night he saw in his dream something away in the horizon like black clouds forming great steps as though they started on the earth and ascended upwards, and from or out of them he saw the Devil coming as though he intended to carry the dreamer off, and would have taken hold of his prey, but for the timely intervention of the little dreamer's eighteen-year-old brother George, who seized the great barshear plow by the end of the beam, and raising the plow up as though it was a walking stick, he struck him (the Devil) a fatal blow, splitting asunder the Devil from head to foot.[19] This relieved the dreamer's fears and so overjoyed him that he instantly awoke from his sleep.

Sometime afterward he had another delightful dream. He thought he was near the bank of the French Broad River, and as he was going from the river to his father's house, his attention in his dream was attracted to an inclined plain just one foot wide, and appearing to start on the earth and just by the dreamer's side, ranging upward at an angle of forty-five degrees and reached to the moon.

On the second day of March 1834, there was a memorable wedding; his brother George was the Bridegroom and Miss Melsena M. Wood was the happy Bride. This was the first scene of that kind the little nine-year-old boy had ever witnessed. Each family prepared a dinner, first at the Bride's house on Thursday, the next day at the house of the Bridegroom.

The first was called the wedding dinner for it was eaten immediately after the marriage, and the second was called the infare dinner [reception for newlyweds], for it was ready on this occasion at noon of the next day after the marriage, and more people came to that dinner than the little boy ever saw take dinner at one house. The fact is they occupied nearly all the afternoon in eating and clearing up the dishes. When the dinner was all over some of the guests wanted to dance but the bridegroom's Mother said no. They tried various ways to get her consent, but it was no use, she emphatically told them that they could not dance in her house, nor did they. Failing to get her consent, the crowd dispersed with very few relatives to enjoy a good night's repose. This wedding was an enjoyable time for the little people because there were many good things to eat.

Another three months school was taught during the summer and autumn of this year by John Edgar, and the boy was again in school for a portion of the three months term.

On September the fifteenth he became ten years old.

2

Death of Grandfather Slover—Birth of his youngest brother—At the old Mill again with his brother Isaac—Marriage of his sister Katherine—A cousin from Illinois visits his father's family—Harvesting wheat—Mowing hay and taking care of it—His Mother makes nurse of him—His Father's family moves three times in three years—Marriage of his sister Sallie—He is hired out to work—His school facilities during his boyhood.

About the month of May A.D. 1835 his Grandfather Abraham Slover died at the age of eighty-five.[1]

In February of this (1835) year there was a Saturday near the first of the month known for many years after as the cold Saturday. This was the coldest day known to the oldest settler of that country. It became proverbial to that generation. One reason why he so distinctly recollects it is because his youngest brother [Thomas H.] was born the 10th day of the same month.[2]

He was permitted by his father to go to the old mill and stay with his brother Isaac during the latter part of the Summer and early Fall of that year. In the Summer of 1836 his sister Katherine was married to Elie Rainwater, but the boy did not have as many good things to eat as when his brother George got married, because it was a quiet wedding and only a few guests were present.[3]

Either in 1836 or 1837 a cousin came from the State of Illinois to visit the family. His name was Raleigh Slover, a son of the little boy's Uncle Isaac Slover of Effingham County, Ill.

It will be proper to state here, for the benefit of the young, the manner of harvesting wheat in that age of the world. It was cut by hand with a sickle or reaphook. Reapers would cut the width of a space between two rows of corn, or four feet to the man. When they cut a through [swath between rows], they would throw the sickle across their shoulder and bind what they cut. Oats and rye were harvested after the same manner and threshed by hand with an instrument called a flail, or trod out by horses on the ground or a barn-floor and the chaff winnowed out with a heavy sheet from the bed or a light quilt. Two men would use the sheet or quilt and one would stand with a riddle [coarse sieve] or some other vessel and let the grain down before the wind-makers; a little later the wheat fan was brought around, and it was a grand invention for the cleaning of small grain.

East Tennessee being corn country, no great amount of wheat was grown. Corn was pulled off the stalk and thrown in small heaps. The wagon would come, and four men or large boys would take their positions, two on each side, and throw up the heaps into the wagon box and tramp in all they could, then away to the crib or some building designated by the old farmer, where the corn was to be thrown preparatory to a big corn husking which would come off some day before or about Christmas. Very often the landlady would have a quilt ready, so that when the men were invited to husk the corn, the young ladies with their mothers were invited to the quilting. The corn would be husked and the quilt quilted and perhaps a half dozen or less of the men would be half drunk, for it would have been remarkable, for an old farmer to have his corn husking and have no whiskey.

The young men would usually keep sober especially if there were young ladies at the quilting, for they would expect a big play after supper. Sometimes, however, they were defeated in the play because the wife would enter her protest to playing in her house.

Sometimes all the corn except bread for the family and feed for the horses, cows, and hogs would be shelled by hand and sold to the distillery before the winter was gone. While the corn was green and before any frost had come, the blades had to be pulled off and placed in between the stalks so as to make it convenient for binding. This was done at night while the blades were damp after being cured. These blades were in common parlance called "fodder," which made good feed for horses, sheep, and cattle.

Hay was mown by hand with a scythe, and every boy and girl were furnished with a wooden pitchfork, and would fall in line behind the mowers and scatter the mown grass so that it would cure. After it had cured or lain in the hot sun for two days, all the force was called out to rake and shock the hay; then it was drawn to the barn or stack. Timothy,

Herds grass or Red-Top, Meadow grass, and Clover were the principal kinds of grasses of which hay was usually made.

In the fall of 1837 his father rented an upland farm on the north side of the French Broad River, and on the waters of Dumplin Creek, belonging to a certain Robert Miller of Jefferson County, and moved the family to it in the early Spring of the next year.[4] Suffice it to say, they only lived on this farm for two years.

Two or three incidents here deserve notice. It was here that the boy became acquainted with the toothache for the first time in life. At the age of fourteen, he was attacked with a pain in one of his lower teeth, and the pain was so severe that he could scarcely sleep. While he was in the kitchen applying hot ashes to his jaw, the dog called Ring began barking toward the sweet potato patch. He went to the door and hissed him because he heard someone talking in the sweet potatoes, and, as the moon was shining, he could see them go over the fence into the county road. Then, after running a short distance, one of them came back and got upon the rail fence and lifted what seemed to be a basket full of potatoes over the fence and then both of them left. They were no doubt close neighbors, and full-blooded Germans, a man and his wife. They did not have any sweet potatoes growing and a few days later some one or two of the Slover family was passing by their residence and saw the sweet potatoes on a scaffold drying.

After the expiration of two years another move was made, to a house located on that part of a farm called a "Hole in the ground" and belonging to a man by the name of Hays Shaddon, where the year 1840 was spent. Another wedding came off while the family resided here. Our hero's sister Sallie S. was married January or the first days of February 1841. She married a certain John Bettis of Jefferson County. No dinner was prepared; perhaps the reason was the family had to move to another farm about six or eight miles southwest of the "Hole in the ground" belonging to Samuel Langston and located on the county road leading from Dandridge, Jefferson County, to Marysville, Blount County, Tenn., making three moves in about three years.

In March of this year, the now sixteen-year-old boy was hired out to a William Mulvany to work on the farm and assist in running a ferry on the French Broad River, known as Allen Bryant's Ferry. Here he worked one month; the wages was five dollars per month. Beginning on the first day of April at the same wages, he worked for three months for a Baptist preacher by the name of William Ellis of Sevier County, Tenn. Ellis needed help on the farm in the erection of a fine brick dwelling house. Here the big boy had to learn how to handle brick. The first thing, however, was to haul sand for the mortar, and dig a cellar and trenches for the walls of the building. Then began the brick hauling with a team of one yoke of oxen and two horses. He had to drive, while his boss helped to load and unload. They were to haul about one quarter of a mile. Before one week's hauling was done, the big boy's fingers were wore to the quick and one or two of them was bleeding, but Saturday night, Sunday, and Sunday night his mother bound his fingers up with tallow plasters on each one, so that when Monday came he was ready for another week's hauling of brick. The three months ended with the thirtieth day of June which included wheat harvest. The sickle had been superseded by the scythe and cradle.

His school facilities were very meager. His parents being poor, his only education was in subscription schools, which lasted three months in each year, but he was so eager to learn, he would study at night especially the long wintry nights by a pitch pine light while all the family but his mother were in bed and asleep. With an occasional instruction from a young man by the name of James R. Henry (who by the way was a fine man) he mastered Pike's Arithmetic as far as the "Single Rule of Three."[5] A number of teachers never knew anything in figures beyond that point.

3

His religious experience—Conversion—He unites with Dumplin Creek Baptist Church—Has a narrow escape for his life January twelfth 1843—His brother Abraham gets married—The winter fever or Typhoid Pneumonia—His first trip down the Tennessee River on a flat boat—Incidents of his return trip—His brother John gets married—Visits his people in Jefferson County with his sister Elizabeth—Is employed by Randals brothers for six months—Mexican War and why he did not volunteer—In school again.

His first religious impressions were in August A.D. 1842. He and his two younger brothers were sent by their father into the cornfield to pull fodder [gather cornstalks for livestock feed] and they had made one round and was about half way on the next through. He was and had been all the forenoon up to about eleven o'clock doing all he could to teach the little boys ugly words, songs, and profanity. While in the height of his folly, a forcible impression seized his mind, as though someone just over his head had said, "Do you know what you are doing?" It was so convincing that he had no more inclination to pursue his folly any longer nor any inclination to talk or speak to his brothers, but Oh, what! what a burden his thoughts brought upon his heart for in a moment all his past life passed through his thoughts, and every thought was freighted with blackness of darkness and evil and forebodings of eternal fire of torment in the abode of the "Damned."

He could resolve to do better, but these resolutions did not seem to effect any good and [in] about a week's time this remedy was abandoned and he resorted to secret prayer. Every evening as he would seek some secluded spot in the woods to pour out his petitions to the Lord, it seemed that the Devil was at his heels.

There were two camp meetings approaching, either of which was close enough for him to attend, one a Methodist to embrace the third Sunday in September, the other was a Missionary Baptist camp meeting to embrace the first Sunday in October. He wanted to go the Methodist, perhaps because it came off first, and he was so anxious, but his mother, being a Methodist, promised her boy if he would stay and look after the home while she attended her camp meeting, he might go to the other and stay as long as he wanted to. This arrangement suited him very well, for a goodly number of his schoolmates and others of his acquaintances would be there. So Friday before the first Sunday in October rolled around in due time, and he left home after dinner and walked to Dumplin Creek Baptist church.[1]

When the services began that evening, he took a seat in the back part of the house, with his heart burdened with sorrow and trouble, but he was exceedingly timid. When the anxious were invited to the altar or mourners' bench, he trembled and wanted to go, but did not, until Tuesday evening, when the preacher called for mourners. Truly he was one and had been for about six long weeks, and had taken a seat this time near the pulpit. He was standing while the invitation was being extended, and very anxious to be prayed for. Presently a young preacher by the name of Helms started to[ward] him. He thought the young preacher was coming after him, and he immediately started for the mourners' bench, met the preacher as he was advancing, who said to him, "Don't you want religion?" He said "yes," and was conducted to the altar and seated on the end of a bench which was about full of the anxious.

As the young preacher left him, his timidity was in his mind again and such was his feelings that if he could have got out of the house without being seen, he would have fled from the place. But this was not possible. The old fathers in Israel exhorted him and prayed for him, but his trouble only grew more severe. Pretty soon his timidity left him and he began to beg the Lord to have mercy upon his soul, then came the darkest moment of his troubles. He reached a point where he was unconscious of the surroundings; he did not seem to know what was going on, neither in himself nor in the house, but when consciousness returned, his burden of guilt was all gone and his heart was full of joy and delight, mourning was turned to gladness.

He raised his head and the first human face he saw was his own cousin, a married woman, Mrs. Allen. She was singing, and he thought she was the loveliest being he ever beheld, but looking at others they were lovely, too, and even the candles looked new, and so everything looked new. He leaped up with a shout, "Glory to God." When the meeting closed for the night, he went with a friend to his tent to sleep, but before he reached the tent something seemed to whisper, "Now you have gone and done it." He thought: What had he done? The answer came: You have left all your associates in the pleasures of the world. A second thought rolled upon his mind: What a burden of guilt you have just been relieved of. Then his soul was all joy again.

    The next day his friend William Langston accompanied him home, and told his mother what had happened to her boy Jim. She was glad and asked if he had joined the church. On being told that he had not, she said to him, "Wait awhile and perhaps you will go with me." He replied, "Mother, you have made me read the New Testament too much for that."[2] He returned to the meeting on Friday and continued to the end Sunday night, at which evening he joined the church, but was not baptized until April A.D. 1843. Then at the regular meeting embracing the first Sunday in April, C. C. Tipton led the willing young man into the water near said Dumplin Church and immersed him in the name of the Father and the Son and the Holy Ghost. His conversion was to him a joyful change from the love and condemnation of sin to the love and service of God.

His father left the Samuel Langston farm and moved the family about three miles to a farm known as the Henry farm. Here four of the family were attacked at once with the "Winter fever" or Typhoid Pneumonia, and the mother was sick with one of her old complaints, called in that day "Liver complaint," so the five had to be looked after by the young man. More than once he had to ride fourteen miles at night for the Doctor and no two of the patients took the same medicine. In March the young man was prostrated with the same complaint; fortunately the others had got able to nurse him. For three long weeks it seemed that it was hard to tell which way the scale would turn, but soon he began to mend; and in a few weeks was all right again.

    In March 1845, Abraham Slover was married to a Mary Calihan who was raised by her Grandfather (Thomas Underwood); she was an amiable young woman.[3] His Mother prepared a nice "infare dinner," and all went off nicely.

In the fall of 1845 the young man reached his majority, and in November after he was twenty-one years old he was employed as a cook on a flat boat for nine men; this was his first trip down the river. These large boats were built principally in East Tennessee waters for the purposes of freighting cotton from Alabama to New Orleans.[4]

The builders would hire some mountain-boomer to get out gunnels [also gunwale; upper edge of a boat] and deliver them to the building place or boat-yard. The gunnels were from ninety to one hundred feet long and from four to five feet wide at the stump end and as large at the other end as the timber would make; it was necessary that they be six inches thick. To make these gunnels the tree is fallen to the best advantage to handle and then measured, cut or sawed off, the bark blazed off the top side, lined from one end to the other, turned over and the other side down the same way. Then it is split in the center; however, it is first hewn on each side until it is one foot thick, so when open the two edges are to hew [even in thickness] and the splinters to dress off on the inside of each piece. Then they are ready to draw to the river.

The builders frame the gunnels with strong sawn timbers, with the bottom side of the gunnels up, then a four-inch "rabbit" [rabbet, a notch in a board] is cut two inches deep on the inside edge of each gunnel. The water floor is pinned on out of two-inch boards twenty feet long. It is constructed on skids on the bank of the river close by deep water. The bottom is caulked, then launched into the river. A foot board is spiked on the outer edge of the gunnel and about two tons of dry dirt is placed all along on the bottom or as much as the foot board will secure. When a sufficient quantity of dirt is on, about ten or a dozen notches are cut in the top edge of the foot board, for the admission of water to saturate the dirt; this causes that edge of the boat to sink in the deep water and the current turns it over, then the water is bailed out.

Studding is mortised into the gunnels two inches from the outer edge of the gunnel and a two-inch board one foot wide is pinned to the studding resting on the gunnel, and the joint caulked like the bottom. The studding is usually ten feet long. A flat roof is put on, raised in the center so as to shed the water or rain.

For one of these ninety-five-feet boats, a pine tree, about twelve or fifteen inches in diameter at the stump and about eighty feet long and not more than six or seven inches in diameter at the top end, is hung on a roller prepared on top of the steam end for that purpose. A two-inch strong board twenty feet long is pinned on the top end and a two-by-four scantling is securely pinned to the stump end of sufficient length to balance the little tree. This is the steering oar, the paddle end floating in the water.

To enable one of these large boats to pass over the Muscle Shoals, fifty miles below Decatur in the State of Alabama, requires a smaller boat seventy-five or eighty feet long, in every other respect constructed like the larger ones; these are called lighters.[5] The party with whom the young man was engaged had two of these large boats and two lighters; a large and a small one were lashed together, and a Pilot placed in charge with three strong men inside to use the side oars. Sometimes it was necessary to double on one or the other of the side oars, hence the extra man. In good water all four boats could be lashed together and float day and night.

There was a fireplace constructed in one of the lighters where they would always find the Cook [Slover], except when the boats would run aground. Then the Pilot would cry out for all hands and the Cook, and once the hands had to pull the Cook in at the bailing hole to save him from deeper water than he could wade in.

The water was low and the weather cold in November. Boatmen called it a hand-spike tide, because when the boat run aground hand-spikes were used to pry it off. Suffice it to say, Gunter's Landing was finally reached in about thirty-five or thirty-six days.[6] A return deck passage was secured for some of the hands, among them was the Cook; he was to work his passage on the steamboat loaded with cotton bound for Knoxville, East Tennessee. When the steamer reached the point called the "Suck," there was a canal without locks for steamers to pass up through this hazardous place.[7]

The Captain had to use the capstan, and "cordell," as it was called in those days. This is done by [using] an iron-bound upright beam with lever holes in it and a strong lever in each hole. A strong cable or rope was made fast on the shore in a huge ring and steeple, firmly fixed in great massive rocks which had been exhumed by the floods of water hundreds of years ago, and the other end placed about twice around the capstan. With one man to hold and coil the slack of the rope, six or eight men pushed on the levers; thus with the help of an engine the steamer would move up the canal. The last rope laid was a three-inch cable but an old one. Now just as the steamer was passing the last hard pull, this old cable severed and as quick as thought, the steamer shot back down the straight passage. The Pilot was at his post or wheel and held her straight, so that she ran stern foremost into the boiling pot below, where it was checked up and another pull was made, but no more old cables were laid but new ones, and the passage was made at the head of the canal about nine o'clock P.M.

It was a very cold night a few days before Christmas. Owing to low water it was about as difficult for the old steamer to make headway as it had been for the flat boats to go down stream. At every shallow bar she had to have help of some kind to drag her over and into deep water. Finally Caney Creek Shoals were reached; these Shoals were near the mouth of a stream of water of the same name. Here she was aground again in early morning. Twenty-one bales of cotton had to be removed ashore before she floated; then this cotton had to be freighted on hired wagons a distance of three miles and reloaded on the Steamer. Seeing what had to be done, the young boatsman proposed to another deck passenger to go ashore and walk, as they had made a favorable acquaintance with each other on the steamer and would be company together as far as Knoxville, which was forty miles east of Kingston in Roane County, where the two agreed to foot it home.

The young boatsman needed new shoes which he purchased in Kingston and put them on immediately, and Mr. King, his new friend, and he took the road about eleven o'clock A.M. of a rather gloomy day. When night came, they had made nineteen miles and stopped at a farm house for the night, tired and footsore. The young boatsman called for hot water for his feet and they both had a good footbath and felt relieved somewhat of the soreness.

Next day neither of them felt like they could walk. The family sympathized with their guests, bills were settled, and the road was again tried. They hadn't gone but a mile when it began to rain and just then a large empty wagon came up going to Knoxville. One of them inquired of the teamster the distance to the city and learned that it was nineteen miles and also ascertained that they could ride all the way for ten cents apiece. It was at once paid and the wagon boarded. About four o'clock P.M. the city was reached and the travelers separated.

The young boatsman was soon across the Holston River, and on the road to his home. He was invited to ride behind a man going the same way and for two or three miles he did so. After reaching the home of the gentleman who showed the kindness to let the boatsman ride, he started on tired and lonely in the sprinkle of rain.

It was dark as one of those lonely Tennessee hollows could be of a moonless night, and after plodding his way up that hollow for a quarter of a mile or more, he concluded to turn back to a farm house at the lower end of the hollow, but directly he heard horses' feet coming towards him. As the sound drew nearer, he discovered that there were two persons and a female voice was one of the two. As quick as they came close enough he hailed them, and told them the circumstances that brought him there on that strange road. The lady said, "You can go to my father's and stay all night. It is seven miles, and my little brother-in-law on that horse can ride behind me, and you can ride his horse." The boatsman got into the saddle, and during the seven-mile ride he learned that her father was an old boatsman.

Finally her father's gate was reached and he was called out and told that she had picked up a young boatsman on the road and that he wanted to stop over night. The old gentleman spoke kindly to the young boatsman and invited him in. His name was Hinds. This was Christmas Eve and the old gentleman felt glad to have a boatsman to spin his yarns to, for he had navigated the same waters in the days of yore.

He and his lovely wife were alone, and he had a lot of eggnog already made; of course it had whiskey in it. He insisted on his guest drinking it with him, but Slover told the old host that he never had drank eggnog in all his past life, and had quit the use of intoxicants for more than three years. Hinds still persisted that his guest should taste the eggnog, saying, "If you never drank any, you don't know how good it is." To gratify his lordship he drank about two spoonsful, but did not think with his host that it was good, for to his taste it was not. Suffice it to say that he was well taken care of free of charge, had a good supper, bed and breakfast, and held pleasant conversation with the host and hostess. After thanking them for such kindness, he gave them a parting shake of the hand, and left for home.

The young boatsman wended his way down the hill into the county road; within sight of her father's old mansion was a neat little cottage which was the home of his daughter that had picked up the boatsman and cared for him the night before until her father's house was reached. She was out in the yard to see the young man pass, and he again thanked her for her kindness shown to him. She was glad when he told her that he had been kindly treated at her father's, and wished him a safe journey home. He thanked her and bid her farewell. The eighteen miles that lay between the young man and his mother was soon measured on that Christmas day by the weary feet of the young boatsman who, reaching home sometime in the afternoon, found his mother enjoying good health &c.

In January A.D. 1846, his brother John got married to a Miss Adaline Wood, half sister to his brother George's wife.[8]

The young man had made an arrangement with Richard and James Randals to work for them six months at six dollars and fifty cents per month. He stayed and labored at several kinds of work. Some days he would run the water power sawmill, cut saw logs in the woods, plow and plant corn, and whatever else was to do on the farm or at the sawmill.

This was the year that President James H. Polk called for volunteers to go to the war with Mexico.⁹ In April at the Battalion Muster ground Col. Dougan appeared with a sixteen-year-old boy, a friend of his, and after throwing the Battalion of five hundred men into a hollow square, the Major was ordered by the Colonel to open one of the lines so that they could enter the open space inside the Battalion. They entered and the Colonel made a short speech about the war. He then told the Battalion that as he and the boy Captain marched around the square followed by the band, as many as would volunteer might break ranks and fall in double column and follow the music.¹⁰

Owing to the intended Captain's nonage [minor status], there were but few of the men enlisted. Had the intended Captain been a man instead of a sixteen-year-old boy, James A. Slover would have answered the call of his Country by breaking ranks and following the band, a volunteer for the Mexican War. But he did not want to be put in the line of battle by that boy. Sure enough, when the Captain boy, as he was called, reached the front and was ordered into line to face the Mexicans, he fled and hid behind the sand hills, and his men were scattered—or at least such was the report that came back to East Tennessee.

When the six months labor with the Randals closed, they could not pay him and he took their note drawing six percent interest from date. To get the money he had to discount it 25 percent or in other words take seventy-five cents on the dollar. He then taught a three months school embracing August, September, and October.¹¹

Then he entered an old field school, taught by one Tobias Lanning, for two months, then changed teachers, also schoolhouses. The first of January 1847 he entered another one of those schools, taught by a certain Alexander Caldwell, a very fine teacher and a gentleman. Here was his first start to study English grammar; he was in this school two months only.

4

His call to the Ministry—Enters Black Oak Grove Seminary near Mossy Creek in Jefferson County, East Tennessee, early in March 1847—Is captured by a young lady, a farmer's daughter—Courtship by letter after leaving the Seminary—His prospects frustrated by the young lady's father—Seeks the heart and hand of another and is married January the seventeenth 1850—Teaches school—Is present at execution of a Negro man in Dandridge—Concludes to go West to Arkansas with his friend Samuel Cook—The building of a flat boat for emigration—Some of the incidents while making the long trip by water—Detained at Van Buren on account of sickness—Reaches Washington County in October—Again in the school room with the "Toothpickers" so-called—Is ordained to the field work of the Gospel Ministry in June 1853—Revivals of that year—Is called to the Pastorate of Missionary Chapel Church—Again in the school room—Teaches his last school in 1856.

Very soon after his baptism in April 1843 he was impressed to take hold of church work, and his Pastor put him forward in the prayer meeting, that is, called on him to pray in public. He answered by kneeling down in the congregation and trying to pray and has never regretted the effort. He is and always was a very conscientious Christian man, so about the time he was twenty-one his mind was exercised very much upon a permanent occupation. As the different kinds of occupations rolled across his active brain, impressions to preach the gospel were very forcible, but then, the human weakness would seem, in his judgement, to stupefy those impressions when he contemplated his inability, his ignorance, and a dozen and one obstacles he would put up as objections. He was naturally inclined to education and was determined to secure at least an English education [as distinct from the sciences] if possible.

Finally his Pastor (Caswell C. Tipton) suggested a plan for him to attend a five months session of school at the Black Oak Grove Seminary fifteen or twenty miles from his home, and located near Mossy Creek [now Jefferson City] in Jefferson County, East Tennessee. He accepted his Pastor's proposal and in the first days of March he took up the line of march for his Pastor's residence as a boarding place while he would attend the high school.

In this school he studied English Grammar, Arithmetic, Geography, Reading, and Spelling or Orthography for four months only and at the close of the term he obtained a certificate from the Teacher certifying that he was competent to teach the above named branches together with writing. The school was closed at the end of four months instead of five, because the teacher punished a grown daughter of one of the principal Directors of the school. Thus ended the young man's education.

He took a subscription school in the fall of 1847 as his first school after leaving the Black Oak Grove Seminary. Such general satisfaction was rendered that he taught in the same neighborhood for two years longer, winter and summer, but never could get money enough ahead to go to College. From a moral standpoint he has long since come to the conclusion that it was better for him that he did not get to College. "And we know that all things work together for good to them that love God, to them who are called according to his purpose."

About a month after entering the Black Oak Grove Seminary he was introduced to a Miss Odel by the Preacher's daughter Martha Tipton. Miss Odel had two sisters and a small brother attending the same seminary. He first met her at the residence of the Rev. C. C. Tipton, where he and another young man by the name of Henry Cate were boarding. Miss Tipton had invited her to come on a certain Saturday to assist her and her mother in finishing a quilt that they had in the frames for several days. On that Saturday, about the first of April, she was made known to him as Maggie Odel.

Whether the arrangement was intended as one of love or not, it resulted in the complete capture of the young student's heart in less time than it could be written by the quickest short hand writer, and to all human appearance the fire of love was mutual. She therefore became his intimate associate, going to and coming from Sunday School and church during his stay at school, and then for more than two years afterward, by a mutual written correspondence until her father got into the secret. He was bitterly opposed to the young man's visits with her.

Whatever was the nature of his opposition, the young man never was informed, but such was the father's antipathy that he even threatened to drive him away should he ever come back. The young man went back all the same more than once after being told what her father had threatened to do. Nevertheless a visit in August of 1849 convinced him of the fact that she intended to abide by what her father advised, for her father was so disgusted with the young man's presence that he would not so much as come into the house when he was talking to Maggie.

A move to Arkansas had been suggested to the young man by his friend [Samuel] Cook sometime previous to this visit with Maggie, who, knowing how her father felt toward the young man's presence with his daughter, told him about it, that same Saturday afternoon. He replied that he was sorry that her father opposed her doing as her father had done in "marrying the woman he loved," but the opposition of her father would not be in the way if she would consent to go to Arkansas with him. After a few minutes meditation she proposed to defer her answer for two months, as the young man had two months of a school to finish in Sevier County. Before his departure he impressed the fact upon her mind that the whole matter was with her, that he was faithful to his promise. So he bid her farewell, also stepped into another room to give her mother a farewell shake of the hand. The mother, by the way, was a fine Christian-hearted woman and thought well of Maggie's beau.

Revolving the situation over and over again as he rode away from the old farm house, he wondered what Maggie's answer would be two months hence. Finally his cogitations settled down, determined to abide by her answer, be it what it might.

His school ran through September and October. On the ninth of November was the time fixed by the Court for the hanging of a Mulatto man in Dandridge, the county seat of Jefferson County, to which the young man desired to go. He therefore deferred his visit to Mossy Creek (where Maggie lived) until that time.

Now since the execution of criminals by hanging was then and there so widely different to what it is here on the Pacific Slope, he deems a graphic description of that event of importance just here. Reaching Dandridge in due time Friday morning, the ninth day of November, 1849, he saw more people than he had ever seen in any town previous to that day, but it was his business to watch the movements of the Sheriff and his posse. In due time that officer approached the jail with a hundred armed men following a cart or wagon drawn (he thinks) by two black horses. The vehicle was backed up to the Prison door, the hundred men forming two columns about twelve feet apart. Suddenly the Sheriff emerged from the Prison door with the prisoner arrayed in a long white shroud as white as bleached muslin could be made and he was seated on his coffin. A young Baptist Minister, Rodgers by name, was seated by his side.

When all was ready, the Sheriff ordered a march. The cart and the guard on foot took up the line of march for a distance of one and a quarter miles, to one of those noted Sink-holes, as such basins in that country were called. On reaching the place of execution there were about five thousand human beings assembled in that Sink-hole, men, women, and children of all sizes, black and white. The guard formed a hollow square around the gallows pole. The prisoner had requested the Sheriff not to break his neck, so all the platform that was erected was goods boxes with an elevated seat and stand for the Preachers and the Prisoner to sit down. There were but five men besides the prisoner inside of the guard, that is two Preachers, one Doctor, the Sheriff, and his Deputy.

About noon Rev. Rodgers, Pastor of the First Baptist Church of Dandridge, arose and announced his text in the following words, "The wages of sin is death but the gift of God is eternal life through Jesus Christ our Lord." He preached for nearly one hour.

The prisoner talked a few minutes, neither denied nor confessed his guilt; his crime was that of rape committed on a white woman. Precisely at one o'clock four men lifted the board on which the condemned man stood while the fifth man removed the boxes and the sixth one swung out to into eternity. He swung there by the neck fifty-nine minutes, then he was cut down and the Doctor tried or pretended to try to bring him to life again but it was a failure. He was dead.

In a short time the mass of human beings dispersed and the scene was over. The young man, alone and solemnly impressed with what he had seen, wended his way to the residence of his old pastor as a stopping place for that ghostly night, for when dark came, anywhere that he would go in the dark he was confronted with that white shroud dangling in the air. Even in his bedroom, when he would put out the candle, there it was as plain as could be by imagination, for he knew that it was nothing more than a phantom caused by the impressions made upon his mind by the hanging he had witnessed that day.

He did not see Maggie until Sunday, the eleventh day of the month. Her answer was given, after two months' meditation, at her father's gate for he met her at church and accompanied her home. However, he did not go inside the front gate. She told the young man that she had concluded not to go with him against the will of her father. Being prepared for whatever decision she should come to, he said, "Well!" Now said he, "Maggie, when you do marry, be sure that you marry a man because you love him." She replied, with tears in her large blue eyes, "I never expect to marry." He replied, "You will perhaps change your notion." He bid her farewell and made his way back to his old Pastor's residence where he had left his saddle horse. Thus ended his first courtship.

Suffice it to say she did marry and was not a great while about it, either. They had acted friendly and parted the same way. Now after that Sunday afternoon they were free from all prior obligations.

His Father's family had moved from the Lanning farm to a farm that was known as Jessee Langston's farm, about two miles directly east and on the same big road, making the move in the winter of 1846 and 1847, where they resided until March 1848.

Having finished the five months school as stated, there was a plan started to secure his services during the spring and summer. Dumplin Creek divided the neighborhood into north and south sides. Each side had a schoolhouse, but neither could make school sufficient to justify the young man to teach. To settle the question as to which side would have the school, two school articles were drawn up by the teacher, exactly similar, with the understanding that the one having the largest number subscribed was to have the school. When each side of the creek was canvassed, it was found that the south side had the greater number. This located the teacher in a new neighborhood, to begin his school on the twenty-fourth day of April 1848.

His Father's family had concluded to move to Long Savanna Creek in Hamilton County, East Tennessee, and the teacher was desirous for a visit to Northeastern Georgia to see his brother, G[eorge]. W. Slover. Accordingly passage was secured on one of those flat boats as described earlier in these pages. A move was made to the boat lying cabled at Underdown's Ferry at the mouth of Dumplin Creek, and about the 10th of March the boat was set afloat for Blue Springs Landing where the teacher's Father and family disembarked. The teacher continued on board to Chattanooga, where he left the boat and walked to Tiger Creek in Georgia near Ringgold. He spent three or four weeks visiting his brother's family, then turned his steps toward Sevier County, Tenn., by the way of Long Savanna Creek to see his Father's family. On reaching their home in that new place he found his Mother prostrated on a bed of affliction, from which she never recovered.

This was a time of trial for the teacher; he had to leave his Mother or lose his school, and thinking her complaint was one of her old spells and that she would be up in a few days, he bid her good bye and was off for his boarding house, Payne McClerry's in Sevier County. About the last week in May his Father notified him of the death of his Mother. She died May twenty-second 1848, and, among other things, his father said, "She died as she lived." Knowing something of the way she lived religiously, he was satisfied that his loss was her eternal gain.

On the twenty-fourth day of April he began his school as per contract, with about forty students, and taught in the same house three five-months and one seven-months sessions, finishing about the first of November 1849.[1]

At this time he began to seek the heart of one of his students with whom he had been acquainted for four or five years. She had been his pupil for two years, and was the oldest daughter of a widow, Elizabeth Ingram. The young woman's name was Harriet M. The young man had formed a good opinion of this girl when she was sixteen years old. She was now nineteen. They were united as husband and wife by Samuel Cook Esq. on the seventeenth day of January 1850 at the residence of her mother.[2]

The long-agitated subject of emigrating to Arkansas was made a fixture at the end of his school in November previous to his marriage. The trip was to be made by water as far as Van Buren, Ark., then across the Boston Mountain by team and wagon to Washington County.[3] A house to float on the French Broad River was to be built. A point on the north side of the river, and near the residence of Cook Esq., was selected as a building place. The size of the craft was to be fifty by twenty feet, and eight feet high on top of the gunnels, making the rooms ten feet high inside.

The material was all soon put on the ground and a few days after the young man's wedding, the boat was ready for turning. As they anticipated being towed up the Arkansas River by a steamer, the boat was raked at both ends, which, when it was pushed into the water, made it hard to handle. They could not move it up stream at all, so with a grapevine for a cable they loaded on the dirt and notched the top edge of the boards that held it. The boat turned far enough to be on edge, struck bottom and back it went bottomside up. It floated around and broke the grapevine cable, and down the river it went to a shoal just above what was called the "Hanging Rock," rather a dangerous point to pass with boats. There it stopped, and seemed to grow fast to the bottom in water about two feet deep.

The weather threatened rain and consequently a rise in the river. So they got together about nine or ten men and went into the water with handspikes to try to move the boat but not one inch could it be moved—the air was all gone from beneath and it consequently stuck to the bottom. They then procured two strong ropes and erected a couple of windlasses on the bank. They made the ropes fast to the gunnel farthest out in the water, for it was located horizontally with the bank, and worked the other end around the windlass, but the bottom of the river still held the boat. It held it for several days.

The parties were about at the end of their wits when one of the men suggested that a blacksmith bellows would have to be erected on the bottom of the boat in order to force the air underneath the stuck boat. The suggestion created a smile in the crowd of men, but his head was level. They erected the bellows and had nine men on the boat's bottom, with a canoe lashed beside the boat as a life boat. All hands being ready, the newly married young man began to blow the bellows, and to the astonishment of all, the boat rose as the wind was forced underneath, and deliberately floated. Bearing up the nine men, it passed the hazardous rock and four miles down the river to Brabsone Ferry where there was thirty feet water, and was soon right side up. The water bailed out, the generous crowd pushed it back home with poles.

The canoe was a borrowed one and had to go home late in the afternoon, so the newly married young man had to go down the river by that ugly "Hanging Rock" in that canoe alone. Before he got control of the little craft after passing the "Rock," it took a sheer by the blowing of the wind, against his wishes, and run under a willow brush. Had he failed to throw down his paddle and lay flat down on the bottom of the water craft and let it go at the mercy of the waves, he would have been drug overboard in deep water and doubtless never would have got out. And it would never have been known whether he was accidently drowned or had committed suicide by drowning, but he reached his wife's house about one hour after dark all right.

In about one week's time the boat was finished, ready for occupancy, and the parties moved in, consisting of Samuel Cook, wife and seven children—one, however, was a bound boy about fifteen years old; Moses Knight, wife and one or two children; the newly married man, wife, her mother, three children, and her mother's brother (Murrow Scruggs)—eighteen or nineteen souls all told, and all bound for Arkansas but the Knight family.

On Friday, February the fifteenth, 1850, the boat was uncabled and a start was made. All was cheerful as could be expected of a company of men, women, and children leaving their native state. In a few days this boat was joined by another similar one from a few miles higher up the same river, and occupied by Allen Bryant and family bound for Missouri. Then after floating into the Tennessee River, they were reinforced by two other moving boats, also going to Missouri, but would be company for each other as far at the mouth of the Tennessee River, at Paducah in Kentucky. The last named addition had a music teacher on board and several music books, and others of the boats had some books also. More or less of the company were religious and a goodly number of the young people were pretty good singers, so that when they were in good water, especially on Sunday, they would make melody and those that could not sing were delighted with the singing. This was the order of the day for amusement, except when in uncertain water; then all hands were on the alert and ready for every and any emergency, especially in waters where a Pilot had to be employed to take the boats over, as at the Suck and Muscle Shoals. Consequently, while the company was together, they made the trip that far very pleasant by being social and friendly as well as singing.

Some of the incidents occurring during the nine weeks journey on the water will be of interest. When the Cook and Slover boat arrived at the Blue Spring Landing fifty miles above Chattanooga in Hamilton County, Tenn., the newly married couple made a trip on foot four miles to visit the young man's father and family, going one day and returning the next; it was a hard trip on the little woman, his wife not being accustomed to making so long journeys on foot and, having been shut in the boat nine or ten days, her feet were blistered and limbs sore.

Those left in the boat thought it hard to have to lie ashore for a day and a half but he got to see his Father, two sisters, and two brothers, and one brother-in-law, and was told that his youngest sister (Rachel Jane) was to be married in about a week afterward to W[illiam]. B. Bettis of Hamilton County, Tenn.[4]

The next place on the river of note was the "Suck," or where the river passes through the Lookout Mountain.[5] It is rightly named, especially when viewed from a flat boat sailing down the river while passing through the mountain. On the south side was then a stage road, and it was so high above the water that a Concord four-horse stage looked to be about the size of a common one-horse top buggy. The next rough water below the Suck is the "Boiling Pot" where the river widens out to about twice the width of the Suck above and the whole of the channel is rolling and boiling up as though it was hot sure enough.

It is said that a Pilot got off the shoot in this water (attempting to pass it at night), and his boat circled around the Boiling Pot. On the south side was a house and there was a dance in that house on this particular night. One of the boat hands heard the music and dancing. As the boat would make its regular trips around in the "Pot," of course it passed the house every time. He said, "They are dancing in every house we pass."[6]

The next place below the Pot is the "Skillet Handle." The water is not very rough at this place. The next and last of the passage through this Lookout Mountain is the "Frying Pan," where the water blubbers similar to a frying pan when frying doughnuts in plenty of lard.

After passing all four of these traditional localities, the river spreads itself out to about six or seven hundred yards in width and calms down to a deep and smooth body of water. Gunter's Landing was the next place of any note, which is in Alabama; Decatur and Whitesburg were the [other] towns of any note between the Lookout Mountain and the Muscle Shoals. These water crafts stopped at Whitesburg or Dittoes Landing and employed a Pilot to take them over these Shoals. Perhaps these Shoals are the most noted for wrecking flat boats of any place on the Tennessee River. The water spreads out to a width of two and one half or three miles, while fifty miles above at Decatur the river is not more than one half mile wide and when it rises at Decatur one foot, on the Shoals it will raise one inch. This phenomena was closely observed by cotton freighters in those days.

Having employed a man by the name of Crow as the Pilot for the four boats at seven dollars per boat, the boats were then moved down to a point designated by the Pilot, and separated into pairs and each pair was lashed with ropes closely together. The Cook and Slover boat was lashed with Allen Bryant's boat. The Pilot then told the newly married man that he wanted him to handle one of the steering oars, and if any of the young women wished to set on top of the boat, they could take chairs up for them. There were but two; the wife of Slover and a daughter of Mr. Cook took seats on top to see the sights.

The distance by water was much further than by land from the starting point to Florence Bridge below the Shoals. It took two days for the Pilot to complete the job. Suffice it to say, he landed each pair safely at the bridge below the Shoal. Only the women on top the boat got the water thrown upon them as the boats passed "Greens Bluff," which was considered the most difficult point to pass on the Shoals.

The balance of the Tennessee River was as a general thing nice going except the last hundred miles which was back water from the Ohio. The boats had to run by the use of the side oars over this hundred miles. Arriving at Paducah, every boat took its own way, and a final separation took place.

Alone the Cook and Slover boat sailed out on the bosom of the grand old Ohio River, almost bank full, and pulled over to the Illinois side to take in the seeing of a sawmill running by steam power, the first sight of the kind that any one of that boat-load had ever seen.[7]

At the mouth of the Ohio is Cairo. The whole city was submerged in water, and the country also for fifteen miles. Here the little boat entered the "Father of American Waters," the Mississippi. The wind blew the boat ashore on Island Number Ten at a point where the high banks were daily caving in.[8] In a short time after landing, a cottonwood tree fell—when the bank caved—across the steering oar of the little boat, striking it just behind the boat, and the water was so deep that the tree sank the long steering oar and slid off, doing the oar no harm, but had it fell directly across the boat, it would have smashed it and killed more or less of the inmates, and the survivors would have been left on the Island.

Soon after leaving Island Number Ten, they hauled in at the City of Memphis where the craft landed and several of the emigrants walked upon the bluff to visit the city. Here was the last sight of Tennessee soil; on the opposite side of the great river was Arkansas dirt, the first of the State that the emigrants had ever seen. After leaving Memphis, Helena City loomed in sight, the first Arkansas city that ever greeted the eyes of these Tennessee home-seekers.

Some distance below Helena, Alpha Cook was taken bedfast with pneumonia, and it was necessary to cross the river for a Doctor. The task of rowing a little skiff across the river fell on Slover. The Doctor was found at home and was soon in the little yawl, with the sun almost gone down and that great river to cross as quick as possible. When the bank was reached, the doctor said, "You are about one and a half miles below your boat." And it was after dark, up the river along the brush until the sick girl was reached. This was an incident with all the fun knocked out of it, but hard work was woven into the trip. The Doctor stopped in the boat all night, then another trip was made across the river to take him home—the girl got well.

The boat soon sped away for Napolian at the mouth of the Arkansas River. Again the wind blew a gale quartering down stream, and the boat had to go ashore. Cook was on top at the steering oar and Slover took the short cable, and the only land in sight at that place was about two feet around a pine stump. Slover made a leap for that spot that he might be able to get the rope made fast around the pine stump. The bark being off, the stump wet from a mist that was falling, and the rope short, he failed to fasten the cable, and away went the boat, leaving him at the stump with the river on one side and a slough full of water and drift-wood on the other. The boat floated around an old log fast on the shore and projecting quite a ways out in the river, causing an eddy and a semicircle in the bank, and was landed and fastened, but the newly married man was still at the stump about fifty yards above and no way to cross the slough but to wade and no means to ascertain the depth of the water. He was not long in determining what to do, so into the water he went, cold as it was in March. It was pretty deep wading but by the help of the logs which were afloat on the surface of the water, he made the shore.

But this is only half the joke of that landing. Just about the time the wet man had changed his clothes, Mr. Cook had walked ashore on the old barkless log which projected quite a ways out in the river. He was returning into the boat when both his feet slid off the slick log and down he went to the bottom—head and ears all went out of sight. Directly up he came, seized the old log and managed to get on it and as he did so exclaimed, "Slover, that's twenty feet deep."

Cook had laughed at the cableman's misfortune a few minutes before his plunge changed the scene, and all were at liberty to laugh at his calamity.

Finally the long looked for City of Napolian at the mouth of the Arkansas River was reached about the twelfth of April. It, like Cairo, was all under water. The fact was soon learned that the hope of being towed up to Van Buren was vain. Therefore the boat had to be disposed of at whatever the Napolianites saw fit to give. Ten dollars was the best bid made, although the material cost the builders about fifty dollars, but such is the world when they have a man where he cannot help himself. The first steamboat that was bound for Van Buren that came after the sale of the partnership craft was boarded, fare settled, and in a few hours an up stream move was made. A last long look at the little boat which had been the dwelling of the emigrants for more than eight weeks were made as the Steamer wheeled the home-seekers out of sight.

Little Rock, the Capital of the State, was reached at about five o'clock P.M. Mrs. Ingram went ashore to spend the night with relatives, and about noon the next day she took sick. On Thursday, the eighteenth day of April, the steamer pulled in at Van Buren, and the sick woman had to be carried ashore on her bed and had to undergo a long siege of sickness under Dr. Brown, then resident Doctor of the town.

Consequently, the Cook family made their way to Washington County.

Being detained at Van Buren on account of sickness in the Ingram family, it was not long until the young preacher Slover [here Slover starts referring to himself as "Preacher"] was employed by G. W. Knox, along with his two little brothers-in-law, Isaac and James Ingram, to go eight miles below Van Buren and on the south side of the Arkansas River, to attend a wood yard and cultivate or plow a thirty-acre field of corn which had been planted by another man who had deliberately gone from the place. Wages as well as everything else was very low; the three worked for twenty dollars a month and worked three months. Mrs. Ingram recovered her health in the meantime and moved down to the same house, and in July her brother Murrow Scruggs bought one hundred and sixty acres of land from Mr. Knox, including the wood yard, field, and house with the growing crop of corn for fourteen hundred dollars spot cash.

In August the young Preacher started for Washington County (the county for which he was bound when he left Tennessee) in company with a gentleman and his wife going to Missouri on a visit. The man had a two-horse team, and one of the horses had never been worked but little. The second day it fagged out and the Preacher and wife with their effects had to stop off. They were dumped off at the house of an old man by the name of Kirk, and in a few days the Preacher bought an improvement on forty acres of Government land with a growing crop of corn and cotton from Hampton Kirk, a son of the old man named above.

Not long after making the purchase Slover took the chills. Kirk made a trip to Madison County, under pretense of seeking a location to move to, but returned in about six weeks and unbeknown to the Preacher, he went to the Land Office and entered the land upon which the improvements were that he had sold to the young Preacher six or eight weeks before.

Such an act was too mean and low down for any gentleman to be guilty of. The fact is none but a thief would do such an act, for he took the money that he got from the Preacher and entered him out of a house to live in, but the poor guilty pup came to tell the Preacher what he had done. He returned all the property, that is a gun, saddle and bridle, that was given in the trade, and he gave a saddle horse, which he valued at sixty dollars, in lieu of the amount of money paid him in the trade. Of course the Preacher was at the mercy of the scoundrel and had to take what he offered. Then in the month of October his friend Cook, having knowledge of the facts, came down with his team and wagon and hauled the Preacher's and Mrs. Ingram's family to Washington County.

5

His first school in Arkansas—The character of this school—School closes with little credit to teacher and less to the Patrons—A new field sought—Teaches a summer term of five months and cultivates a small farm—The new location—Finds a Baptist church—His wife is baptized—Buys a young black mare as a saddle animal for his wife—The mare threw her Mistress—Also her sister—Smart "Ellicks" and Wise-acres—Locates near Elm Spring on forty acres of Government land—Enters the same under the graduation law—Again in the school room—His first child is born—Changes his church relationship—Is ordained to the full work of the Ministry—A protracted meeting is held—Good results—Is met, at Mount Zion Association, by a delegation from Missionary Chapel Church—Becomes its pastor—Compelled to teach school again—Secures a good school near Evansville—His second child is born there—Returns to his little farm in January 1856—Teaches his last school in that year—Incidents at Latties schoolhouse.

He resumed teaching after a respite from the school room for twelve months. Through the influence of his friend Cook, a three or four months subscription school was made, but he soon found that he was not teaching in East Tennessee.[1] The students were, as a whole, good as other or Tennessee children were, but the parents were more like a hornets' nest when a school boy would throw a finger stone into it, than anything else that they could be compared to. So he was very glad when the term ended.

Some of the patrons either had the "Bighead," or extremely little heads—so extremely little that they thought they had a soft head for an instructor of their children. One of them had an old sow that had a defective head, caused no one knew how. Yet as he defect became a running sore, he fattened her, but the head didn't heal. He told his neighbors that he intended to pay his school subscription with that hog. The teacher got wind of the diseased hog as well as the intentions of the owner. Sure enough, about hog-killing time or Christmas, here he came with the porker already dressed with the bad place on the side of the head smelling badly. He had to take the hog back home with him, for the teacher would not receive it. The school closed with very little credit for either the teacher or the patrons.

Now a new field had to be sought for spring and summer employment. He made a trip to a neighborhood known as Walnut Grove southwest of Fayetteville, the county seat of Washington County. He learned that they desired a school to be taught during the spring and summer; also he found a small farm to let, belonging to a widow Johnson. A subscription school was soon made and the small farm rented, which suited the teacher. The widow had a boy at home about fifteen years old that could be hired at seven dollars per month to do the plowing. His services were secured. The teacher then returned, got his wife and household goods, and moved to Walnut Grove early in March 1851, and located in one room of Mrs. Johnson's dwelling house. The land was all put in oats and corn by the tenth of April, and about the middle of the same month the school begun. This was decidedly a better neighborhood than where he taught his first school in Arkansas. He made a fine crop of corn and oats and taught a No. One good school for five months.

He had his church letter from Dumplin Creek church, East Tennessee, and there was a Baptist Church about nine miles away on the waters of the west fork of the White River, so he sought and obtained membership by giving the church the letter.[2] In the fall of the year, his wife, who had been a Methodist, joined. A place was sought in the west fork of White River where there was sufficient water to baptize her, and C. H. Boatright immersed her.

Sometime during the Summer he bought a young black mare three years old and broke her to ride, then gave her to his wife as her riding animal. In the month of September she rode the mare to a protracted meeting in company with her husband, returning late in the afternoon. They came upon a prairie and the mare took a fright, made one jump and the girth broke and off came the rider. The mare ran with the halter rein around the horn of the saddle, until it was all gone but the saddletree. She stopped and the Preacher relieved her of her trouble. But the woman did not ride the mare home nor never rode her again.

Another incident of some interest shows that all the "Smart Ellicks" were not dead nor that they all lived near Mount Comfort, where the Licensed Preacher taught his first Arkansas school, but in the neighborhood of Walnut Grove there were a sprinkle of them. One of these "Smarties" held the office of road overseer as they were called in those days; so he intended that the school teacher should work one or two days on the public highway. So that the Overseer might have a witness to prove that the teacher was legally notified, he sent a man to warn the hands along the road. The teacher knew enough of Arkansas law to know that he was exempt from such labor, and he gave the gentleman to understand that he did not work on roads. When the ten days expired and the teacher did not answer, the Overseer brought suit against him in the Court of an acting Justice of the Peace. At the trial all the teacher had to do was to make affidavit that he was a Licensed Minister of the Gospel. This settled that difficulty and the Overseer was responsible for the cost.

Another of these "wiseacres" concluded not to pay the teacher his tuition bills. This fellow was one of those Cumberland Presbyterian preachers.[3] The teacher brought suit before the same Justice of the peace, and got his debt and cost from the Cumberland Presbyterian preacher.

As soon as the corn crop was gathered and disposed of, the teacher found it necessary to look out for a new location and found a small improvement on forty acres of Government land near Elm Springs for sale. He traded for it on good terms, giving the black mare in exchange for the place and moved into the cabin about Christmas 1851. There were about ten acres under a good rail fence. A few years later he entered the forty acres, under the graduation law and got it at seventy-five cents per acre.

He was not long on this place until he received a proposition to teach during the spring and summer of 1852 on Brush Creek, better known as Jones' Mill. A good schoolhouse was made and a dwelling house built near the schoolhouse, where he taught ten months. This was one of the good neighborhoods of Arkansas.

When this ten months school closed, he returned to the forty-acre farm and raised a crop of oats in 1853. On the thirtieth of March of this year the first child, a boy, John E., was born to the loving mother and father. He concluded to make a home on this forty acres of land, and Antioch church in Benton County being much nearer to his home than the one near White River, he called for a letter of recommendation and united with Antioch. In June of the year 1853 he was ordained to the full work of the ministry, having been licensed in East Tennessee in the month of May 1849 by Dumplin Creek church, and he made his first attempt to preach on the fourth Sunday of August 1853.[4]

Another man by the name of Asaph Brown of the same church was ordained the same day, a noble young man, too, but with a limited education.

In July a protracted meeting was held by these two young ministers in a very small schoolhouse in Robbom's Prairie, in Benton County. In a few days the congregation became so large and interesting that the grove had to be resorted to for room. For three weeks the meeting grew in interest; a rest was thought advisable, and in August another long protracted effort was made. The two meetings resulted in about seventy-five converts, fifty-one additions to Antioch Baptist church. The Methodist and Presbyterian Societies, of course, took a number of the converts. Mount Zion Association, of which Antioch church was a member, convened that year with Sugar Creek church in the north part of Benton County and in the vicinity of the since-noted battle ground of Pea Ridge or Elkhorn Tavern.[5]

At this annual session, the delegates of Missionary Chapel church were instructed by their church to look up a Pastor. The newly ordained J. A. Slover was invited to visit said Missionary Chapel church that the church might hear him, and call him to the Pastorate if satisfied with him. He set an appointment to preach for that church Saturday before the third Sunday in September.

Following the association [meeting], he went twenty miles from his home to the western part of Benton County, and met a few people in an old dilapidated cabin on a deserted Methodist campground. The congregation consisted of the church Clerk, Deacon, and eight nonprofessing men, not a woman present, for it was raining lightly. At the close of the sermon the Preacher called for seekers of religion and to his surprise every one of the eight came forward, much concerned. A grand and glorious revival ensued and for ten days he preached day and night.

A change of place was made to the unfinished Baptist log church house without floor, but straw was soon substituted, and temporary seats arranged. The church was organized two years before this meeting with thirty-two members. At the end of one year's labor on the part of the pastor, the membership was trebled, numbering ninety-six and nearly all by baptism.

The pastoral year closed with September 1854, which year was a fearful dry one in that region. Corn crops were a signal failure. The church called her pastor for another year, but the drouth cut their crops so short that they could not pay enough to keep him. Four bushels of corn was all that could be secured for the year's services and that was equal to four dollars. Again the Preacher was compelled to teach.

He made a school in the vicinity of Evansville in the southwest portion of Washington County, Arks., and taught ten months in the Lattie Schoolhouse. In the early part of the year 1856, he returned to the little farm near Elm Spring, and made a crop, principally corn. And in the closing of said year he taught his last school in his own neighborhood. He never engaged in teaching any more.

In the early part of May 1852 a fearful hurricane or tornado passed near the schoolhouse where he was teaching, leaving desolation in its wake. It leveled to the ground three strings of the fence on his little farm; houses were blown down and wagons carried away and torn to pieces. It traveled from west to east, and was about two miles wide. No one was killed to his knowledge.

He had kept up a regular preaching service while teaching at Jones' Mill on Brush Creek, and a Methodist preacher by the name of Thornburg also preached at the same schoolhouse. He challenged the Baptist preacher for a debate on the mode and subjects of baptism, which Slover accepted. "Immersion is the only scriptural mode of baptism," the Baptist affirmed, the Methodist denied. "Infants are scriptural subjects of baptism," the Methodist affirmed and the Baptist denied. The people were the judges and while the Methodists were well pleased with the effort of the Champion of their favorite principles, the masses said the Baptist produced the best arguments on both propositions. The debate was friendly and well attended by all denominations, as well as by those not belonging to any denomination, but with what results the Lord alone knows.

In November of 1853 his (Antioch) Church settled the Alien immersion question.[6] A council had previously been called consisting of Bros. Heath, Jehue Chastain, and T. B. Vanhorn; the last one named was an educated man and was a school teacher of fine ability; he was from the North somewhere. Heath did not come. Chastain and Vanhorn were present with the two newly ordained ministers, namely Brown and J. A. Slover. Vanhorn was in favor of "Alien immersion," but the only argument for it that he produced was that some of the churches in the North practiced it. Chastain replied to him and said, "Because my brethren err that is no reason that I should; I want 'thus saith the Lord' for what I do."

Speech after speech was made by the four ministers present until the day was well nigh spent. Finally the Rev. Slover suggested to the Church Clerk (privately) to make a motion to rescind the act of the church in September previous that had raised the issue. The motion was instantly made and seconded by the Preacher that suggested the same. It needed no debating. When the question was called for vote, about nineteen-twentieths of the large church rose en mass in favor of the motion, which act of the church ended the question and sent it where it belongs, that is outside of a Baptist church, and never be entertained for a moment by any Baptist church.

While he was teaching near Evansville in the Lattie Schoolhouse, a Baptist Association convened with Vineyard church which held its meetings in said Schoolhouse. As he was pastor of the church, he was appointed a corresponding delegate to this association. On Saturday evening he preached from Hebrews tenth chapter, twenty-first and twenty-second verses: "And having a high priest over the house of God; let us draw near with a true heart in full assurance of faith, having our hearts sprinkled from an evil conscience and our bodies washed with pure water."

At the close of the sermon an opportunity was given for persons to join the church. A young Cumberland Presbyterian preacher came forward, and after telling the church his experience of the work of Grace in his heart, he related as the reason for leaving the Presbyterians substantially the following:

> This day was the day set by the Presbytery for me to read or preach my trial sermon at Cane Hill before that body, and when called on for it, I told them I did not have any. The President asked me why; I told him: in writing a sermon on the text given—"For the Son of man is come to seek and to save that which was lost"—it went well until I got the sinner saved in Christ; then the question arose instantly in my mind: "What does Christ require of such believers in him?" and in my searching for an answer to this question I found that the Scriptures required him to be baptized; this led me to look in the New Testament what baptism is and found that it was the immersion of a believer in water. Reaching this conclusion I quit writing my sermon. I could not conscientiously write that sprinkling and pouring was baptism and I would not write that immersion was because I knew the Presbyterians held and taught differently and I respected their feelings. The President asked me what I was going to do; I told him

I was going to find a church which baptized according to the New Testament by immersion.

Then he said he desired to be baptized and become a member of this church if he was thought worthy. He was received and immersed the next day. On that bright Sunday about noon in the month of November 1855, the Pastor, in the presence of a large congregation (among whom was the President of the above named Presbytery), buried him with Christ in baptism. After this association closed its annual session, the year was soon gone and school closed.

With January the seventh came another boy into the family and they called his name Thomas Jacob Conway, the first part of his name for his uncle Thomas H. Slover, the second for a cousin who had spent a portion of the winter with the family, and the third part for a brother of his mother.

Before Slover left this neighborhood, there was a marriage in the little town of Evansville which was peculiar. One of the patrons of the school just closed had two grown daughters; both had been students in the Preacher's school and the whole family was very friendly and sociable with the teacher's family. On a certain Saturday the two girls made a visit with their sister in Evansville, perhaps a distance of two miles from their father's home. They spent the night with their sister. About 9 o'clock the Sunday morning, Amanda, the older of the two, appeared at the door of her teacher's house alone and said, after usual salutation, "Mr. Slover, you will have to go home with me." He said, "Why so?" She replied that Exira, her youngest sister, is gone to get married, and no doubt is married before this time. He asked, "Where is she gone?" She said, "To Esquire Stouts, and I am afraid to go home alone; father will blame me for it." Enough was said; her teacher said he would go with her; he put on his overcoat for it was cold and a little snow was on the ground.

One half or three quarters of a mile brought them to her father's house, and found him with his boots off and lying before a nice fire. As soon as he saw that his youngest daughter was missing from her sister, he instantly said, "Where is Exira?" and became agitated as though he suspected that she was off to get married or that the Preacher then present had officiated at the marriage. The Preacher spoke for the half-scared girl and said, "You had just as well be quiet for your daughter Exira is married and gone." He bounced up, pulled on his boots and said excitedly, "Did you marry them?" The Preacher laughed and answered, "No sir, but Esquire Stout has married before this time of the day." "She is not of age and I will have Stout arrested," he exclaimed. "Oh," the Preacher said, "you had better let that alone, for you will have to submit to it." By Slover constantly talking to him and laughing at his folly, he was overcome and soon began talking of other things, and the Preacher soon saw that the storm had passed and there was a calm and he went home.

In about a week or ten days the old folks invited their new son-in-law to come home with his wife; the newly made wife was asked how she managed about her age, she said, "I cut the number eighteen out of a newspaper and put it in the inside of my shoe. When the Esquire asked me if I was over eighteen I said, 'Yes,' and that was all that he said." There was no license for marriage in Arkansas at that time, but simply a certificate of the officiating officer had to be filed in the County Clerk's office within thirty days after the marriage.

Another incident in connection with the last school that he ever taught must be allowed a place upon these pages; to wit: The school term involved Christmas of that year and the school had some half-grown boys and large of their age, so they concluded to have some apples as a Christmas treat from the teacher. Somehow or other the teacher got wind of their game and concluded to humor the joke and bought two bushels of fine winter apples about two days before the morning set by the youngsters for their fun, and deposited with a friend near the schoolhouse.

According to their arrangement, on the twenty-fourth day of December, they were at the schoolhouse bright and early and barred the door. On the arrival of the teacher they demanded apples or a promise of them or admittance would be refused, and furthermore the teacher would receive as a further punishment a dip in cold water, head and ears. The only water in any reasonable distance was a well, where the school got water and that was about three hundred yards, and the only chance to dip him at that well was to fill the watering trough three parts full and put him in. He told them that he would dismiss the school and go home; out they came and had the teacher in strings in less than half the time it takes to write it, but they had no wagon to haul him in and he refused to walk. They deliberately picked him up and carried him to the well and had the vessel filled with water.

The trip from the schoolhouse to the well was the teacher's part of the fun, so seeing that they intended to put him in that watering trough, he said apples would be forthcoming and the day made up at the end of the school. The boys then liberated the teacher and a large boy was dispatched to the house of the teacher's friend for the apples. Soon the messenger came with the treat and all had plenty of apples and lots of fun. Thus ended the young preacher's school teaching with the year 1856.

6

He accepts an appointment from the Southern Baptist Convention through the Domestic and Indian Mission Board located at Marion, Alabama, to preach to the Cherokee Indians—His visit to the Chief for an Interview in regard to locating in the nation—Moves to Tahlequah—Begins operations as a Missionary—Cold snap in April—Russel Holman, Corresponding Secretary, visits the field—The Missionary is interrogated as to his plan of operations, touching the vexed question of Slavery—His answer is well received—A girl baby comes to his home to stay—His first year's labor closes—Indians give him a name—Incredulity of the Natives.

While Slover was teaching his last school, a brother Baptist, Joseph Land, whom the teacher knew at the Lattie Schoolhouse, wrote from the Creek Nation and made inquiry whether the Preacher would accept an appointment to preach as Missionary to the Cherokee Indians. If so, he (Land) would have H. F. Buckner, Missionary to the Creek Indians, recommend him for appointment to the proper Board of the Southern Baptist Convention.[1] He answered his brother Land that he was ready and willing to accept such appointment, after Antioch church had been given proper notice.

In a few weeks a correspondence was opened with him by the corresponding Secretary of the Domestic and Indian Mission Board of that body as to the desired time to begin work, an am't of salary &c &c. He replied that he could begin work the first of January 1857 and that he would begin the labor at a salary of five hundred dollars, and at that time he had his wife and two little children depending on him for support.[2]

In due time his commission came, duly authenticated with the act of the Board making the appointment and a promise that the amount above stated would be paid quarterly.³ Receiving this commission, he set about to get someone to occupy the new house he had just erected on his little farm. Samuel Cox, who had married his wife's sister about three years before, was found and the little farm turned over to him. His mother-in-law was to remain with her youngest boy, James C. Ingram, in the house.

The next step was to make a trip to Park Hill in the Cherokee Nation to visit Chief John Ross in regard to locating in his country.⁴ There Slover found that no land could be owned by Missionaries, but that they were permitted to locate upon some Native's lands. The Tribe was in favor of all denominations being allowed to preach among them.⁵

The Missionary secured a Baptist Deacon, James K. Green of Evansville, to accompany him. Now the weather was very cold with the crusted snow about six or eight inches deep on the frozen ground, which made the trip disagreeable. It took four days for the Missionary to make this trip.

Then another tour was made to Tahlequah when the ground was in better condition for horseback traveling.⁶ On reaching Tahlequah he stopped at the hotel of Johnson Foreman, whose wife was a Baptist.⁷ He conversed with her in reference to Indian Missions, among other things asked he (before he made himself known as a Missionary) if she thought that a good place for a missionary to locate. She looked him in the face and replied, "Yes, if the Southern Baptist Board would send a man, he could do a good work, no doubt." The Missionary surprised her happily when he told her that he was that man and that he was looking for a house to move into and circulating an appointment to preach in town the next Sunday. She seldom failed to attend his services held in the town of Tahlequah.

He was not long finding rooms to move into, belonging to one Thomas Foreman, at reasonable rates. He then returned to Elm Springs in Washington County and as soon as was possible made the move to his field of labor. Being somewhat comfortably situated in the rented house he at once began operations; his first work was to look up the few scattering Baptists nearest his location, as well as to look for localities where he could preach without an interpreter, for hundreds of the inhabitants could understand the English language, as well as the Cherokee.⁸

A cold snap came over that section of the country sometime in April, perhaps near the middle of the month—peaches and apples were nearly as large as marbles. It happened on Sunday night. The wind blew all day and in the afternoon the snow fell and drifted on the prairie in heaps against every object that was large enough to hold the drifting snow.

Monday morning every drop of water along the road in horse tracks and other small cavities were frozen into ice and all the fruit was frozen. Consequently there was no fruit in that country that year.

Sometime during that summer, Russel Holman made a flying trip in the territory from the Board of Missions of which he was then Corresponding Secretary. He only preached one sermon in the Cherokee field. He was a good preacher and a pleasant companion, and knew how to sympathize with a poor Missionary. He saw the situation of the employee of the Board, which no doubt led the Board to increase his salary to six hundred dollars for the next year and to the erection of a dwelling house for him.

While locating his respective preaching places, he was very often interrogated as to his practice in regard to the vexed question of African slavery, and the Indians wanted to know whether he did like Rev. Jones, who under the requirement of the Boston Board had dismissed all slaveholders who would not emancipate their slaves from membership in any of the churches he had constituted among the Indians.[9] Slover invariably answered no, that he would baptize a slaveholder or the slave as soon as any one else, and that he had nothing to do with the question of slavery; that it was his business to preach Christ and Him crucified. This answer was well received by all classes of Indians, especially by the better informed that understood the teachings of the Scriptures—that politics and religion are separate institutions, the latter is of God the "Infinite," the former of finite man.[10]

On the third day of September of this year a girl baby came into his home to stay and by consent of parties the name Elizabeth Jane was given her. Her Grandmother's name on her Mother's side was Elizabeth, also an Aunt on her Father's side had the same name; and another Aunt on the same side bore the name of Jane.

The Indians, as was their custom, gave him a name, "Gilstaugah," which means in their language a large bird of that country which flew around between sundown and dark. When they made a dash, they swept down almost to the ground and rose with roaring noise. As the Indians called it, "Gilstaugah" applied to the Missionary, meant that he traveled everywhere and preached.

This Missionary being the first one in the Cherokee Nation under the patronage of the Domestic and Indian Mission Board of the Southern Baptist Convention, the people were very incredulous and anxious to know or find out whether or not he would take the same position upon

"That vexed question, slavery," that all other Baptist Missionaries in the Nation did. Not being able to ascertain this fact from the tenor of his preaching, they would at their firesides approach him upon this subject and ask such questions as the following: "Do you belong to the same Board with Jones? Do you take the same course that Worcester does?[11] How do you manage when those having slaves want to unite with your church?" &c &c.

To the first questions he gave a negative answer and to the last he told them he did not preach politics nor make stump speeches upon political subjects, that he considered that the question belonged to another body of men, and not to the church of Jesus Christ; and that he found no distinction made in the new Testament; therefore he had no right to make any. Consequently if the master wishes membership, if the non-slaveholder wishes for it, and the servant, they can all have it upon the same terms.[12] He preached the same gospel alike to the rich, the poor, the bond, and the free. And as there is "One Lord, one faith, one baptism," he desired to know nothing among them save Christ and Him crucified. For one long year he traveled, preached, and labored under these embarrassing circumstances with little or no visible effect.[13]

In the meantime he was represented by someone as a newcomer, signifying that he was a new kind of Baptist, allied to the Mormons.[14]

Many impediments were thrown in his way to impede the progress of his ministry. But in this he can now say, "All things work together for good to them that love God."

During the latter part of the first year the Methodist circuit riders began to attack his doctrine at almost every point where he preached, crying down the Baptist denomination as close communists and narrow hearted.

7

Encouraging prospects—Travels and preaches—Makes a trip to Fayetteville, Arks.—Takes sick—Narrow escape from drowning—Dwelling house built—A Cherokee Lawyer interprets His sermons—Family increased by one—Churches organized—Association formed—A Judge interprets for him—Incidents—The Civil War begins—Actual hostilities or first gun is fired April the tenth 1861—He is employed as Chaplain for the first Cherokee Regiment under Col. Stand Watie, Confederate Mounted Volunteers, serves eight months—Cherokee Nation secedes in the fall of 1861—Terms &c &c—He concludes to abandon the field.

The second year was begun with somewhat brighter prospects, and a more encouraging element was felt all around. He took new zeal and as soon as the winter was over, he began to travel and preach in different parts of the Nation. In the month of July he traveled five hundred miles and preached forty sermons.

Immediately after this month's labor, he made a trip to his old home near Elm Springs, and also to Fayetteville where the District United States Land Office was located, and paid for the forty-acre tract of land at seventy-five cents per acre, it having been in market for more than fifteen years.

On the day that he left Tahlequah to make this trip he took the bilious fever and on arriving at his old home, where his mother-in-law lived, he had to call in a physician to treat his case. In a few days he was able to get out; his friends in that neighborhood were anxious to hear him preach, so he consented (even when he ought not to have done so) and preached two sermons the same day. The weather being very warm the result was a relapse and a whole winter's siege of the chills, but he continued preaching when he was able to get out.

The day after Christmas, the Missionary had a very narrow escape with his life from drowning. He had bought a lot of dressed pork from Jacob Bushyhead on the east side of Illinois River and he employed a two-horse team and wagon.[1] A Negro boy was sent to drive the team. On reaching the ferry (the Missionary being on horseback) he found that the wagon and team with the driver were all that could be taken at one trip. He then asked the ferryman if the river could be forded. The ferryman said the river was quite full, but still some people forded it.

A mile down the stream brought him to the ford where he found the water all over the bank at the going-out place on the opposite side, but some full-blooded Indians happened to be at the ford. They told him how to go, but he did not understand them and thought they meant for him to go out at a high bank some hundred yards below where he used to ford when the river was low. So understanding them, into the river he rode with his eye fixed on the only dry land he saw on the desired shore. After riding about twenty yards, his horse was in swimming water. Knowing the animal was a fine swimmer he let go the bridle, guiding the horse with his hands. He soon reached the bank and found it was a bluff bank. His horse threw his front feet upon the top of the bank and made an effort to ascend, but the girth severed. As the saddle began to slide on the horse's back, he aimed to seize hold of the mane, but failing to reach it, caught the rein of the bridle and turned the horse over backward into the deep water.

Believing that if he held on to the rein he might drown the horse as well as himself, he instantly let the rein go. No quicker did he do this than the horse leveled himself up in a swimmer posture and turned his head back toward the west side of the stream and swam back. Meanwhile the Missionary was struggling for dear life in deep water, not being able to swim and having on heavy overshoes, leggins, and a winter overcoat, with gloves on his hands—also hat on his head. In a few moments his saddle was kicked from between his feet. Yet he never sank entirely under the water. He knew that he could remain in that condition but a few minutes at the most. The thoughts of his wife and three little children passed rapidly through his mind. Quickly he turned them to the protection of the God whom he served, yielding his all into His hands. He struggled to get to the bank which was not exceeding ten feet from him, but with all his efforts he could only keep his head above water. He was between the main current and the bank in water that made regular evolutions down, and then up stream. He very sensibly felt its force against his back and it moved him about three feet directly toward the bank.

Then he was able to see in the roily water an old log about six inches under the water and on the second loop he discovered a limb about twelve or fifteen inches long beneath the water and on this old log. He seized hold of this old limb and saw it was solidly fast to the log. He helped himself on to the log; and looking in the direction his horse had gone, he saw him just in the shallow water going out on the same side that he had left.

By this time the saddle was just being floated out into the current, the blanket had sunk or washed away ahead of the saddle. The Indians who had watched the whole scene caught the horse. He thought there was a chance to get the saddle and suiting the action to the thought, he ran down the river fifty or sixty paces, picking up a long dry pole with a crooked limb at the small end. By the time he overtook the saddle, the water was shallow enough to wade in a few feet, so as to reach the saddle and hook the crooked limb over the horn of the saddle. Thus he was enabled to land it pretty quick. He then threw it on to his shoulder and made his way back up the stream.

He told the Indians to take his horse above the ford where the water was about twenty feet deep and put him into the water and force him to swim over to him. This they did, but he (the horse) would not be caught until he ran about one half mile to Mr. Beans where he had been used to stopping. By the time the Missionary was in the saddle, the wagon was in sight returning with the pork, and as soon as the river was crossed at the ferry, he left the wagon and put the whip to the horse and run him four miles home for both were cold. Suffice it to say there was nothing but the saddle blanket, for which he had paid a dollar the day before, lost.

Early in the year 1858 the Missionary asked for aid from his Board to build a dwelling house, and his petition met with favor and about one thousand dollars was appropriated for that purpose, so a carpenter and a stone mason were engaged and the work begun in that year and finished in the early Spring of 1859. The house was thirty-six feet by sixteen, one story high, a frame weather boarded outside and ceiled inside, had a stack chimney in the center with two fireplaces, also a long porch on one side with banisters. The house was painted white on outside, making a comfortable dwelling for a Missionary's family.

He soon found it necessary to have an interpreter.[2] No Native preacher could be found that could be employed, so he engaged a Cherokee lawyer. Unfortunately the lawyer made no pretensions to religion; still he was well disposed to the good work, and was competent. His name was Thomas Taylor and he was a native of Georgia.[3]

In October [10] 1859 there was another boy added to his family, and he was named for the Corresponding Secretary of the Domestic and Indian Mission Board of the S. B. Convention, Russel Holman.

He had gathered and baptized a goodly number of converts, and organized three churches in different parts of his field of labor, and also had employed three or four Native preachers before the close of 1859.[4]

The year 1860 dawned with still more encouraging prospects. The full-blooded Indians began to get their eyes open on the doings of the Northern Board of Missions touching the question of Slavery in the Indian Territory. They were aware that for many years that Board forbid its Missionary to baptize or receive any slaveholder into the churches under their jurisdiction, unless such person would emancipate their slaves.[5] But the Indians, that is the full-bloods, did not understand why. Hence they began very soon after the arrival of the representative of the Southern Baptist Convention to make inquiry as stated in the preceding pages of autobiography.

A statement is appended here of a Native preacher when he applied to the church of which he was and had been for several years a member in good standing, that he might join a church under the care of the Southern Board. Statement of Thomas Wilkinson:

> When I called on the church for a letter in order to join the Southern Board, John Jones asked me what reason or cause I had for wishing to withdraw from the Northern Board; I told him that I thought it was nothing but right for me to join and work with the Southern Board. Jones asked me again for my reasons for thinking so. I referred him to the 28th chapter and 19th verse of Matthew. In this passage of the gospel we are required to baptize all that repent and believe; according to my opinion, if a slaveholder should desire baptism and we find that he is worthy, &c. Jones asked me if that was the only reason I had for changing my connection with the church. I said that was not all. He then asked me if it was not because the Southern Board would pay me for my labor? I told him that was part of my reasons. He asked me what my pay would be; I told him three hundred dollars. He then asked me if that was not all the reason I had? I told him it was not. I referred him to the Constitution of the Cherokee Nation which I had great respect for; that it has been a usage and custom of our forefathers to worship God according to the dictates of their conscience and I had often told him under the requirement of the

Northern Board we found at times that we could not do so. He then asked if the Constitution opposed emancipation of slaves, or that if the Nation was to emancipate her slaves and become a free Nation, if it would affect the Constitution. I told him it would, that it tolerated slavery, and that the Northern Board was doing everything they could against it &c. He said the slaves were whipped until the blood run to the ground from their backs, and that the money I would get would be bad money, being the price of blood. I then referred him to his public collections that he very often made at camp meetings; and told him that the gambler, the drunkard and other wicked persons contribute, so you see that perhaps the larger amount of your contributions are from wicked persons. Some win their money at the gambling table, some get it by unlawful traffick—the sale of whiskey in the Nation. Ah! said he; these things cannot be compared with the evils of slavery. Now said I, if you were to call upon the people to contribute sometime and I was present and should cast in a dollar or two of this money I had gotten from the Southern Board, would you take it? "Yes," he said. He could not refuse it coming from him; said I, it would not be bad money then, would it? Thus ended our talk, and I had to leave my church without a letter. Jones said if he granted me a letter to join the Southern Board, he would be aiding and abetting slavery. I left and am now laboring under the employment of the Southern Board and some of my brethren left also and many others have their eyes open upon that subject.

Tahlequah C[herokee]. N[ation].

May 10th 1859

(signed)
THOMAS WILKINSON

About the close of the year 1859 the Mission was reenforced by the arrival of the Rev. Isaac Reed, who was cordially received by the Missionary on the 19th day of December. His arrival greatly encouraged the work and especially the heart of the Missionary.[6]

In the early part of 1860 three more churches were organized in connection with the Mission, and in September of the same year an Association was formed of the six churches then organized, known as the Cherokee Southern Baptist Association. Shortly after the formation of the association, one of the Associate Judges of the Supreme Court was employed to interpret his sermons (the lawyer having declined); his name was [Jesse] Russel [of Tahlequah].

The Methodists became jealous of our success and, highly exasperated, began to lay schemes to thwart the Missionary's progress, one of which is here given.

His regular monthly meeting on Saturday before the fourth Sunday at the Bayou Manard public schoolhouse had been established for twelve months [about 20 miles southwest of Tahlequah] and during that year quite a number had been baptized and a Baptist church organized. At the June meeting 1859, a woman was to be baptized who was a member of the Methodist church, so called.

To the surprise of the Missionary, an appointment had been made by the presiding Elder of the Methodist Episcopal Church South, embracing the fourth Sunday in June which was the time of the meeting of the Baptist church.[7] The time came; both the quarterly conference and the Missionary with a portion of his numbers were at the schoolhouse. The Elder was preaching when the other parties reached the house. It was plain to everyone that the Elder intended to hold and keep, if possible, the congregation and rule the Baptists out of hearing their minister preach.

The Elder never said a word about his appointment conflicting with the Baptists' regular meeting at that place. He asked the Missionary as a casual visitor or attendant at his meetings to preach Saturday night, but he declined. Then one of the circuit riders, Rev. Delano of Tahlequah, delivered a brief discourse, after which the Missionary, by permission of the rider, told the people that he would preach the next day at 3 o'clock P.M. one-half mile away at the residence of Mr. Stearns and immediately after would baptize a waiting candidate, saying "this will give us an opportunity to be at the meeting here tomorrow morning." Sunday came and the congregation assembled; the Missionary took a seat far back in the congregation to hear the Elder preach upon the subject of baptism. Many people who came to the ground, finding there was a confliction of appointments, took no interest in the meeting.

Now while the Elder was preaching, a beef was being barbecued on the ground, to be ready for eating as soon as the preaching services were over. The Missionary and his church sat and heard themselves exposed and then the Elder had the impudence to invite them to commune with him. After announcing four o'clock services for that afternoon, they dismissed to take their repast. The Missionary immediately started to his three o'clock appointment and after dinner to their utter astonishment, scarcely any but their own members (which were few at that place) stayed for the four o'clock preaching. Their whole effort to supplant the Baptists evidently resulted in a perfect flash. They closed sine die and never made war on the Bayou Manardians since.

In the summer of 1860, another incident of opposition occurred in connection with the labors of the Missionary. He was called to the Verdigris River about eighty miles northwest of Tahlequah to assist some Native preachers organizing a Baptist Church. The meeting was to be at the residence of David [McNair] Foreman, a Native minister supported by Coosa Association of Georgia.[8] On arriving at his house, the Missionary and his wife were told by Foreman that a meeting at his house was not safe, because his neighbors of the Northern or abolition party had notified him that such a meeting as was anticipated could not be held in that neighborhood. Foreman made no explanation but simply told the Missionary that he was going to leave home that afternoon and accompany him on his return to Grand River, a distance of thirty-five miles in the direction of Tahlequah. This was rather frightful news for a Missionary to hear while on a mission of peace to the souls of men.

But such was the beginning of the pending difficulties that were in store for the Missionary of the Southern Baptist Convention. Suffice it to say that a start from Foreman's was made at five o'clock P.M. on Friday before the fifth Sunday in July, Foreman in his saddle, the Missionary, wife, and a baby in a spring wagon with a team of two horses. After traveling about ten miles to a fine spring, a halt was made, horses picketed to graze, and a luncheon prepared by the wife of the Cherokee preacher was dispatched in haste by the fleeing party. Then between sundown and nightfall the journey was renewed across a twenty-five mile prairie.

Directly after dark, a dark cloud arose in the northwest with lightning and muttering thunder. The night was so very dark that the only times the Missionary could discern his Indian guide were when the forked lightning would flash from the upper elements. Fortunately the storm lingered until Grand River was reached and the party was housed in the dwelling of Mr. Alberty and the horses stabled and fed. Then the rain fell in torrents. Certainly the lingering of the cloud was a Godsend to the wife and babe of the Missionary, for it rained as it can in that country.

The next day (Saturday) was spent in visiting and notifying the people that the fleeing party would preach at the dwelling house of Alberty. A respectable congregation came together and the Missionary preached

Sunday morning and evening, then on Monday drove forty-five miles to his home in Tahlequah.

In another neighborhood in the northern part of the Cherokee Nation, the Ministers and Deacons meeting had been broken up by forty men styling themselves the Delaware soldiers. Four of the forty feigned themselves drunk, but they were not. They claimed a certain hollow about ten rod north of the church house, "Dickson's Hollow," meaning Mason's and Dickson's line which was the southern boundary of Missouri. In a short time after this difficulty, the whole country was full of reports as to what these Delaware soldiers were going to do in the future. They called themselves "Delaware soldiers" because they belonged to a district known in the Cherokee Nation by that name.[9]

Another incident came in the way of the Missionary, no doubt to defeat his purposes as an employee of the Southern Board of Missions. This incident grew out of the attempt the Presiding Elder of the M. E. Church south made to defeat the baptism of one of his sheep who became convinced that sprinkling was not Scriptural baptism.

Sometime after that attempt the Missionary was called to Park Hill near the residence of the old Chief [John Ross] to preach the funeral of the wife of a Cherokee Presbyterian minister, who had been dismissed from their employment because he would not set his Negroes free. After the funeral was over, the Chief invited the Missionary to go home with him for dinner. He went and after dining with the Chief and his amiable wife and daughter—the wife was a Wilmington Lady from the State of Delaware—the Chief and the Missionary repaired to the spacious parlor. The Chief then called up the circumstance of the conflicting appointments referred to in these pages. Evidently someone had misrepresented the Baptist Missionary to the Chief because he charged the Missionary with disturbing the Elders' quarterly conference at the Bayou Manard schoolhouse. He also reproached the Southern Baptist Convention, saying the object it had in having Missionaries among the Indians was to secure the Indian Territory and make a state out of it. I told him if the Southern Board had any such design I knew nothing of it, that my commission forbid me to know anything but "Christ and Him crucified." Then as to the Presiding Elders' meeting the Missionary told the facts in the case, that the Elders' appointment conflicted with a Baptist church's appointment which had been established for more than a whole year. He abruptly replied, "Differently is reported to me, sir." The Missionary told him he could not help that, for he knew that the Chief had been misinformed.

About the close of 1860 the political elements in the United States of America began to smack of war between the Southern and Northern States. As soon as the presidential election was over in November and the result ascertained that Abraham Lincoln, the Republican or Abolition candidate was elected, the Southern states began preparations for forming a Confederation preparatory to leaving the union and forming a separate government.

The Indian agent of the Cherokees, holding appointment under President Buchanan, was a Mr. Post from the State of Georgia.[10] The Missionary interviewed Mr. Post on the situation of the political aspects of the United States. He replied, "O there will be a Confederacy formed." True enough; it was only a question of time that the seceded States of the South were formed into the Southern Confederacy, and a provisional government organized by appointing Jefferson Davis President. The seat of Government located at Richmond, Va. Armies were rapidly formed both North and South, ostensibly on the part of the latter to set up a new Government, and on the part of the former to defend the Union.

But the great underlying object of the fire-eaters of both sides was that on the part of the North to free the four million slaves of the Southern States and that on the part of the South to hold them in bondage.[11] The war raged for four long years, resulting in overpowering the South with one half million of men and billions of money expended by the North, and rivers of blood on both sides, with the freedom of "Four Million of Negroes." That wonderful "Proclamation" of the President of the United States [Lincoln's Emancipation Proclamation] was a clear evidence of the purpose of the North. Although it was hypocritically claimed that it was a war measure, the North could put three men to one for the South in their armies, and they were backed by the money power of the world—especially by Her upon whose Dominions the Sun never sets. If she showed any favor to the Confederacy, it was alone for the gold that was in the contract, for she long before this war goaded the United States with the idea that they claimed freedom of their citizens from a kingly monarchy, and at the same time held millions of Negroes in bondage. "Bosh."

If African slavery was wrong, the Southern States were not alone responsible for its existence in the United States, because twelve of the original thirteen Colonies were slave states when the sacred document called Constitution was adopted. Rhode Island alone went into that compact with a constitution asserting that all citizens of her little insignificant domain should have free and equal rights to life, liberty, and the pursuit of peace and happiness.

As the years rolled by, the time came when the "Yankee" saw that he could hire European serfs for less money than he could keep African bondsmen. His conscience began to soften, as it always does when gold is in sight. But it (his conscience) did not get soft enough to give the Negro freedom. He found it to his financial benefit to drive with profit the slave trade, collecting the darkies in droves and driving them to the great cotton growing plantations of the South and selling them at the highest bidder. Little he cared for separating husband, wife, or children so he could fill his pockets with coin or United States Bank notes.

About the same time, 1843 or 1844, the American Baptist Missionary Society took a dive into politics, and declared that they would not knowingly employ a Home Missionary who was a slaveholder. Just here let it be said that Baptist churches very materially differ from all and any other religious body calling itself a church in the fact that they, the Baptists, are independent local bodies, so that Baptist churches have no common fund as churches, but the Missionary Societies are creatures of volunteer acts of the churches. Whatever is contributed by the volunteer act of individuals or churches to the treasury of said Missionary Society becomes the funds of that Society and is used by the Board of said Society as its constitution provided. Now let us see the result of this declaration of the American Baptist Home Missionary Society. It was soon known all over the South how that Society had said it would not knowingly employ a Missionary who was a slaveholder.

The State Convention of the Baptists of the State of Georgia recommended a Minister for appointment as State Missionary and in a note or postscript (it being no part of the qualifications of the man for the position, but a mere matter of information), they—knowing the grounds the Board had taken on the slavery question—said he is a slaveholder. The Board on receiving the application construed the item of information (that he was a slaveholder) into a test question, and after debating the subject of his appointment during five successive meetings of said Board, the question came to a secret vote in that body. When counted, it stood six for his appointment and seven against. This was the first secret balloting of that Board on record.

The Baptists of the South arose with holy indignation at this step of that Board to dictate to the churches whom they should have to labor among them as Missionaries, and called a convention to meet in one of the cities of the South for the purpose of organizing a Southern Baptist Convention, which was done in 1844 or 1845.¹² Soon after these religious bodies were divided, slavery became the great bone of contention. . . .

[Here Slover borrows from history textbooks to recount some of the politics and events leading to the Civil War.]

The first shot of the Civil War was fired April the 12th at four o'clock thirty minutes A.M.

Soon after the capitulation of Fort Sumter, the two great sections of the United States were in arms against each other. Volunteers were called for by both the President of the United States and of the Confederate States. A regiment of Confederate troops was raised in the Cherokee Nation by a half breed Indian called in the English tongue "Stand Watie" (Tek-ah-talk was his Cherokee name) and mustered into service under General [Benjamin] McCulloch of Texas Volunteers for Confederate service.¹³ Under the adverse circumstances which surrounded the Missionary, he sought the position of Chaplain of said Cherokee Regiment, for, about this time, no money could reach him from the Board of Domestic and Indian Missions at Marion, Ala. He thought this step necessary to secure a support for himself & family while the horrible war continued. He, however, only was permitted to remain in that service about eight months.

In April 1862, a little girl babe came into his Tahlequah home to stay; she was permitted to bear the name of her Father's Mother and a cousin of her own Mother. So her christen name was Rachel Malvinie. She was not permitted to live but a little over five years.

An interesting incident occurred in connection with his ministry in the month of June 1862. He was invited by E. L. Compere, the pastor of the first Baptist Church of Fort Smith, Ark., to assist in a protracted meeting in the first part of the month of June. He went, thinking he would only be gone for a few days, but the meeting became so interesting at the close of the services of the first Sunday that the pastor and church thought proper to protract it from day to day for nineteen days; during that time the pastor baptized thirty-six persons. As soon as the last day's services were ended, the Missionary left Fort Smith for his home in Tahlequah about four o'clock P.M., wending his way on a strange road the nearest way through the Indian country, anxious about his family, the distance being sixty miles. Of course night came before half the distance was told. He traveled on until about three o'clock A.M. when he became so sleepy he could scarcely retain his position in his saddle.

Not knowing how near he was to anyone's house nor how far, nor whether, if per adventure he should come to a house, it would be the house of a friend or that of a Pin Indian—and at any rate he could not talk Cherokee—so he dismounted and felt his way a few feet from the road, made his horse fast to a sapling, took off the saddle, and spreading his saddle blanket on the ground and committing himself to the care of his Heavenly Father, was soon in dream land, and did not awake until the sun was shining on his hastily provided resting place.[14]

About breakfast time of that morning he rode up to the house of one of the Native preachers of his Board's employment—his name was [Jesse H.] Owens. Here he knew the road for he had been at that Native's house before; moreover he was kindly received and he and his hungry horse hospitably entertained. After some pleasant conversation with his friend and brother preacher, the Missionary made the remaining twenty-five miles to his home where his anxiety and fears subsided because he found the family all well.

Secession among Indians of the southern part of the Indian Territory began in the Spring of 1861. But when General [Albert] Pike, Confederate Commissioner, first entered the Cherokee Nation in May 1861, he was threatened by a mob of what was called the Pin Cherokee Indians (A Secret order of the full-bloods) who opposed secession, but the Missionary's interpreter, Thomas Taylor, met them and dissuaded them to not fall on Pike and his sixty men, until they (the Indians) could communicate with Chief John Ross.[15] They yielded to his proposition, and sent five or six men to interview the Chief who told them to go home, that he would not give Pike any kind of an audience, neither of the Council nor Committee in Council; let him pass to the Creek Indians.[16] So he did; Pike passed unhurt to the Creek, Choctaw, and Chickasaw Indians, and treated with them.

But the defeat of the Federal Army at Wilson Creek [also called Oak Hills] south of Springfield, Mo., caused a reaction in the mind of the Cherokee Chief and his people. A convention was immediately called to convene in Tahlequah; and an ordinance of secession was framed by some of the lawyers of the Nation and read section by section and each section voted on by about five thousand Indian men from every part of the Nation; not a dissenting grunt was heard. A messenger was at once dispatched after Gen. Pike, bearing an official request for him to return, that a treaty might be made between the Confederate States and the Cherokee Indians.[17]

In October following the Convention a treaty was ratified between the two parties.[18] The terms of the treaty in short were about as follows: The Confederacy agreed to return or give the Annuity which had failed to reach them for about two years; the coin was in the Mint in New Orleans, La., which had been seized by the South. Perhaps there was something over one hundred thousand dollars of this annuity which of right belonged to the Cherokees.[19]

Also the Confederacy proposed to buy a tract of eight hundred thousand acres of land known, and held by the United States for the Cherokee Indians, as "Neutral land." It was located on the western boundary of Missouri, fifty miles long north and south, and twenty-five east and west, which the Cherokees took in lieu of five hundred thousand dollars in a contract made between the United States and the Cherokee Indians in 1835, for which the Confederacy agreed to give the five hundred thousand dollars with interest at six percent from 1835 to the time the Secession treaty was ratified by the contracting parties, and pay in Confederate money, and three hundred thousand dollars down. Which was done. The Indians were required to muster into the Confederate service one thousand mounted men armed, which they did.

The Missionary was a looker on on the day the treaty was returned from the Confederate Government at Richmond, Va., and the one thousand Indians were received as Confederate soldiers.[20] He saw the white flag with a blue half moon sewed on it with a red star located just between the two horns of the moon. The red star represented the Cherokee Nation, the half moon represented the Confederacy. A Cherokee lawyer walked around gazing at the flag thus arrayed and said, "I would not give a D-mn for the star when the Moon fulls." The whole, however, was hailed by the Southern Indians and the Confederate officers as the dawn of brighter days for the Cherokee people. But alas! How soon their hopes were blighted.

The Treaty Regiment (as it was called) under the command of Col. [John] Drew, took up the line of march for Gen. McCulloch's headquarters and was received, equipped, and mustered into service.[21] Gen. [Douglas] Cooper was placed in command of the Indian Division.[22] The first and last fight this Regiment was in as Confederate troops was the battle of Pea Ridge in the northern part of Benton County, Ark.[23] After this battle, in which Gen. McCulloch and [James McQueen] McIntosh were picked off their horses by sharp shooters in the Union army and the Southern troops then commanded by Gen. Sterling Price of Missouri retreated through the mountain passes of White River, the Treaty Regiment retreated to Park Hill, the then residence of Chief John Ross, and grazed their Indian ponies on the wide prairies in that vicinity.[24] The Union forces fell back to Springfield, Mo.

The war elements in the Cherokee Country were somewhat calm until July. In the meantime the Missionary made the visit to Fort Smith referred to in the foregoing pages. The latter days of June E. L. Compere, the Pastor of the first Baptist church in Fort Smith, made a visit to Tahlequah and was with the Missionary up to the time he came to the conclusion that it would be better for him to abandon his field.

8

The Union Troops under Gen. Blunt on Cherokee Territory—Stand Watie's headquarters burned and his staff made prisoners—Gen. Blunt's letter to Chief Ross—Ross's ingenious answer—Mutiny of the Treaty Regiment—In company with his brother preacher E. L. Compere, the Missionary visits Chief Ross for information—Temporarily abandons his field—Three hundred Union soldiers make a raid on Tahlequah wanting the Missionary and seventeen other men—He stops outside of Indian Territory with Deacon J. W. Greer's family—His anxiety and mental trouble—His hazardous trip to Tahlequah and final abandonment of the Mission.

About the last of June 1862, Gen. [James G.] Blunt came down from Missouri into the Indian Territory and established his Headquarters on Wolf Creek, forty miles Northwest of Tahlequah in the Cherokee Nation.[1] On the first day of July he captured Stand Watie's headquarters in that vicinity where they had been foraging since their return from the battle of Pea Ridge. Col. Stand Watie with his Regiment were out on scout, and were not captured, yet all their camp equipage were burned and the men at headquarters were made prisoners, among whom was Wm. Penn Adair and several other noted men of that Nation.[2]

On the second day of July Gen. Blunt sent a special letter to Chief John Ross. The messenger that bore the letter was a surgeon in Blunt's command by the name of Kirkpatrick, and to secure his safety against Rebel soldiers, two young women, sisters of the prisoners, were forced to ride with the messenger as his bodyguard.[3] They were particularly charged that if they suffered Rebel soldiers to molest him while gone, their brothers would have to suffer to atone for the death of the surgeon. Truly this was an unreasonable charge and an unjust position to place two innocent young women who would have been powerless to defend their escort had he been met by a squad of Rebel Indian soldiers, but it so turned out that the trip was made unmolested.

The contents of the letter were an invitation to His Excellency, the Chief, to come to Gen. Blunt's headquarters on Wolf Creek, some forty miles away, that they (the Chief and Gen. Blunt) might adopt some plan whereby the unfaithful part of the Cherokee Indians might be put under his (Gen. Blunt's) command.

Chief Ross was at that time an old man more than seventy-five years old, and he had seen much political trouble among his own people when the Ridge party and the Ross party were at dagger's points. He had for a long time been Chief [since 1828]. Although he owned about sixty Negroes, yet personally he was opposed to Secession. But, he said, "The United States has withdrawn all the Regular Soldiers from the Indian Territory." Fort Gibson was evacuated in 1858; this Fort was in the Cherokee Nation.[4] He further said that when Missouri and Arkansas seceded that he then was without protection from the United States. Therefore his alternative was to go with the South. Hence the secession ordinance of 1861. Therefore, he realized the fact that he was between two great fires: The South and the North.

This may account for his ingenious answer to Gen. Blunt's letter. He said, "Am I not one of the unfaithful ones." The tenor of his answer partook of the spirit of the answer the Mayor of New Orleans gave Farragut when he asked him to surrender the city.[5] But there was doubtless an underground communication that reached Blunt on the return of the messenger, because the next day after the surgeon and the young lady escort left the Chief's, the Treaty Regiment of Confederate soldiers which were in camp on the Prairie nearby mutinied. Their Colonel had to flee for his life with ninety of his men, and he lost his hat. The whole of the Regiment except the ninety raised a white flag with a red star in the center and marched in single file to Gen. Blunt's headquarters.[6]

On their arrival, enquiry was made of certain men in Tahlequah and especially about Slover. The Indians reported that there is nothing against him except he is a full-blooded secessionist. This was imaginary and grew out of the fact that he was the employee of the Southern Board of Domestic and Indian Missions. Had they reported that he is a full-blooded Southern man, they would have made a true report. As a further evidence of the Chief's duplicity, a company or two of Blunt's command came down and camped near the Chief's residence and guarded him and [his] family for three weeks while he and his treasurer, Lewis Ross, a brother of Chief John Ross, could get everything in readiness for a final trip to Washington City. Accordingly, when the necessary horse-shoeing and repairing of carriages and wagons were through with, the caravan moved off quickly for Blunt's headquarters; from there they were passed on through the Union lines to Washington.[7] If they ever returned, this Missionary knew nothing of it. His impression is that the chief died there or at Wilmington, Del.[8]

On the day the Treaty Regiment mutinied, E. L. Compere and the Missionary rode out on the prairie west of Tahlequah to look after some young horses, and just as they were ready to return, they discovered the fleeing Indians with the white flag &c. Three or four of the Indians were dispatched to intercept the two preachers but when they discovered the Missionary and that they had no arms, they at once returned without molesting them.

The next day the two preachers made a trip to Chief Ross's for information, and found him in great excitement over the meeting of the previous day. Evidently he thought himself in imminent danger. In conversation with the preachers he said the Negroes turned themselves loose in wild confusion, some got guns, some pistols, and those of them that could not get a gun or pistol got clubs and took horses and in fact every thing was at the mercy of the mob. He gave the preachers the information about the Treaty Regiment's mutiny, the colonel's escape with ninety men, and the departure of the soldiers for Blunt's headquarters on Wolf Creek.

The Missionary interrogated him as to what he thought of his remaining in his field of labor; he knew of no other white preacher in the Cherokee Nation. The Chief replied, "I cannot tell whether any one is safe or not, not even myself."

As the Missionary and his companion returned to Tahlequah, somebody met them and told them that it was reported in town that the Negroes intended to kill every white man living in Tahlequah and burn the town that night. Under the circumstances, this report was calculated to give alarm to the Missionary, and he, in consultation with his brother preacher and his family, set about to devise a plan of protection in the event the darkies should attempt to slaughter the white men and burn the town.[9]

It was first thought the Missionary had better temporarily leave the Nation, so everything was hid about the premises except what was absolutely necessary for immediate use, except the wearing apparel. Blankets, fine quilts, sugar, and coffee were stowed away in the garret by opening a scuttle hole overhead in one of the wardrobes beside the stack chimney and passing the articles up, then fastening the hole. Bacon and salt were secreted in another place, and meal and flour in another. Then in the second place a plan was adopted for the night; the two preachers concluded not to sleep inside the house and to make their saddle horses all rigged for travel if need be. So they each took a loaded gun and repaired to a thicket of blackjack bushes [probably *Quercus marilandica*] near the yard fence, and tied their horses, having first told Mrs. Slover (who with her five children was to remain in the house) to lock all outside doors and not to open them, unless the party seeking admittance first made themselves known.

The house was a one-story building thirty-six feet long, sixteen feet wide with a stack chimney in the center and a fireplace in each of the two rooms, and a long porch on the east side of the building, with banisters, and one entrance at the center with stone steps. The preachers were close enough to hear or even see if any one should approach the house, and they did not sleep but very little that Fourth of July night. The moon was right at the full, and consequently shown all night in the clear sky.

Saturday morning the fifth dawned bright and lovely, but no darkies had ambled around the building, nor no white man nor Indian was killed nor the town of Tahlequah burned. Horses were put in the little barn and fed, then breakfast was eaten and about eight o'clock A.M. the horses were saddled, and the parting hand given to the little children and their Mother. Mounting their horses, the preachers were off for Deacon Greer's in Washington County, Ark.

After one night at Greer's, Rev. Compere journeyed on for Fort Smith on the Arkansas River. Here at Deacon Greer's the Missionary stayed for nine or ten weeks without hearing anything definite from his family.

On Sunday morning the sixth of July and the next day after the Missionary's departure, three hundred Union soldiers of Blunt's command made a raid on Tahlequah, having a list of eighteen names of men whom they had come to arrest and take to their Headquarters.[10] The Missionary's name stood at the head of the list, but he was absent. They found eight of the eighteen and took them with them; as these eight men were citizens and not Confederate soldiers, they were permitted to come home, but no doubt they were forced to take the oath of Allegiance to the Union. As soon as the Chief and his party were ready to move, which took about three weeks' time, Gen. Blunt withdrew from the Indian Territory.

Then for a time the people were at the mercy of what was called the Light horse or home guard of Union men.[11] They were home thieves to all whom they suspected of being Southern families. They came sixteen in number to the Missionary's house and carried away every article of clothing except what the family had on, and took all the sheets and pillow cases from the bed. One Cherokee got a suit of the Missionary's fine clothes, hat and boots, went to the barn, put them on and came into the house, strutted across the room and said, "Slover Stand Watie man." Mrs. Slover got alarmed and sent the oldest boy to a neighbor woman's house and told her what was going on at his home; the woman could talk Cherokee, so she went with the little boy and shamed the Indians for robbing a poor helpless woman, and they took their prey and left. All the bacon the family had except one side—they had been using off that—was placed under the floor of an Indian cabin, in a place where dirt had been taken out to make a hearth and fireplace in the little cabin. A loom being was placed in its proper place immediately over the hidden treasure. No one would ever dream of anything being under that floor.

When the robbers came, they went into that cabin and saw the part of a side of bacon, hanging in its place on a pole at one side of the cabin. They asked Mrs. Slover if that was all the meat she had; she of course told them yes. They said that being all, they would not take it from her, but clothing was scarcer than bacon at that time so they asked no questions as to whether she or the children had any other clothing but unceremoniously took all they found, and the dear mother had to cut up the pink window curtains to make some kind of dressing for the children so she could wash the clothing they were wearing when the protective home guard came— not to guard her in the peaceable possession of what little she had, but to distress her and children by taking the little supply of clothing that they had.[12] This happened while the husband and father was thirty-five miles away, and not being able to hear from the dear ones, he was in mental trouble, yet otherwise well cared for by the Greer family.

Some rumors were afloat that Blunt's command had gone from the Nation and that the Confederate commander, Gen. Cooper, had moved north to Tahlequah and Park Hill and was in possession of the Cherokee country with his command. These rumors were calculated to make the Missionary anxious to go back to Tahlequah and get his family. While he was thinking over the situation, about four hundred Confederate soldiers came to Greer's en route for Tahlequah, headed by Lafayette Adair, a half breed Cherokee, as a pilot. The Missionary asked the commander if he could go with them. He said, "Get in your saddle and fall in line."

It was Sunday morning, perhaps the seventh day of September. All was nice sailing until about eleven o'clock A.M. when the Pilot (Adair) told the Commander that he wished to take seven men and go a mile and a half off the road to a grist mill in search of a fine horse the Pin Indians (Cherokees) had stolen from him sometime before that; the command could stop about a half mile ahead at a large spring. The Commander detailed the seven men to accompany the Pilot. On reaching the mill he found his horse and about twenty Pin Indians; they all fled into a willow thicket but seven who were captured.

The Pilot got his horse and with the seven prisoners set their head toward the sprint to join the command. It seemed that two of the Pins that had come to the mill that Sunday morning had gone to a peach orchard. Seeing the soldiers pass, they left the orchard and took an Indian trail for the mill which crossed the road that the Pilot was traveling. These two returning Indians crossed the big road a short distance behind the Pilot, and they shot him, inflicting a severe flesh wound just below the breast bone on the left side. The seven prisoners got away. The Pilot was carried by the seven soldiers and taken to the command at the spring; a litter was constructed and the wounded Pilot placed on it, and the line of march resumed about two o'clock P.M. Consequently they did not reach Tahlequah that day, but Monday morning the Missionary made the eight or nine miles alone and reached his home in the forenoon, to behold and meet his wife and children looking sad and forlorn and destitute of clothing. Gen. Cooper had turned the fine residence of the Chief into a hospital. The wounded Pilot was taken there and cared for; he got well but never soldiered again in that war.

The Missionary now concluded to abandon his field of missionary labor and leave the Cherokee Nation. He secured the use of two wagons and teams of the Stand Watie Regiment, sold to them his standing crop of corn—about sixteen acres—for a Confederate Voucher of the value of nine hundred dollars, which he afterward sold for six hundred dollars in Confederate paper money. Milch cows and hogs were disposed of to the best advantage. The household goods and all supplies that were hid two months before in the garret loft of the house and what bedding the

Indians had left, and the remains of the circulating Library, together with the kitchen fixtures and a loom, were loaded into the two Confederate wagons, and his family with some camping equipage into his own two-horse wagon. Then with an escort of a few soldiers, the first "Skedaddling" trip was begun late in the afternoon.

The little train headed for Wilsonville [Washington County, Arkansas] where his friend Greer resided. The only thing dreaded was a raid of the so-called Cherokee Pin Indians; therefore the greater part of the distance was made in the darkness of a moonless night. About 2 o'clock A.M. of the next day the wagons halted, a thorough inspection of the roads were made and the guard reconnoitered the premises for a considerable distance in front and rear, and finding no traces of an army or advance guard thereof, a camping was ordered until daylight.

Daylight soon appeared and about fifteen miles were yet to travel. This was done safely and unmolested. Deacon Greer's house was generously offered as a temporary resting place for the Missionary's family, where they abode for about four weeks or until the twenty-fourth day of October, when the fall campaign was in motion and every one on the "Quieve" [on the alert].

A second "Skedaddling" expedition was arranged. Deacon Greer, his youngest son James, two or three Negroes and all the horses he had with a camping outfit and the Missionary with his wagon and team with a saddle animal and a yearling colt, and a lot of blankets and quilts with camp equipage, started for the Arkansas River.

After about two and one half days, they pitched tent seventeen miles below Van Buren in a switch-cane brake [overgrown tall, bamboo-like grass] on the north side of the River. This tent, however, was not of canvas, but an improvised one constructed with poles, posts, and clapboards. It was so arranged as to be closed to the ground on the back side, with high and open front and closed sides; then a log heap was made the whole width of the camp, and fired of a night so as to keep the camp warm. Here they lived for two months in dread, for their families were at the mercy of their enemies fifty miles away.

An incident of deer hunting occurred while the two months were slowly passing. The Deacon claimed to be somewhat skilled in the art of hunting and killing wild deer, but the Preacher knew nothing about the business, notwithstanding he had a good old flintlock gun in camp and wanted to try his hand at it. He first set down to get all the points he could from the Deacon. One point in particular he wished to understand: that is to know how to get in shooting distance in case he should be so fortunate as to get the sight of a band or even one deer. The Deacon said, "If you are in a position where the wind is blowing from you and there should be any deer near, they will smell you and then run the other way, but if to the contrary, they may come very close, provided they do not see you."

So the Preacher cleaned up his old flintlock rifle and carefully loaded it and primed the pan and closed down the freizen; his powder-horn and shot-pouch were adjusted so as to hang under the right arm.[13] Thus equipped, he strolled off in a northerly direction, while the wind was coming briskly from the North and withall pretty cold. After passing the switch cane, he came to an open forest of big trees, mostly cottonwood, and in the midst of this forest was a dry slough. There on the north side of that he saw two deer slowly moving from him. Directly they parted; the one carrying a head of horns led off north, but the hornless one turned to the right, forming a semicircle.

The Preacher put a large cottonwood tree between him and the deer and prepared to shoot as soon as the deer would stop, and to his astonishment the animal circling around came within fifteen feet of him and stopped still. He thought it would be impossible to miss such animal as it appeared to be. The gun was fired without seeing the sights on the gun. At the report of the gun, the deer leaped into the air unhurt and away it went in the direction its mate had gone. Beside that old cottonwood stood a preacher with an empty gun in his hands, while the deer went skipping away through the forest.

Disappointed and sad he had to return to camp where the Deacon accosted him with the usual interrogation, "Where is your venison?" The Preacher replied, "The legs carried off the meat." But the thing was too good not to tell the Deacon, who, when the Preacher related the circumstances of the deer coming so near and missing it when he shot at it, said, "Buck ague, buck ague."[14] The Preacher told him no, but because it was so close and looked so large, he thought it impossible to miss it and shot without seeing the sights of the gun.

Before Christmas another battle of the civil war was fought in Washington County, Ark., known as the Prairie Grove fight. Gen. [Thomas C.] Hindman commanded the Confederate forces and Blunt and [Henry W.] Halleck commanded the Union army.[15] After a desperate fight both parties fell back, Hindman crossed the river at Van Buren, Ark., and made his way down the Arkansas River to Little Rock. Gen. [Earl] Vandorn was left for a time in Van Buren with a few men to care for the sick and wounded of the Prairie Grove battle.[16]

The Preacher became exceedingly anxious about the dear ones he had left two months before at the house of friend, Deacon Greer. Learning that some wagons were going to Washington County under a flag of truce, he interviewed Headquarters as to whether he could send his wagon along with the Lieutenant who had charge of the small train which was going to carry supplies and clothing to the wounded Confederate soldiers. He was told by the Commander to be on hand at sunrise Sunday morning, the twenty-eighth of December, 1862. Accordingly, the wagon and team were ready as ordered, and the Preacher's brother-in-law, James C. Ingram, who had fled from Washington County to save his life, was placed in charge of the wagon to drive the team.

As he (Ingram) had borrowed a horse from a Cherokee Indian to ride to the camp of Greer and the Preacher, it became necessary for the Preacher to take that horse over Lee's Creek into the Indian Territory and deliver him to Mr. Star, the owner of the animal. In order to spare a barefooted saddle mare, the only one he had left aside from the team, he borrowed a good, well-shod gray mare of a friend he had living in Logtown on the hill one mile from the city of Van Buren, and, leaving his own animal in charge of a little boy, a son of Mr. Cox where the Preacher had stopped the preceding night, he started early in the forenoon on his errand.

About 10 o'clock he forded said Lee's Creek. As he arose the west bank, he saw two Confederate soldiers going post haste toward Fort Smith. He inquired what was the matter. They quickly replied, "General Blunt made us kick the sand out of our saddles in a hurry early this morning." These two men belonged to a picket guard of a squad of men who had been at a place on the big road called Dripping Spring. The Preacher enquired further if Blunt was coming to Van Buren. They said, "He is there by this time." This was rather startling news to hear at that time, and all the circumstances considered, the Preacher was awe stricken because he supposed a flank guard of Cherokee Indians would be sent down through the Territory to look out for Rebels.

He did not ride more than a mile until he met Mr. Star, the young man to whom the borrowed horse belonged. The horse was quickly delivered, and as the decision had already been made to return to Logtown as soon as possible, he turned his face in that direction thinking, well, if he must be arrested, he would try to escape the Indians because he knew they were treacherous. After recrossing the same Lee's Creek, he took the blanket that he was using instead of an overcoat, and folded four square and spread it over his saddle, that everybody he met might be able to see that he bore no arms.

Pretty soon he reached the stage road over which Blunt's Cavalry had passed a few hours gone, and he saw about fifty Union soldiers; each one was carrying a drawn saber, a gun, and a brace of pistols swinging to the horn of their saddles. They didn't seem to notice the Preacher who turned to the right on a trail that saved at least one quarter of a mile's travel, and at the junction of the trail and the stage road, he met [Mrs. Wood] the wife of his friend bearing a cup of water. She said, "Aren't you a prisoner?" He said no but he did not know how soon he might be. He asked her where she was going with the water. She replied, "There is a Confederate soldier wounded down the hill at the roadside and I am going to take this water to him," but before she reached him she met the Union soldiers which the Preacher had passed and they told her the Confederate soldier was dead.

The Preacher had asked her what he should do with the gray mare, and she had told him to tie her behind the house for they, the Union soldiers, would get her anyway. On reaching the house, he tied the mare as directed, behind the house, and went into the setting room of the dwelling house and set down by a window where he could see the road.

It was now noon. Presently the armed squad of the Union soldiers passed their way to the city of Van Buren, and Mrs. Wood returned from her errand of mercy to her house and related the scenes of the early forenoon. She said every citizen, no matter how old, was driven into Van Buren from their homes by the Union soldiers. Also she told him about seeing a certain blacksmith take the mare from the little boy and leave Logtown with the straggling Confederate fleeing soldiers. Then it was settled that the Preacher was minus his animal, and, by the way, this was the first one he had lost. When interrogated about Mr. Wood, her husband, she said he went, too, but she did not know where he was.

That lady and her children were kind and friendly to the Preacher, who had concluded to abide his fate until moon down, which would be about midnight. Then, if he escaped arrest, he was going to make the effort to escape. For twelve long weary hours of suspense, he took in from his standpoint the sights as they transpired that afternoon and half the long night.

First about one o'clock he heard the report of a cannon apparently on the south side of the Arkansas River (Gen. Hindman had located one piece of his artillery about three miles south of Van Buren). The report was from that battery; they had thrown a bomb into the city of Van Buren which fell on the roof of a dwelling, but did not kill any one. About ten or fifteen minutes after the cannon's roar, a scene came in sight that made the hair of the Preacher's head stand on end. It was to all human appearance a perfect stampede of Blunt's Cavalry, and it seemed next to an impossibility for the officers to stop them, but finally they succeeded in checking them just in full view of the Preacher from his window.

Now the second scene of the panorama occurred, as quick as the fleeing cavalry was brought to a standstill, about one-half dozen of officers in full uniform, going on double-quick time, passed northward on the by-road. They had been gone but a short time when four pieces of artillery came in sight. Evidently this part of the command had been hurried up by those officers, for the artillery horses were in full speed with a man in a tight jacket and whip in hand on each horse. They were unlimbered about one quarter of a mile south of where the Preacher was setting. Then the roar of cannon was the order of the balance of that Sunday.

The third scene occurred just as the sun was sinking behind the western hill tops. The infantry came tired and hungry; two of them came to the door of Mrs. Wood's house and called for something to eat. She gave them bread and meat in their hands, told them the well was not fitten to use—there was something dead in it. This was done to prevent them from bothering her premises during the evening, as well as to secure the Preacher from being arrested. These two infantrymen, while dispatching their luncheon, said they had been on a forced march ever since three o'clock A.M. without anything to eat and that the commissary wagons would not get there before midnight. They said they were after Rebels and if they didn't catch them pretty soon, they didn't think they ever would. The Preacher was inside the house taking in all their conversation and thought as they made the last remark, "You are on a cold trail now, for they [Rebels] were all across the Arkansas River en route for Little Rock."

When nightfall came, the moon was high in the heavens, pouring down her silver light. Everywhere on the south, east and north could be seen soldiers' camp fires, even in the garden there was a fire and the men were talking. After the family had eaten supper, the Preacher, being conscious that, as soon as the soldiers had done with their supper, they would likely some of them be in the house to gas about the war, said to Mrs. Wood, "What are you going to do with me, for they are sure to come in?" She said, "I will lock you up in the 'Dining Room.'" Into that cold dark room he went, no light nor fire.

Presently he heard loud talking in the room he had just left. Sure enough, two of the soldiers went to Mr. Wood's empty storehouse where there were a few apples the family had put away for the winter. The door being locked, they smelled the apples and began tearing off the boards. Then Mrs. Wood went to them as quick as she could and found two of her neighbor men pulling off the boards. (They had left early in the war and joined the Union Army.) She asked what they meant; they told her that they thought they would get in the store and take the apples to keep the soldiers from stealing them. She understood that kind of talk and told them not to break the building. Be it said to their credit for once they did not enter the old storehouse and her apples were safe. But being acquainted with her they came in with her and talked for hour or more.

The Preacher had set the hour of one o'clock A.M. to make his escape. The gray mare had escaped the soldiers' eyes and still was tied behind the house or on the west side, which fortunately had no camp fires burning, the nearest one being in the garden not more than twenty yards from where the hungry gray mare had stood since noon without anything to eat.

Finally the long wintry hours passed and the moon was sinking behind the Western hills, but still there was some conversation heard in the garden. The hour of one A.M. had come; the good woman opened the dining room door and let the prisoner of hope out. She filled his saddlebags full of bread and meat, told him to take the gray mare, and then gave him instructions how, and where, to go about seven miles to a Southern man's house by the name of Seegraves, particularly telling him not to stop at any house until he reached Seegraveses. Everything being ready he thanked the kind woman for kindness and gave her the parting hand, and she wishing him a safe trip, he untied the halter rope or leather rein.

Now the first thing that confronted him was a rail fence which he had to lay down or open a gap in it so that the mare could get through with as little noise as possible, for he could still hear someone talking in the garden. Through the fence, he found a second difficulty: that was a cornfield with the stalks about all knocked down by the army the forenoon of Sunday "Ride." Now he could not think of riding two hundred yards over dry corn stalks on a gray animal with soldiers so near to him as that garden. Quickly he struck a plan, that was to throw his saddlebags as across his right shoulder, take the halter rein in his left hand, and then in a half bent attitude walk under the gray mare's chin across the field, feeling sure that every step increased the distance between himself and the soldiers in the garden. In that position the field was soon crossed.

A third trouble confronted him—a rail fence with a lot of blackjack brush on top of it. Brush was cut green in the summer and was dry with the leaves on. This fence had to be opened or laid down, and just such rattling of brush he dreaded, lest the wakeful soldiers in that garden would hear and come after him.

Outside the fence, a fourth difficulty was before him—great rocks two and a half and three feet high and appeared as large as a forty-gallon barrel. It being dark he could not ride, for he had to feel his way up that hill for a short distance, then wind down on the northern slope. After reaching the base of the hill, the ground was clear of rock, so now adjusting his saddlebags on the saddle, he mounted and through the woods he made his way.

Forming a semicircle around Logtown, on the north he came to the big military road. An imaginary trouble came upon him as he imagined a picket sentinel might be stationed in the dark somewhere about that distance from the camp, and if so he would stand a good chance to a get a ball sent toward him for he had no countersign. But the way seemed clear, so thrusting both spurs into the sides of the gray mare, that big road was crossed at about two leaps of the animal, thence across the dry bed of Rock Creek, and he was in the neighborhood road that led, as the good woman had directed, from Van Buren to Frog Bayou, and to Seegraves' at whose house he arrived about three o'clock A.M., and called. A man came to the door; the Preacher interrogated him as to his name. Finding him as directed, he asked if he would feed his mare and let a Baptist minister sleep in his house until daylight. He said, "Who are you?" "Slover," the Preacher replied. "O yes," Seegraves answered. "I know you. Get down and come in."

The gray mare was stabled and fed and the rider put to bed. He omitted to state the narrow escape he made at the crossing of the big road. He had only got across the little dry creek and fairly in a leap, when he heard the rumbling of the wheels of the train of commissary wagons. Of course this train was heavily protected by front and rear guards, and had he been a few minutes later he would have encountered the advance guard and been made a prisoner, and carried back to headquarters with the loss of the gray mare, but he was very thankful to his God that such was not the case.

A good rest and sleep were enjoyed under the roof of his strange friend.

After a nice hot breakfast was dispatched, the gray mare was saddled and bidding his host good bye, the Preacher started for the camp, but another imaginary difficulty lay across his way. He knew there was another thoroughfare coming from the north to Van Buren called the Frog Bayou route, and thought it more than likely a heavy flank guard would be on this road to look out for the movement of Hindman's Rebel soldiers, lest they should make a flank movement and cut off Blunt's return to Fayetteville north of the Boston Mountains. He knew he had to cross this big road about two miles below Seegraveses. Down the creek he rode, fully determined what he would do should he be so unfortunate as to meet Union soldiers.

Sure enough when he came to the dreaded crossing, he saw the evident sign that at least one hundred cavalry had crossed the creek but a little while before, because the water was rapidly running down the road from the south side of the stream, showing beyond a doubt that soldiers were on their way to Van Buren. But the Preacher thought of the old adage, "A miss is as good as a mile," and passed on somewhat assured that he would reach his camp unmolested, and so he did.

But his friend, Deacon Greer, had put everything into his two-horse wagon that very Monday morning and started down the Arkansas River. While the Preacher was looking at the fresh wagon tracks to ascertain the direction the wagon had gone, young James Greer and the Negro boy came in sight following one of the Deacon's young animals which had left them a short distance below. On learning that the Yankee soldiers had not visited the camp, he felt a great relief. He with the two boys overtook the outfit at Big Mulberry Creek where it enters the River. The creek was somewhat deep, but cross it they must, and the only way was to ford the stream. The water was about half side deep to the horses. All was over by noon and a stop was made and a luncheon ate, for the Preacher had plenty in his saddlebags which he brought from the good woman in Logtown the night before.

A little while before one o'clock P.M. a start was made with four horses hitched to a two-horse wagon with a joint tongue and the Deacon to drive. At the first curve in the road, the lead horses swung around briskly and broke the wagon tongue off at the double-tree. This mishap blighted the hopes of the Deacon especially, and he exclaimed in despair, "What shall we do!" but as soon as the Preacher could look at the broken tongue, he answered the Deacon's question, saying, "We will mend it," and suiting action to the answer, he tied the gray mare to a sapling, laid off his coat, and having some tools along, he fell a small hickory sapling, cut it off the length he wanted it, then split it. Using one half of it he fitted it on the underside of the broken tongue and bore holes with a three-quarter auger both behind and in front of the double, and drove good pins in, and in just sixty minutes from the time it was broken, it was ready for traveling again.

The Preacher turned the gray mare over to young Greer and got on the seat with the Deacon and said to him, "Give me the lines." He did so, and again the party resumed their run, or as it was called then, a "Skedaddling." Ten hours drive in haste brought the party into the town of Ozark, the county seat of Franklin County, and about one or two o'clock A.M. Tuesday the party pulled up to the residence of a preacher by the name of Miller with whom the Preacher and Deacon were acquainted for Miller was a Baptist minister. With this family the party were refreshed and received kind treatment, but they would not be content to stop on the North side of the river. So moving on down the river they came to Roseville at the head of McClain's bottom, where they crossed the river by private ferry, and traveled up the south side several miles, where they found forage for their hungry animals, and pitched camp and learned that Blunt had only spent one night in Van Buren and then fell back to Fayetteville.

The party rested here until Friday morning, then the Preacher concluded that it was time for his family to be nearing Van Buren. He saddled the gray mare and bid the Deacon good bye. This was the last time they ever had the pleasure of meeting for not long after he (the Deacon) went back to his home, the Indians killed him. The Preacher wended his way up the river, stopping over night with a friend about three miles from Van Buren. Saturday he rode to the river where there was, ten days before, a ferry, but the Yankees had burned it together with two steamboats loaded with corn. On reaching the South bank of the river, he saw his returning wagon driving down the bank on the other side. There were no means of crossing but in a small "Row Boat," that was put to use, and soon the family and their goods were on the south side all safely.

The Preacher had deposited a box containing all the fine quilts and blankets, with a trunk containing a lot of old letters, a pair of fine boots, and a hat box with a silk hat in it, at the residence of Mrs. Southmaids, one half mile out of Van Buren. They had been in the attic room of her house all the while he was camped in the cane brake, so he took the wagon and went after those articles. On arriving at the residence of the lady above named, he soon found that the Union soldiers had forced the door to the attic chamber, and broke the trunk, stole a watch and took the silk hat, but the boots being in an old sack they left them. They pried the lid up on the box containing the quilts and blankets but did not take them.

Being thankful that they left as much as they did, and thanking the good woman for the kindness she had shown to him in storing his goods so long, he made his way back to the crossing of the river. He made another trip across the river with the rowboat, but that team and wagon had to be driven across at the fording place a little below the ferry landing. The water was low, but quicksand was the difficulty, so leaving the family with all the goods on the south side, he returned in the little craft to the team and all alone he drove into the water. Having seen other men, long before that time ford the stream, he had learned the track by observation, and with some difficulty with the sand he made the trip, while the dear ones looked on with anxious thoughts. The goods and chattels were carefully reloaded, and the family, the wife, her five children, their grandmother and her son, all on top, constituted all the property he had left.

Now a start was made for Grand Prairie, twenty or twenty-five miles down the road toward Little Rock, where he secured a house and occupied it for about one month. On the last days of January 1863, Thomas H. Compere, a brother of E. L., came to the house and reported that the Union troops were then occupying the city of Fort Smith, and that he thought the Preacher had better make another move. It did not require much time for him to decide to do so. An arrangement was speedily made, Sunday as it was, for another skedaddling expedition. And early Monday teams and wagons were rigged for a move. Compere's team were oxen, and the plan was that the Missionary's brother-in-law take his team and the Missionary's family and go through the hill country with Compere, while the Missionary went on horseback direct to Dardenelle, in order to see Rev. E. L. Compere who was to start to Alabama on the third day of that month.[17] It was important that the Missionary see him before he started.

As soon as all things were ready, the wagons rolled out for Danville through the hills, and the Preacher found himself mounted again on the same gray mare of his friend's in Logtown, with a little something for himself and mare to eat. Sixty miles had to be traveled in twenty-four hours in order to meet Rev. E. L. Compere who was going to start for Alabama on Tuesday morning.

The Missionary had two thousand dollars due him for two years' service as Missionary to the Cherokee Indians. The means of public communication had been stopped and the Board of Missions could not send safely any money to their Missionaries. He wanted to send an order to the Mission Board by Rev. E. L. Compere for the money. This was the reason that he turned the family over to Thomas H. Compere. He rode until noon, stopped and fed the gray mare and ate his own luncheon, and then was soon in the saddle. About three o'clock A.M. Tuesday, he found it necessary to stop and sleep. He called at a house near the roadside, and was permitted to lie down on the floor before the fire. As quick as it was daylight he was up and off for Dardenelle, got there on good time, but it began to rain very early in the forenoon of that day and Compere did not go, so there was a disappointment.

The rain was the beginning of a fearful rain and snow storm, especially in the hills where the family was, and nothing but a wagon sheet to keep the rain and snow off. The wagons and family were in that fearful storm with the front axle of the Preacher's wagon broken out. This detained them for more than a half day, but finally they got through. After being exposed for about four days in the wet and cold with lots of snow on the ground, the Missionary's wife never was well any more.

After stopping a few days with the T. H. Compere family, he got a house about three miles below Dardenelle near the Arkansas River and lived in it for one month. No doubt the exposure in the above-mentioned storm was the cause of the death of his wife, together with the fact that there was no medicine in the country in reach of the physician. Be this as it may, he had been in this last named house but a short time when his wife was attacked with typhoid pneumonia. A doctor was called from Dardenelle, who, after exhausting what medicine he had, said he could not get the medicine that he needed and the case was a critical one. In a day or two more he told the Preacher that he had to give up the case and that she would not live very long, that there was no medicine to be had in the country. And on the twenty-seventh day of February 1863 she died, leaving three small boys and two little girls to mourn the loss of a mother.

It now became necessary for him to make another move, and looking around he found a farm for rent, belonging to the County Judge, three miles due south of Dardenelle. Early in the month of March this move was made, with nothing to feed his horses and but little for the family, but he heard there was some corn on a large barge or flat boat lying alongshore in the Arkansas River a short distance below Dardenelle, which could be bought for one dollar and fifty cents per bushel. It had laid there in the wet without a cover until it had soured, and having the husk on it begun to swell and come off the cob, but this was the only chance for grain for his horses.

Everything considered, the surroundings looked gloomy and drear. Directly across the big road from this dwelling lived an old planter, a Union man. He was continually bemeaning [demeaning] the Southern Confederacy although he owned sixteen Negroes and a pretty good upland farm. He had no family but the Negroes, and he was seventy-five years old. He was once married but his wife only lived six months. He rode down to a neighbor's house whose name was Ross, who had once lived in the same dwelling that the Missionary had rented, and said, "Mr. Ross, who do you think is living in your old house?" "I don't know," said Ross. "Well," said the old man, "he is a d—m—d preacher. I'll have him to support, I reckon." Such was the old planter's conviction of the industry of a preacher but this time he made a mistake.

The Preacher wanted to buy some fodder for his horses and seeing that the old planter had a good lot on hand, he walked over one day to purchase a dozen bundles, but the old planter told him he had no fodder to sell. A few days after this he borrowed a plow of the old planter and was plowing some ground to plant early potatoes. The old planter came over on his milk-white farm horse which he said was twenty-five years old, and stood and looked at the Preacher handle that plow and team for a while, then said, "Come over and get some fodder for your horses. It will resuscitate their stomachs and give them an appetite for the corn you are feeding them." "Thanks," said the Missionary, and at noon went to his barn and got a dozen bundles. He asked the old planter how much he wanted for the fodder; "Nothing" was the answer. The old planter went to Ross's again in a few days and told him that Preacher was the best worker he ever saw, and that he knew exactly how to plow. After that, it was no trouble to get help from that old planter, whose name, by the way, was Thomas Waters.

A man never knows the value of a wife until he loses one and is left with a lot of little children to take care of, but fortunately for the Missionary, his mother-in-law lived with him at the time of the death of his wife, and had been for several years. There were five children—the oldest was about ten years and the youngest eleven months old—to clothe and feed, and there was nothing in the clothing line that could be bought in any store. A plenty could be found to eat, but how to get clothing was the problem to solve. A winter had just passed and consumed all the clothing the family had provided for that winter, and another winter would soon be at the door. Finally he fell on a plan. His mother-in-law was a good weaver and spinner, and his own mother had, while he was quite young, taught him a good deal about making cloth but he never wove any, but finding a flying shuttle loom in the neighborhood that could be bought for twenty dollars in Confederate money, he made the purchase.

So it happened that the summer of 1863 was the time for a host of Southern people to leave Yell County and go to Texas and there was a demand for cotton material. There was at Norristown on the north bank of the Arkansas River a spinning factory that would exchange thread for raw cotton, and a certain planter had left and gone to Texas and let a large quantity of raw cotton in the lint-room of his cotton gin, in charge of a Negro man who said he was authorized to sell the cotton for twenty-five cents per pound in Confederate money and that was the only kind of money he [Slover] had. So learning these facts, the Preacher and his mother-in-law soon arranged a plan. He found that he could do very good work in the loom and sell all the plain cotton cloth he could weave.

By this means he managed to furnish clothing for the children and himself. By the help of his mother-in-law he could weave four treadle jeanes, and she was good with scissors and needle, so they could make heavy clothing for winter. He would preach of Sundays at different places.

Suffice it to say that things politically moved smoothly until September. By this time the Southern soldiers had about all gone south to Red River and Texas, Fort Smith had been taken in the summer by Blunt and Little Rock by [Frederick] Steele, so that the Arkansas River was the base of operations for the Yankees.[18] On the ninth day of September A.D. 1863 Col. [William F.] Cloud took Dardenelle and held it and established winter quarters and a post at that place, and as a matter of course the Missionary had to submit to be under the protection of the United States soldiers.

The incidents and events of the twenty-one months he resided in Yell County will here be given in the order of their occurrence so far as can be remembered by the Missionary.

On the taking of Dardenelle by the Yankees, the horse thieves that belonged to the command or followed it came early Sunday morning to the residence of the Missionary. As well as remembered, there were eight of them all told, four white men and four Negroes. However, one of the Negroes (and an important one for the Preacher) was not with the other seven on their arrival, but came during the conversation. They were all on horseback, led by a good-looking, fair-complected young man, appearing to be about twenty-five or thirty years old. He approached the yard gate where the Preacher met him with ordinary morning salutations, after which Captain as they styled him (Captain Brown) said to the Preacher, "Have you any good horses here? If you have them, we want them; if they are not good, we do not want them."

This was the first time such thieves had ever made this kind of a demand on the Missionary, and he thought the best way to answer was to tell the truth to the letter, and at once told the thieves that he had two horses and only two, that one of them was a good one and the other was a good Cherokee or Indian pony, but said that these are all the horses he had and did not want them to take them. The Captain said, "Where are they?" "Down in the pasture," was the ready reply. He said, "You have them hid, have you?" "No, sir," said the Preacher. "They are running in a stubble field where they have been ever since the oats were taken off the ground." Just as the Preacher was making his second plea for the party not to take the horses, the Captain said, "You're a d—m—d good Southern man, I suppose." "Yes," said the Preacher; he was never anything else, for he was born and raised in the South, but being a minister of the Gospel, he was not nor had been a soldier.

Just at this juncture the other Negro man rode up as big as heck and said, "Good morning, Parson," and deliberately straightened himself up in his stirrups, and seeing the situation in which the Parson, he called him, was placed, said "Captain, I don't think you ought to take Parson Slover's horses, for," said he, "the Parson has been here about eight or nine months preaching to the people, both white and black, and works hard and attends to his own business." "Very well, is there not another house close here?" "Yes," said the darkie, pointing across the County road to the Preacher's old friend, Waters, who happened not to be at the house at that time.

The Captain then ordered his men to go over to Waters' and just such destruction, O my! The captain ordered the Negroes belonging to the old man to yoke up the oxen and put them to the wagon, and load it with their bedding and told his men to force the smokehouse door, which they did by means of a large stick of firewood. This gave access to all the supplies the old man had laid in for himself and sixteen Negroes. Then they (the thieves) went into the residence, pulled up the fine carpet from the floor, tore it into saddle blankets; even took the wheels out of the clock and every particle of bedding but one feather bed and one quilt. An old Negro woman who was housekeeper for her old master refused to leave the premises, but they forced all the rest to go. They (the thieves) went to the barnyard where the mules and horses were and drove them off as if they belonged to them.

The old man came in pretty soon after these robbers had left, and the old Negroes told him the lamentable story. He followed after the thieves and went to the Commander-in-Chief and succeeded in getting back one yoke of oxen and two mules. The poor old man was miserably treated by his friends, for he was to all intents and purposes a Union man. But the visit to the Preacher's house did not satisfy the thieves. They had been in Dardenelle but three weeks when they conceived a plan to steal the Missionary's horses.

In the afternoon of Saturday about the first of October, two officers arrayed in their uniforms came into the Preacher's house and conversed socially and freely. During the conversation the Preacher turned to his two small boys and told them to go out and water the horses. The boys went into the orchard where the horses were that forenoon, but could not find the horses. Pretty soon they (the boys) came in and one said in the presence of the two offices, "Pa, there are no horses in the orchard." Immediately the officers made an excuse to leave, and the Preacher went out and surveyed the situation, and soon found that the horses had been stolen and passed out through a back gate which led into the woods or commons. The yoke that the big horse wore had been cut off and left lying at this back gate and the gate was open. Also there were tracks showing that shod horses had just a short time before been there. "Well," thought the Missionary, "the thieves have got my horses at last." He has never been able to find them. Now the visit of the two soldiers was explained. They entertained the Preacher while some of the soldiers stole the two horses and got away with them.

Here more trouble looked him square in the face. Winter was close at hand and the Preacher had no time to draw wood nor horse to ride to the preaching places, but his old friend Waters had a yoke of oxen and a good saddle mule. He had traded the other mule for a saddle horse for himself to ride. So he came over to see the Preacher and told him he could use the oxen for a team, and the extra mule to ride for their feed. He kindly thanked him and was glad to accept such an offer, for he had a fine crop of corn and oats and some hay and fodder, but the Yankees took one stack of fodder and they didn't as much as lay up the fence of the cornfield where they come in, and they went out another way, leaving gates and fences open, and killed one of the old planter's hogs and lashed it on top the load of fodder, but they were very careful of one thing, viz., not to say a single word about pay, either for fodder or hog.

Things run smoothly during the winter 1863 and '4, and the Missionary was quietly preaching at two or three churches, one church in Pope County in the town of Russellville, another about ten miles down the Arkansas River on the south side, and occasionally in Dardenelle and other places. In the early part of March 1864 an event transpired at the church on the south side of the river which was somewhat amusing as well as interesting. The church had an important conference meeting on Saturday, and consequently there was a good turnout and there seemed to be an unusual number of mule teams at church that day. One wagon had four of these animals to it, and several long-eared creatures with saddles on, among them was the Deacon's daughter's (Miss Lizzie Holland) and of course the Pastor's donkey was on hand.

It so happened that the Commander at Dardenelle issued an order that Saturday morning, and sent out a squad of men to take all the mules they could find that was over two years old and bring them to headquarters at Dardenelle, and just as the Pastor had got well underway in his sermon, he observed that his congregation was agitated about something transpiring outside the house, and he saw, on looking out at the door that there were several soldiers with blue coats, and casting his eye out at a window behind the pulpit, he observed one of these soldiers about to untie his saddle mule.

By this time his congregation had all arose to their feet and were moving toward the door, but to no avail. The soldiers had the harness and saddles off all the mules in a very short time, except the old gentle mule the Deacon's daughter had rode to the meeting. They left the Preacher an old pony to ride. The Deacon's daughter was crying and begging the soldier that had her mule not to take it. He told her he would go and tell the Lieutenant to come. Presently he came and she again renewed her appeals for the mule. The soldier was holding the halter rein and both he and the Lieutenant were in their saddles ready to go, but the tears of the young woman overcame him in good degree, and he straightened up in his stirrups and said, "Madam, I have a wife and two little babies and if the Rebels hurt her, I never will quit killing them; bring on the mule." The soldier holding the rein also popped to his saddle horse. The old farm mule threw up its head, but did not move, and the soldier let go the halter and cried out with an oath, "I can't lead this mule," so the young woman saved her riding mule.

As the soldiers went up the road with the stock of stolen or captured property, they met Deacon Holland returning from the office of the Provost Marshal, where he had been to get a permit to sell his cotton. He said to them, "You got the Parson's mule, I see." "Yes," they replied. "What did he say?" inquired the Deacon. They told the Deacon that he was preaching and looked out at the window and saw one of the boys taking the mule, and never took time to come down the steps of the pulpit, but closed his Bible, leaped over the book board, and said, "I'll be d____d if they haven't got my mule." Then they raised a huge laugh and on they went.

This report that the Deacon heard about the Pastor was too good a joke not to tell him, so when he got home he found the Pastor at his house and told him what the soldiers had said. This does very well to laugh over even until this day. But the Pastor's saddle mule was gone and he was riding a very indifferent pony instead. Nevertheless, he had taken the oath as administered by the Provost Marshal, and was determined to have that mule or know the reason why, so just five days after his mule raid, he heard that the Scout had returned which had rode the mule into the country.[19]

The Pastor went down to the Commander's headquarters and demanded the mule. The Col. said to him, "Have you taken the oath?" The Pastor told him he had. The Col. turned to his secretary and said, "Write this man an order upon the quartermaster for his black mule." The order was presented in less than five minutes time after it was written. The harness was on the mule, but the Quartermaster told the driver to unharness that black mule and turn him over to this man, which was done without a word. The Preacher road the mule home.

In the month of May Gen. [Joseph O.] Shelby made an attack on the Union soldiers at Dardenelle on a Monday morning before daylight, and completely routed them, burned up their winter quarters, and took their supplies, and all the horses that they had to leave in their stampede.[20] He held his men in the place for three days. Then he moved on toward Missouri. Pretty soon after the departure of Shelby, a new phase of the war trouble appeared, viz. bushwhackers had command of the whole country. There were about seventy-five Union men and about the same number of Southern soldiers. First one party would raid the farms for supplies and then the other. But before these companies were formed, the Preacher had another interview with about four hundred Yankees. It was on this wise:

About three weeks after the "Feds" had been routed by Shelby, they came back up the north side of the Arkansas River to Norristown, one mile and a half above Dardenelle. The Preacher had drove his ox team down to town to mill and was waiting for the grist to be ground, when suddenly there appeared two good-looking young women at the mill and enquired for the ferryman. No such man could be found, and there were no men in town but the Miller and Negro Jim by name, and a Mr. Thompson who had been a Rebel soldier and was discharged because he had lost his speech.

The girls insisted on crossing the Arkansas River at the ferry which was a mile above town. They said they had the money, either greenback or Confederate money. They said they had a wagon and one yoke of oxen and their little brother and was going to north Arkansas to bring their sister south where she could be better taken care of.

The Missionary listened at these appeals for a good while; finally his sympathy was aroused for the young women, though strangers, and he said to the old Negro Jim, "Jim, let us go up and put the ladies over." Old Jim agreed, and the party set out on foot for the ferry. On reaching the boat, behold, the top floor had been thrown into the river by the fleeing Union men on their flight from Dardenelle three weeks before.

There were sure enough the wagon, oxen, and a ten-year-old boy; the wagon was empty. The Missionary turned to the women and said, "Are you willing to risk the team and wagon in that old boat?" "O yes," they said; they thought it was safe. He again said to them, "Is the team gentle?" One of the women responded and said they were very gentle. "Well," said the Missionary to old Jim, "if they are willing to take the chances, we ought to be." He then told them to drive in; they did so and the boat was taken to the other side of the river in quick time, and as the team was driven out, a young lady by the name of Stout appeared on horseback and wanted to cross over to the south side. She was invited to ride in. She did so and remained in the saddle on her horse. Just as this point the Missionary began to "smell a mouse," in reference to the mission of the two women going north and Miss Stout going south.

The south bank was gained as soon as the oars could make the boat run across, running aground some twenty feet before dry land was reached. The young lady was told that she would have to ride out into the shallow water, and the two ferrymen soon followed by stepping into the shallow water and drawing the boat after them as far as they could, and left the craft on the sand bar, and it was at least three hundred yards across a heavy sand bar to the timber.

It seemed to the Missionary that it behooved him to get to the timber as soon as possible, but he failed to do so before he heard horses' feet pitapat on the other side of the river. Looking around, the Missionary said to the old darkie, "Jim, look at the blue coats coming on the other side." Jim said, "Rebs." The Preacher said, "No, sir, they are Union men." They were coming about as fast as their horses could bring them and before they had walked one hundred yards a voice was heard from the rushing crowd of horsemen, "Bring that boat over here." The darkie and Missionary stopped to think what answer to make, but the soldiers were in a hurry, and sent another voice over the river accompanied with the explanation, "I will shoot you if you don't bring it."

The two ferrymen, as they now saw they were doomed to be for all the time the gathering crowd wanted their services, hastened back to the boat and applied the oars, and very soon was nearing the other bank. When close enough to be recognized, the old Provost Marshal (Capt. Smith) yelled out, "Hard down on it, Parson." On hearing this, the Preacher said, "Hallow, Captain. What brought you here," or something to that effect. He immediately began to ask where there were any Rebels over in Dardenelle. "Not when I left there," said the Preacher. "Are you sure of it?" he rejoined. The Preacher said, yes, not when he left, which was about eleven o'clock A.M. and it was now after twelve.

As soon as the boat was landed he (Capt. Smith) said, "I want you to take twenty of us without horses over." Into the boat rushed the twenty armed men, and away the boat was pulled by the Preacher and old Jim. As quick as the craft landed, the Captain said, "Take the boat back to the men on the other side," and they, the twenty, made their way to secure a place behind a huge rock known there and then as Dardenelle Rock. It stood at least twenty feet high and about thirty or forty long and lay just on the edge of the high bank at the timber.

The boat was taken back and by this time there were about four hundred men gathered, and at Dardenelle a half dozen Rebel bushwhackers showed themselves. The boat was made fast and the ferrymen had gone up to mingle with the crowd of citizens that had been brought there under arrest by this body of soldiery. It was but a short time when a [Union] Lieutenant inquired who was ferryman there. Someone in the crowd pointed out the old darkie and the Preacher as such men. The Lieutenant said to the Preacher, "I want this ferry-boat run up the river one quarter of a mile." The Preacher said, "Those Rebels over yonder will shoot us if we go into the boat." The Lieutenant drew his sixshooter and leveling it at the Preacher's breast said, "D—m you, I will shoot you if you don't go into the boat and run it up as directed."

Suffice it to say the Preacher had no more to say that afternoon, but without dinner or supper, he and old Jim run that boat back and forth, putting six or eight men with their horses over at every trip until after dark. Not a soldier offered to touch an oar. When dark came the soldiers told the Preacher and the darkie that they might go. They were now put to their wit's end as to how they would manage to go down to Dardenelle in the dark, not knowing where a picket guard might be placed, and, of course, they had no sign by which they could make themselves known. Neither did they know but the town was full of Rebels. Finally they thought of a small skiff that lay along shore a short distance below the place where they had toiled that afternoon, and they resolved to get in it, and silently float down the current of the river to Dardenelle, fearing to make any noise with the oars, lest the soldiers might be somewhere in the dark, in hearing, and shoot at the noise, and they knew that bullets had no eyes. So into the little craft they stepped and set her afloat and floated silently down to town.

They found everything as silent as the grave, could see no soldiers nor no one else anywhere on the streets, so the darkie and the Preacher bid each other goodnight, and the Preacher concluded to go into Mr. Thompson's house and see what he could learn about the news of the afternoon. When he entered the door of Thompson's house, Mrs. Thompson exclaimed, smiling, and said, "I never was to glad to see a man in my life." The Missionary said, "Where is Mr. Thompson." "Oh!" she said. "He is gone and will not be back tonight," and went on to say, "Why Mr. Slover, there is not a man in town." He then told her he would have to drive home in the dark. "No, sir," she said, "you will not leave here tonight. I want you to stay with us for we (meaning her children) are alone."

She further told him to go and get his team and put it in the lot and feed the oxen, and so he had to stay. She got him some supper and furnished him a good room to sleep in. She said the Union men came down on the streets and rode around and went off, said there were but five or six Rebel soldiers or bushwhackers in town that forenoon and they did not stay but a little while.

In early fall, the Missionary was holding divine service in Dardenelle on Sunday, and having preached in the forenoon to an attentive congregation, principally women, made an appointment for four o'clock P.M. same day, and just as he was bringing the sermon to an end, a yell of the bushwhackers was heard as if they intended to make people believe that there were a thousand of them, but there weren't but seventy-five of them, but in less time than half an hour they were in every street in town.

The Missionary had rode a young mule to church that day for which he paid four hundred dollars in Confederate Money but a short time before. The mule was in an inclosure made of boards about seven feet long and stood on end and nailed close together. Therefore, one had to look over the top of the fence to see what was inside. While the bushwhackers were raiding the other parts of town, the Preacher walked over to the house where he had stopped, and as the sun was getting low he concluded to saddle the two-year-old mule and go home. As he entered the corral, one of the men on the outside on horseback said, "Captain, here is a good mule in this corral." "Yes," the Preacher responded, "and I am going to ride him home."

The man, seeing at the second look what the Preacher was about doing (saddling the mule), said bring him out. The Preacher said, "I intend to and I am going to ride him home." On passing through the gate, the Captain said, "Get into your saddle and go with me." He began talking very roughly to his prisoner and with one of those big oaths so common among soldiers said, "Why are you not in the army on one side or the other; you are a hale-looking man." The Preacher answered him mildly and said, "I am a Minister of the Gospel and did not wish to go into the Army." He then spoke kindly and said, "You stay here until I get away with my men."

The Preacher began to fear that the men in the rear would take his mule, and so when the Captain blew his horn for a move, the Preacher moved with him. Down the river they went. Presently they put their horses in a gallop. Then the Preacher turned his mule to one side and began spurring him to make him cut up, and finally got his head back towards town and still digging him in the flank to make the men as they passed him believe that he was very fractious.

One of the men said, "You are breaking him, are you?" "Yes," said the Preacher, "but he may break me." He felt very much relieved when he passed the last of them to know that they had not taken his mule. He made his way home, and about midnight he was called by the Captain of the Rebel bushwhackers. He answered, for he knew the Captain's voice. The Captain (John Orr) said, "Were you in Dardenelle today (meaning Sunday)?" "Yes," the Preacher said. The Captain talked about the Union men being in town and asked where they went. The Preacher replied, "They started down the river." The Captain and his men started for Dardenelle but somehow they learned that the Union whackers had come back to town and were entrenched in the old stockade. Then Orr turned aside to a thicket of underbrush and lay down on the leaves until morning.

The Union party was up and off very early Monday morning and rode down the river about twelve miles to the Baptist Deacon's farm (Holland). Deacon Holland was not home; two white women, daughters of the Deacon, and a Negro woman were there. The Union men demanded dinner and that the Negro woman prepare it for, said they, "You white women might poison us." While the dinner was being prepared they searched the premises for money.

The Rebels pursued them to a certain point where the road forked, and anticipating the movements of the Union men, they left their track and made their way to a certain crossing of the Petit Jean River where they (the Rebels) knew the other party had to cross if they went to the hills, but the Union men were slow in getting there. The Rebels got impatient and moved down three or four miles further near the mouth of this little river and while there the other party made the crossing and escaped to the hills.

[John] Adams had been from home as a refugee, and his church had called the Missionary to preach for them. In October of 1864, Adams came home and was with the Missionary at the Saturday's meeting of the church, and took him home with him to spend the night. The Missionary observed that Adams did not sleep on a bedstead but lay on the floor with the door open. Sunday morning at the proper time, the Missionary, Adams with one of his small boys behind him on horseback, and fourteen others, principally women and a few old men, were on their way, all on horseback. Adams and the Missionary were at the head of the little company going to church. When within about one-half mile of the schoolhouse where the preaching was to be, they saw two men with guns, and a niece of Adams standing at the junction of two roads. The niece was on foot, the men on horseback.

As the church-going party drew within about seventy-five paces of the two men, the young woman yelled out and said, "Uncle John (meaning Adams), don't you come here." Instantly one of the two men cried out, "Halt!"

The Missionary instantly halted but Adams popped the spur to his horse and wheeled to the left, placing the crowd between himself and the two men, but as soon as they saw that he did not halt when they cried a halt, they came as fast as their horses could lope and by the time Adams rounded in sight at the rear of the crowd, they fired at him on shot each. He bowed at the report of the guns and was in the brush. His boy fell off, and some of the little company thought he was wounded. The ball lodged in his coat collar. After shooting at him they pursued and caught him.

The little company all scattered into the brush but the Missionary and the two ladies, who said to the Missionary, "What shall we do?" He replied, "Stay right here with me." Pretty soon eleven more ruffians, all disfigured with some kind of paint, came from the direction of the schoolhouse. One of them approached the Missionary and said, "What was that shooting about?" He replied that they were shooting at a man. "Did they hit him?" "Can't tell," said the Missionary. "Which way did they go?" The Missionary pointed to the direction, and the eleven rode on in single file, like so many Indians for whom they evidently wanted to pass themselves by being painted like Indians. They put Adams under arrest and started off, rode a mile or two, and two of the painted band were sent (in pretense) to report to Col. Fuller and to get instructions what to do with Adams. They were gone but a few minutes when they came into the road and reported that the Col. said, "Being that he is a preacher, and has no arms, take his horse and saddle and send him home to his family." So two of them rode with him nearly home, dismounted him, took his horse and saddle and went their way.

Just one week after this, the man that had Adams' horse was killed by a party of Rebel bushwhackers; the latter came upon seven or eight of these Union whackers in a cornfield with horses and guns outside the fence. The horses and guns were captured and one man was killed. The others got away in the cornfield.

9

Another Skedaddling necessary—Preparations for a move to Texas—Has charge of an old preacher and family—Rainy weather—A breakdown in the mountains—Missionary fills the old preacher's wagon wheel at night—Stops at Richmond near Red River—Learns of the death of two brothers in Cherokee County, Texas—The Civil War closes—Is made acquainted with Mrs. Josephine M. Rodgers, a Rebel soldier's widow—Whom he afterward marries.

As time rolled on with these two parties roaming over the country, it became unsafe for non-combatants to live at their homes. Even some old men were shot down near their doors, others were tortured in one way or another to make them tell where their money was. This latter mode of carrying on a warfare of destruction was inaugurated in Yell County while the Yankees held the post at Dardenelle, but it will never be known who the perpetrators were, as they always went under cover of night and usually masked so as to escape detection.

There was a Mrs. Williams, a widow who in the spring of 1864 sold her cotton for two hundred and seventy-five dollars. She had used perhaps seventy-five dollars of the Greenback, and had the rest in the house. On a Saturday night a party came to her house and said to her, "Did you not sell some cotton a few days ago?" She told them she did. "Well," they said, "we want the money." She told them she had used the money, but they told her she had lied to them. She had gone to bed before they came. She tried to get them to go off without the money, but no, they were going to have it, so they uncovered the woman and took her in their arms and set her bare feet on the coals of fire that were still burning in the fireplace. She then told them were the balance of the money was, but she did not walk for a month.

With such dangers as these, and having five small children to care for, the Missionary concluded that he had better prepare for another skedaddling expedition and take his children to his brothers in Texas. The team was the first requisite. During the previous summer and spring, he had become the owner of a young Claybank mare, but had let Deacon Greer have her about the time they were together on the Arkansas River. It had been brought to the Missionary by the Deacon's son James in early spring of the year 1864. Also Gen. Shelby gave him a little Spanish mule while he was in Dardenelle. The Claybank had been stolen by a Southern man because he was laboring under the delusion that the Missionary was a Yankee. More about the Claybank further on. This left him with the little Spanish mule and the sorrel one that cost him four hundred dollars in Confederate money, but the road was too rough to start with these two small mules. Another one was bought in selling some things—the loom, corn, hay, oats, and some other things.

With the three mules, he thought he could make the trip. A wagon-sheet was made and supplies for the trip were laid in. Now there was an old man (a Baptist preacher by the name of [Lee] Compere, the father of the two Comperes mentioned earlier) who with his wife and daughter wanted to go.[1] He had a team and an ambulance, one wheel of which was tied up with ropes. The pilot or captain said that wheel would not stand the trip through the mountains, but go the old man would, and he looked to the Missionary to see after his welfare. The old man was very feeble at times, for he was seventy-five years old; his wife was younger (being his second wife) but the daughter was young and handsome. Unlike her father, she was, to all intents and purposes, a regular Rebel, full of vim and ready at all times to do her part, and more, too, to get to Texas for her fellow was there whom she afterward married.

All being ready, a point was designated where the several families were to get together. It was now the month of November, and Thursday was set for starting. The company drove a few miles after crossing the Petit Jean (or more commonly called Pettyjohn) and camped for the night. The day had been a kind of hazy day but pleasant and warm, but Oh! what a rain fell on the skedaddlers at night and not a tent in the company.

For days it kept raining but not so much as on the first night; consequently the journey was slow. But all were cheerful and made the best of the wet weather that they could, until the party had got a ten days' travel into the mountainous region of country lying between the Arkansas and Red Rivers [the Quachita Mountains]. Saturday late afternoon, within one quarter of a mile of the camping place, the old man Compere's wagon was disabled by every spoke in one hind wheel breaking off at the hub save one.

Here was trouble. It was still drizzling rain and was cold. The old preacher was placed in a saddle on horseback to ride to camp. By the time he got there he was nervous and a partial paralysis was the result, and he was a statue on the horse but was soon lifted down by careful hands. Then wife and daughter began their usual remedy, and in an hour or less he was all right again. His wagon was soon brought to camp, and the Captain said to Slover, "What are you going to do with that broken wagon?" Slover answered, "I am going to fill that wheel," and to the happy surprise of all hands, there happened to be, lying by the roadside at that camping place, the very timber needed—a two-inch by twelve piece of white oak about twelve feet long. It evidently had been left by some parties who had split it out for wagon timber, and it was well seasoned by wet from the recent rain. Looking at it the Missionary went on to say, "And here lies the timber to make the spokes."

As soon as supper was over and all things arranged for the night, the sound spoke was drawn for a pattern, and a young man by the name of John Grace was put to cleaning out the broken spokes from the hub. By midnight the Missionary had the wheel ready for the tire. Some of the boys were still up assisting what they could, and he said, "Now we will go to bed and in the morning while the women are getting breakfast, we will set the tire."

Sunday morning an extra fire was built and the tire heated. Young Grace and the Missionary dropped it on the newly filled wheel, and the water was applied. When cooled, it was pronounced a good job under the circumstances, but when the wheel was thrown down on the ground, from the cooling process it dished the wrong way. Then the boys, in fact the whole camp, began teasing the Missionary, for on examination it was found that every spoke was driven wrong side front.

They traveled one day with the wheel dished the wrong way, and the clouds cleared away and it began freezing before night. This change in the weather admonished the company that they had better stop in the first vacant house they come to. Sure enough, just after emerging from the mountains and foothills, in the farming country in Montgomery County they found a pretty good empty house, and into it the little skedaddling company went, without leave or license, and raised a good big fire in the yard.

Pretty soon after supper it was discovered that the camp was surrounded by Rebel soldiers who had seen the fire and thought perhaps there were a Yankee fitout there. Three or four of the soldiers came with a white flag to learn the facts in the case, and finding some friends, they came to the fire and chatted awhile pleasantly, and left for their quarters.

Early Monday morning the Missionary got hold of an oak rail and sawed out four braces. He threw the dish in the crazy wagon wheel and then cut his braces to fit and placed one on each of the four sides of the long shoulder of the hub opposite each other. He nailed them fast to the shoulder end of the hub and had a crotch sawed in the other end to fit the felley [felloe or felly—the circular rim of a wheel]. When this was done, the old preacher had a good wagon for the balance of his trip to Texas.

Pretty soon the little company reached a neighborhood in Sevier County called "Red Colony," where Rev. T. H. Compere lived.[2] Here the old man was left by the Missionary and the rest of the party scattered and found homes for the winter. The Missionary crossed Little River and got as far south as the little town of Richmond. Learning from some Rebel soldiers that his brother George W. Slover was dead and also his brother John, and the weather was cold and the mud was desperately heavy, he was advised to stop in Arkansas, so he traded for a house and located in the town of Richmond.

In May 1865 the Civil War was terminated by the surrender of the Confederate forces to Gen. U.S. Grant, Commander in Chief of the Union forces, by Gen. Robert E. Lee, Commander in Chief of the Confederate troops in Virginia. Thus ended a four years civil war between the free States and the seceded Southern States of the once United States of America.

The Missionary soon made the acquaintance of many friends, among them was Mrs. Josephine M. Rodgers, whom he afterward married. She was a Rebel soldier's widow.

10

The Missionary and widow's courtship and engagement—His visit with the Domestic and Indian Mission Board—Southern Baptist Convention in Alabama—His sickness in Marion, Alabama—Returns by Crystal Springs, Mississippi—Archibald Fitzgerald and what his brother Aaron said of his copper—Sees the Rev. E. L. Compere and wife—Chances for courtship while making this visit—Is appointed Domestic Missionary by the Board—And finally reaches home in November and finds his affianced suffering from a fall from a horse—They get married in February 1866.

The first introduction the Missionary had with Mrs. Josephine M. Rodgers was at the residence of Col. Hamiter in Rocky Comfort, Ark., which event happened about the close of the year A.D. 1864 or the first of the year A.D. 1865. Of course, the Missionary was not at this time on a courting expedition; nevertheless he was favorably impressed with his new acquaintance, and determined to cultivate it further. Not long after this he met her at church on Saturday and concluded, if she had no objections, to go home with her. Objections on her part were waived, her mule was brought to the stiles and soon she was in the saddle.

There was quite a contrast between the animal she rode and the one the Missionary rode, for his was the little Spanish mule that Gen. Shelby gave him at Dardenelle, and she was mounted on a large one. Of course he had to look up to her to see her face and eyes. But they got along nicely for part of the way home when they came suddenly upon a piece of very muddy road, and all of a sudden she rode off and left the Missionary in the center of the road with his little mule, all under ground except the saddle and the mule's ears. He walked off of the mule and out of the mud. The mule floundered around and took a fright and was out directly, and started on after the big mule. Now he thought he would have to walk the balance of the way, but she took pity on him, and between the two they caught the deer-legged mule, and soon they were on the go again as jolly as if nothing had happened.

She was well acquainted with the road; he was not, but whether she let him drop into that quagmire to test his affection for her or not is still a mystery, although she pleaded innocence. As he had come through the time of the war and had been buffeted and knocked around from pillar to post and from post to pillar again, he could stand it. Rest assured, he went on home with the widow, she making all kinds of excuses for fear he would turn back and go no further on account of the accident.

Time passed on and e'er it was long, the balmy days of spring came, when it was nice to go fishing. Now the widow Rodgers was so constituted that she hailed with delight these days of fishing parties, but like most women, she did not like to have to bait her own hook, especially when the bait was angle or red worms. She told her Pastor (for such had the Missionary become) that there was going to be a fishing party at a lake at a certain time in the near future and invited him to go with her. He being very fond of fish after they are ready for eating, said yes, he would go, but he did not tell her that it was more to be with her than for the pleasure of catching fish or eating them after they were caught. He could afford to handle the red worms, bait her hook and take the fish off the hook when she would catch one, all for the sake of being with her. So they had a grand good time at the fishing party, lots of fish were slaughtered that day, but the widow caught the biggest sucker that was caught.

Blackberry time came in July. These berries grow spontaneously all over Arkansas in greater or lesser quantities, and young and old parties would go out to pick the berries. Sometimes there would be a dozen or more together with their vessels in one of these large patches of blackberry briers. Now of course the widow wanted to see whether or not a preacher could pick these berries and proposed that they go with some others who were going. He agreed; she prepared the vessels and together they made their way to the place designated by the part, and that afternoon satisfied her that there was one preacher that could gather the fruit from the blackberry briers and get as few scratches as anybody else. But whether this made her think any better of him than she did before, he never was able to find out.

The final result—just before he started to Alabama to visit the Board of Missions, she told him what he had been trying for four months to get her to tell yes or no, she said yes. He now could go satisfied and afford to delay the time at her own option, for he considered the engagement consummated.

During the month of July of this year 1865, he heard of the stolen Claybank mare, and that a man by the name of Mathis near Center Point in Sevier County, Ark., had her. This information was brought to him by an old acquaintance of his who lived at Russellville, at which place the Missionary was Pastor in 1863 and 1864. This friend happened to come south in the early summer of 1865 and stopped at Mathis' and saw the mare. The friend made a trip to Texas, and on his return stopped at Richmond and told the Missionary where his stolen mare was. Slover took with him James Ingram, his brother-in-law, and rode over to Mathis', got there at noon, and at the dinner table the Missionary told his mission, namely that he was on search of a certain mare which was stolen from him at Dardenelle, and he had heard that Mr. Mathis had such an animal. The Preacher further said he would describe his animal, and if the description did not suit the one he had, he did not want her. He described her exactly and then told Mathis that she had the faint resemblance of the letter "G" on her left hip. Mathis instantly replied, "She is yours," so there was no further need of proof, but Mathis asked to keep her six weeks to make one more trip with his wagon to Texas. His request was granted, and then he delivered the mare at Richmond.

Mathis then gave an account of the manner by which he became in possession of the mare, viz. A soldier came there in the early spring of 1865 with the mare jaded down until she would no longer do to soldier on. He left her in Mathis' possession, and took an old mule belonging to Mathis. The mule was in good fix, however. He said the soldier told him that he swapped a horse with very sore back for the mare with a citizen going south in the fall of 1864.

Having secured the promise from the widow that she would marry him on his return from a visit to Alabama, and having found the stolen animal, he was ready for the trip. He made the visit in consideration of the fact that he had been under appointment from the Domestic and Indian Mission Board of the Southern Baptist Convention, in the Cherokee Nation Indian Territory from the year 1857 to 1862. Two years of this time he had received nothing from the Board. Therefore, the better to adjust matters of the past and to arrange for future work, it was desirable that the parties be together.[1]

Arrangements were soon made, and about the twentieth of August, the four-hundred-dollar sorrel mule was saddled (for the trip to Shreveport had to be made on mule back or on foot) and the Missionary was soon off for Shreveport, La. Two days ride brought him within thirty miles of that city, and lodging with a family whose relatives lived in Marion, Ala., where he was bound for. The son of this family agreed to take care of the mule and convey the Missionary to Shreveport on a wagon. He thought he would return about the first or middle of October, but was detained a month on account of sickness.

He got to Shreveport on Thursday evening, and whom should he find running a hotel but a native of the Cherokee Nation, Archibald Wilson. The Missionary had officiated at the marriage of him and his brother Alexander's widow, Rebecca Wilson. Here he had to stay until four o'clock Sunday following his arrival. Money was scarce with the Missionary, but being a Master Mason, and meeting some of his Cherokee Masonic brethren, he did not lose anything by having to lay over here two days.[2]

Sunday morning he talked to his host about a Baptist church and found there was no such organization in town. The Catholic church was suggested, so he thought as he had lived about forty-one years and never had witnessed the service of the old mother of Harlots and Abominations of the earth, he would go that forenoon. Now he never was, neither before that time nor since, in a theater, but had read of theatrical plays. The services as conducted by that Priest and two little boys just filled the bill as described by what he had read. It looked to him solemn mockery.

About four o'clock P.M. he secured a stateroom on board the steamer bound for New Orleans, heavily freighted with cotton bales. It looked as though every inch of room on her deck was filled with bales of cotton. The guard floors were closely packed with bales of cotton, up to the cabin floor. He inquired of the mate how many bales aboard; he told him fifteen hundred.

The water was somewhat low, and consequently many sand bars were dry and upon these he discovered the alligators in multitudes [that] were lying in the hot sun. The passengers who had six-shooters would pour a volley of bullets among the hideous monsters just to see them slide off the bars into the water.

The boat hadn't been afloat for but two or three days when on nearing the falls above Alexander, as the steamer was passing an old wreck of a steamer, she struck it a glancing stroke. Did the vessel no harm, but seventy-five bales of cotton tipped overboard. The Captain instantly called to all the passengers to get on the light side which they did just in time to save seventy-five more bales from falling from the other side. The steamer was run ashore and the pilot discharged, and the floating cotton bales were rescued and reloaded.

In a few days she pulled into the wharf at New Orleans and her live freight put ashore. The Missionary was conveyed to the Saint Charles Hotel where he had to stay at three dollars per day for two days, it being Thursday when he arrived and Saturday at five o'clock P.M. when he left for Mobile.

His voyage from New Orleans was either down the Mississippi and then on the gulf of Mexico, or a five miles ride on the Rail Road to Lake Pontchartrain and then aboard the steamer Mobile; he preferred the latter. Saturday, quarter of an hour before five, he boarded the train and at five he was shown a stateroom in the cabin of the steamer *Cherokee,* and soon she was far out on the bosom of the Lake Pontchartrain. About eleven o'clock A.M. Sunday, the *Cherokee* pulled into the wharf at Mobile, Ala. At four o'clock P.M. he boarded a train for Meridian, Miss., which station was reached Monday evening. Tuesday morning he again boarded the train for Marion Junction, but after traveling about a dozen miles or more, something got out of fix with the engine and the train was dropped. There it sat in the broiling sun until the evening train came down from Selma, Ala., and run it back to Meridian where the eastbound passengers had to stop until Wednesday morning when again they boarded the eastbound passenger which reached Marion Junction about one hour behind time. There the Missionary had to stay about twenty-two hours.

He had begun to get sick while the train was lying in the hot sun; at the Junction he got much worse, but when the Marion train came rolling in, he was at the depot ready. About five o'clock P.M. he was at his destination in Marion and so sick he could not set up. The hack carried him to Rev. M. T. Sumner's house (who was then Corresponding Secretary of the Board) but he was soon conveyed to a brother Lee's residence where there were no children. A physician was called the next morning, and put him through a course of medicine for nine or ten days, and for a month he was confined to the house.

In October he met the Board of Domestic and Indian Missions and was given an appointment as Domestic Missionary in southern Arkansas.[3] While at Marion he was made a Royal Arch Mason and a Council Mason by the Royal Arch Chapter of Marion, Ala. He visited some out in the country, especially with a Rev. Freeman, and preached one sermon to a congregation of Negroes. About twenty-five hundred were present; they met in the grove close to the church house where Freeman preached at the same time.

About the twenty-fifth of October he made a start for home by the way of Jackson and Crystal Springs in Mississippi. At Jackson he preached on Sunday, and at night an attempt was made to rob him. He thought it was done by the young Negro boy that showed him his room upstairs in the hotel. He had belted around him about one thousand dollars in money and checks on New Orleans. Some of it was for a missionary by the name of H. F. Buckner who was under appointment of the same Board, to labor in the Creek Nation.[4] The young darkie showed the Missionary upstairs to his room and instead of going immediately down, he passed out of the bedroom by a side door on to a veranda, and no doubt was watching the Missionary as he undressed himself, and observed him put a memorandum book under the pillow together with his vest which had his watch in the pocket.

Sometime during the night the Missionary awoke and discovered that his book and vest were missing and he arose and found them on the floor. The watch was all right; he concluded that he had by some means pushed the things on the floor, and replacing the things under his pillow he went to sleep again. But when he arose in the morning he found a small piece of currency which he recognized as belonging to himself because it had been torn and a bit of common letter paper pasted on the break. Finding this led him to look in the memorandum book, and sure enough, a little over two dollars had been taken from the book. He never believed that anybody else got the money but that young Negro man, though he denied it and said that robbers had been in town that night.

The down train came in about nine o'clock A.M., and he boarded it for Crystal Springs. Here he stopped with Archibald Fitzgerald, whose brother the Missionary had met in southern Arkansas. The Missionary was in and around Crystal Springs for three weeks, and attended a protracted meeting some distance in the country, where he was again brought in company with his old friend and brother, E. L. Compere. During this meeting he (Compere) was instrumental in securing about eighty-five dollars in money for the Missionary. E. L. had married a fine-looking young lady in Mississippi and was now at his mother-in-law's.[5] There was a fine-looking widow in this family, a sister of E. L. Compere's wife, whom E. L. had picked on as suitable for his friend Slover, and to whom the Missionary was introduced on his arrival at the protracted meeting. But it was no use. By the way, while he was in Alabama there was an old maid, perhaps thirty years old, brought to his notice, no doubt for a similar purpose, but to no avail, for his doom was sealed before leaving Arkansas on this visit, and he could not allow anyone to intrude on the sacred plighted promises.

This protracted meeting over, he returned to Crystal Springs, delivered up the saddle animal which he rode, and bidding his friends good bye, he boarded the train for New Orleans. About eleven o'clock P.M. the same day reached the city and was taken to the Saint Charles Hotel. He lay over here one day and made some purchases of dry goods for his children, &c., &c.

The next day he boarded the steamer for Shreveport and in a few days run was at the last-named city. Arranging shipment on board a wagon for his supplies, he boarded the stage for twelve miles, then the train up to within a mile of where he left the four-hundred-dollar sorrel mule, then on foot for one mile; there he lodged for the night.

The next day he started for his home, and finding H. F. Buckner where he stopped all night, he gave him the check sent him by the Board. He had a pleasant evening with his brother Missionary, of the Creek Indians, who was indeed glad for the aid sent him by the Board. In a few days he was safely at his home in Richmond, and as soon as he could conveniently go, he made his way to Rocky Comfort to see the affianced widow whom he found suffering from a fall from a horse.

She was glad to have him back again. It was not long after his return until he and the widow mutually agreed upon the fifteenth day of February A.D. 1866 as the time for their wedding. The time for his second marriage soon came, and Rev. L. W. Davis having been previously engaged to officiate, he and the Missionary made their way to the old home of the widow's Mother. On Thursday evening, the fifteenth day of February A.D. 1866, he was united in the solemn ties of matrimony with Josephine M. Rodgers, then of Sevier County, Ark.

11

His labor as Missionary of the Southern Baptist Convention ceases—Is appointed to the Office of County Clerk of Little River County—Elected Justice of the Peace in 1868 in Little River County—A serious time in Rocky Comfort on the day he finishes his duties as Clerk—Little River County under martial law—Loses his horse and saddle—Militia soldiers in Richmond—Makes a trip to Washington County preparatory to crossing the Plains to California—Emigrates to California—A whole year on the road—One summer near Visalia—Locates on Tule River in Tulare County.

With the close of 1866 his labor ceased with the Southern Baptist Convention as domestic Missionary of that body because of a depleted treasury. Now the Legislature of Arkansas for the year 1866 divided Sevier County and created a new county between Little River on the north and Red River on the south, and known as Little River County.

The officers of this new county had to be appointed by the Governor; Mr. [Isaac] Murphy was Governor at that time and appointed the ex-Missionary to the office of County Clerk, which position he held until the regular election in 1868, when another man was elected, and he was elected to the office of Justice of the Peace.[1] He was about two months behind with his records in the Clerk's office, when his successor was qualified.

There were serious times in the county seat which was Rocky Comfort at that time [later Richmond]. The Freedmen's Bureau Agent (Mr. Willitts) and the Internal Revenue Assessor (Mr. Andrews) were killed by a band of Texas bushwhackers known as Baker and Co.[2] This occurred about ten o'clock in the forenoon, but the fact was not known in town until two in the afternoon. It seemed that the two United States officers were on their way to Rocky Comfort, riding together in a buggy which belonged to the Internal Revenue Assessor. The Sheriff of Little River County [W. M. Freeman] was on horseback, and perhaps was one-quarter of a mile in advance of the buggy, and immediately behind the buggy was a Negro man riding on horseback, and this party were all traveling through what was known in that locality as the black bottom of Walnut Bayou, about three miles south of Rocky Comfort.

The Sheriff was halted by five men coming suddenly out of ambush, and was disarmed and one of the men was detailed to guard him, whom the Sheriff recognized as Bud Griffin, a citizen of Little River County. The other four ruffians retired to their ambush.

Pretty soon, the buggy drew near and was also halted by the four ruffians, again emerging from their ambush. The officers were ordered to give up their arms. Willitts replied that he would not, but suddenly concluded that he would, and began to unbuckle his belt, when the four ruffians fired and killed both of the white men and also the Negro. The Sheriff, discovering that the man in charge of him turned to look at the horrid murder, leaped into the thick brush and made his escape; the guard emptied his shot-gun at him but without effect. Believing that the murderers would follow him, the Sheriff secreted himself after running for a mile or more, until the afternoon, then made his way into town and reported.

Now it so happened that it was drill day of the militia, which were all Negroes but the drillmaster, Col. Scott, and there were about two hundred in the command. As quick as the news of the killing of the above party was known to the militia, one of the black scoundrels exclaimed, "Now they have commenced on us, let's begin and take the whites from the cradle up—children, women and men." There were only about twenty-five white men in the place, but as soon as this threat was noised abroad, Thomas McGrary from Richmond went to Scott and told him what the Negroes were proposing to do. He also told Scott that he had better go to the Negroes and suppress their threats for, said McGrary, if a gun is fired even accidentally, there will be bad work in the town. Scott went immediately to the militia Negroes and told them to be quiet and to go in pursuit of the Texas murderers and capture them.

A squad of sixty of the militia was placed in charge of a young Englishman to go hunt the murderers. They marched to where the dead men were and looked at them, but were careful not to follow any further.

The whole country was in arms in less than twenty-four hours. Men had assembled at the town of Richmond, fifteen miles east of Rocky Comfort, through which town the militia had to go in going home from Rocky Comfort, and the white men avowed that no Negroes should carry a gun through Richmond. Scott said they would, and the next day after the murder in the black bottom, they attempted it and were halted at the outskirts of town, and an old citizen by the name of Campbell interposed and told Scott that he had tried to get the white men to let the Negroes pass peaceably home with their guns, but was unable to accomplish anything further than that the Negroes could go peaceably home if they would surrender their arms, which they did and went home.

This whole affair was only a prelude to a more disastrous trouble, for it was but a few days until three or four counties, including Little River, were declared by Governor Murphy to be under martial law, and three companies of militia immediately sent to punish the county for what it had no hand in bringing about, viz. the death of the two U.S. officials.[3]

On learning that the militia was advancing toward Little River County, the citizens rallied and in less than three days there were a thousand men in arms and assembled at the crossing of Saline Creek in Sevier County, at which point the advancing militia had to cross said Saline stream. The militia evidently was not so anxious for a fight as they at first would make believe, for had they attacked the citizens, there would not have been one left to tell the story. But their colonel in command devised a more sure way of advance, by sending over his signature a flattering proposition, viz., that if the citizens would disband and go home and let him and his men pass into Little River County, each and every man should be protected in person and property. On receiving this promise, every citizen returned to his home.

As quick as this was known, the colonel's promise was neutralized instead of being realized, for they were no sooner in Richmond than certain men were arrested and a guard-house established. In the filthy place many of the best citizens were thrust and kept for a number of days. In the meantime, the Negroes were armed and the stealing commenced, or rather the taking of horses and mules and everything else that they could destroy but human life. Everything in the county was theirs; they would even steal chickens at night. This state of things lasted for a month—well, as long as there was a good horse or mule left in the County that they could find. Finally after they had got all the valuable property, and exhausted the forage of the citizens, they were withdrawn.

On the ninth of January 1867, the first fruits of the Missionary's second marriage appeared in a well-developed nine-pound girl baby [Mary Ellen].

All was well and the parents were happy. The child grew and made a fine young woman.

In the early spring of this year there was a special election ordered for county officers of the new (Little River) County. For the first time in his life, the Missionary became a candidate for office and was defeated for the office of County Clerk. But the man elected could not qualify. Then the duty devolved upon the Governor of the State to appoint a man, and upon recommendation of a sufficient number of the citizens of the county, the Missionary was entrusted with the clerkship. This was a new departure for the Preacher and a position which he sought solely for the profits of the office, which he felt to be necessary to enable him to support his family and to continue the work of the ministry best he could. It was not a very profitable position after all.

It was a time of experiment by the cotton planters of that county with the freedmen in cultivating their farms. The land owners would furnish land, teams, tools, seed, and feed for the teams, and take half the cotton and corn grown on the land as their part. The freedmen were therefore thrown upon their own resources for bread and butter and all other expenses of the family, and keeping the tools in order. Thus situated, they had to give a mortgage on their undivided half of the crop, and this made business for lawyers and county clerks. He was ex-officio County Recorder, and of course the mortgagee had to pay for recording.

In October of the year 1867, death again visited the Preacher's family and took the youngest of his first wife's children, Rachel Melvina. She died October the 10th, A.D. 1867, and was buried at the Baptist Church below Richmond. She was at the time of her death five years and exactly six months old.

On the tenth day of February A.D. 1868 another baby girl [Fanny Isadora] appeared, the great drama of the Preacher's new married life. This was a fine intelligent babe, but not so large as the first. She had several hard struggles for her life while quite young, but survived them all, and grew to be a very well accomplished young woman considering the limited education her father was enabled to give her.

The most noted reminiscence of the latter part of this year was the coming of the militia which in general has been related, but personally it has not.

The Preacher had a good saddle horse and a new saddle which he had loaned to an acquaintance. Some of these militia thieves met him in the road, dismounted him, and deprived him of the horse and saddle. The

Preacher found out that a certain company, whose Captain was a Mason, had the saddle. He determined to test the Captain, so he repaired to his headquarters and made himself known to the Captain and told his errand. Suffice it to say he was successful—but the horse he never got.

The county was now in a state of confusion and an unpleasant place to live on account of the Blacks appropriating a great many things to their own use which belonged to the white race. Therefore, he, with many others of Little River and Sevier Counties, began preparations for a move to California.

A trip had to be made to Washington County to settle up some real estate matters. In March 1869 he mounted the sorrel mule and made his way to the little farm he once owned near Elm Springs, Washington County, Ark., and made a call on a Mr. Wood to whom he had sold the farm two years and a half before, but could get no money. He had to take a wagon and a mule and harness for the two hundred and fifty dollars due him. It took considerable time to even get this kind of a settlement. In the meantime he got to see and bid many old friends farewell. On his return to Little River County, he took sick south of Fort Smith on the headwaters of the Washita, at the residence of a Mr. Kelley who was very kind to him. Recovering in a few days, he reached his home in Richmond toward the last of March.

The fourteenth of April was the day fixed upon by the company to make the start. Wagons had to be rigged, and supplies for the family laid in. In order to complete the teams the sorrel mule had to be traded for oxen or sold outright, so his wife's brother, Augustus D. Jones, accompanied him across Red River to find a buyer for the mule which was soon done. The mule sold for one hundred and fifty dollars in Greenback money. This was the same mule that he bought in the spring of 1864 in Yell County, Ark., for four hundred dollars in Confederate money.

The sale of the mule enabled him to fit out two small teams of oxen, two yoke to one wagon and one yoke to the small one which was known as the family carriage, and the larger one as the commissary wagon. He had also thirteen head of stock cattle which he intended to drive across the Plains, and was going to work some of the Milch [milk cows] in the event it was necessary.

Now a Vendue sale [public auction] had to be made, to dispose of certain household furniture which could not be transported very easily across the Plains. At this sale a certain man by the name of Hill distinguished himself as a friend of the family by buying a number of articles, and bidding upon others in order to make them bring something like half price.

Wagons loaded, the emigrant family left Richmond the thirteenth day of April A.D. 1869, and drove fifteen miles to the old homestead of the wife's father, where her widowed mother lived and with her family was ready to join the train for California.

He had bad luck, or rather bad management began. As above stated, he intended to work some of the milk cows on the trip, and thinking that it would be a good plan to yoke up a couple and let them wear the yoke all night, so he did. The result was that the next morning one of them had her neck broken, and the other one was so badly injured that she could not travel. This was a clear loss of two good milk cows to start out with, but those who have must lose. The injured cow was given to an old family Negro called Old Uncle Frank.

All things being arranged, the start was made for the final move on the fourteenth of April A.D. 1869. Somewhere on the south side of the Red River the whole company rendezvoused and organized by electing John D. Billingsley captain.

The company consisted principally of the following heads of families, their children, relatives, and friends: Thomas Wright, wife and two grandsons; William Wright, wife and five children; John Wright, wife and child; Wm. Hunter and wife and two or three children; James Caughran, wife, two young men, and two grown daughters; James Wesley Caughran, wife and child; W. L. Caughran and wife; John D. Billingsley, wife and nine children; Amos Wright, wife and four children; Mrs. Fuquay and two boys; Dr. David Taylor, wife and two daughters; Nathan Moore, wife and child; Mrs. Holt and four children; James Pauley, wife and two children; Martin Thomas, wife and child; Mrs. Sarah Jones, two grown daughters and a grown son; Thomas W. Holder and wife; J. A. Slover, wife and six children all told; F. B. Fuquay; Sherril French; John French; old Capt. Moore; William B. Billingsley, Martin Davis, John Thomas, John Gordon, George Dillard, John Taylor, Taylor Dale, and enough more not enumerated in this list to make one hundred and thirty-five souls, counting a young Negro man and a young Negro girl, with thirty-five wagons and about six hundred head of loose stock, besides the teams.

The Preacher was appointed chaplain but there was but little preaching done during the long and tedious journey, owing to the scarcity of grass on the Plains that year. Many of the cattle never reached California and a few of the people were buried on the Plains.

The company remained together, or nearly as practically, until Arizona was reached. Then in search of feed, they traveled more in squads or small bands, and finally in about twelve months all reached their destination.

Here the writer will have to leave this company of emigrants and go back and enumerate and chronicle the incidents of travel more minutely connected with his own family.

At Clarksville, Texas, the Preacher with the rest of the company were told that Greenback or United States paper money would be of but little or no use on the road or even in the Golden State of California, and that the best they could do would be to sell all the currency they had for gold and silver coin. This false impression being made upon the minds of the men, what little Greenback they all had was soon gobbled up by the Clarksville "Sharpers" at the fair discount of twenty percent, or in other words, one hundred dollars in Greenback was given by the poor emigrant for eighty dollars in coin, gold and silver.

Experience taught a dear lesson as a starter, for on the road the company only used money in small quantities and they found that a dollar or five dollars in Greenback would buy just as much as that much silver or gold. But it was too late with the emigrant, except when he would have a twenty, ten or five dollars changed, then he could get only dollar for dollar.

Beef for Nothing—This was another hallucination or false impression made upon the credulity of the company about the time of starting, that is, they were told that the Plains abounded with herds of cattle. All they would have to do would be to tell the herder that they wanted a fat yearling or a two-year-old, and he would tell you to go into the herd and select one, dress it and take the meat to camp.

This experiment was tried one afternoon by the Preacher and some others connected with his family in their travels. Horses and guns were made ready after the camp was pitched for the night, and away to a herd they went, or rather they went to the herder and told him their errand. They were no little surprised when the herder told them to go among the cattle, and if they could find one unmarked yearling or two-year-old "Mavrix," to kill it. They rode out on the hills for two or three miles and finally about one hour before sundown, in a long swale or narrow valley, they discovered the creature they were instructed to take. It looked at though it might not be much more than eight or nine months old. At first sight it was a long way off, but one or two of the hungry party were or had been Rebel soldiers, and they said, "He is all right." Now the next thing was to get in proper distance to shoot him. As quick as the cattle took the hint that one of their number was sought after, away the little band of ten or less went, and every minute took them further from camp. But about sunset, a deadly shot was fired and down came the calf-looking animal, which now proved to be a two-year-old unmarked "Mavrix."

The hide was taken off in quick time and the meat divided between the men to carry it to camp, but where was camp? Dark was soon upon them. They made a start by remembering something of the point of the compass they had come from, and guided their course by the stars for there was not a tree in sight nor road, and the Plains all looked alike. Fortunately it was warm weather, and after an hour or two's wandering, the party espied the camp fire and was soon in all right with their beef.

Arrested by United States Troops—As the Arkansas company (as it was called) drove into Fort Griffin, a Texas company (as they were called) filed out and on the road for California.[4] Here the Arkansas emigrants saw the first Indians; there were about twenty-five friendly Indians who rode into camp at noon while the company were resting. Their nationality is not now remembered. There were some women among them; they did not tarry very long. After traveling one day and a half west of the Fort, both companies were ordered under an arrest by the commander at the Fort that search might be made for army guns.[5]

The particulars are about these: One of the soldiers or a man connected with the Fort got into the arsenal and stole ten of the repeating rifles and sold them to the boys belonging to the Texas emigrants. As soon as the fact was discovered by the commander, the thief left the Fort in pursuit of the emigrants to whom he had sold the guns, to inform them that they must look out for their guns because the soldiers were on pursuit.

On the night before the arrest, the two emigrant companies were camped about four miles apart, the Texans were in the advance and camped on a stream called Dead Man's Creek, and the Arkansans on a tributary of the same. Grass was very scarce.

Friday morning dawned with a clear sky and the sun arose lovely and serene. To the utter surprise and astonishment of all in the Arkansas Train, thirty-eight head of the best work cattle they had were missing. All kinds of conjectures and imaginations were in every mouth and head. Some were positive that the Indians had driven the cattle away. A small circle was made all around camp; all things were right except the thirty-eight work cattle. They could not be seen nor their bells heard anywhere. Amidst this trouble up rode about thirty-five Bluecoats, headed by a Lieutenant of the troops, and inquired for the captain, whose name was John Gordon (he being elected when Billingsley resigned). He was pointed out to the Lieutenant, who told him his company or Train was under arrest. Before you could get a good look at the Bluecoats, they were in every wagon searching for guns, but none of the stolen property could be found. The captain (Gordon) had a gun just like the stolen ones, but had bought it two or three weeks before. The soldiers took it all the same, and every one of that brand found, no matter how long owned by the emigrant, was taken and carried off by the soldiery.

The boys that had bought the ten were too sharp for the Bluecoats and succeeded in keeping their guns, although the trains were kept under arrest from Friday morning until Sunday evening.

About noon on Friday of the disaster, the boys, in search of the stray oxen, found them about four miles up this Dead Man's Creek in a natural corral with stone walls with but one entrance and the finest grass and water imaginable. The boys thought they had been driven there on purpose, to retard the movement of the Train until the gun affair was settled, but this might have been imagination. However, the oxen had fared well and were all safe; not even a bell was stolen.

Monday morning the Train was en route for Fort Concho.[6] Here a night was spent. The Train wandered all day up the Concho River and about five o'clock P.M. struck the dry plains known as the Staked Plains.[7] Filling the water vessels from a western Texas pond, the Train moved off late in the afternoon across the Staked Plains for the San Pechos (pronounced San Pacos) [Pecos River], traveled all night and until noon the next day without wood or water in sight. San Pechos is a narrow stream but very deep and banks generally abrupt, and at this (middle of June) time level full of water and muddy. The only way to cross this little river on the Plains was in a skiff or small rowboat.[8] The Train remained in camp all night, and early the next morning the job of crossing thirty-five wagons was undertaken. All hands were in good humor and assisted each other like men and women. The program was to drive one wagon down at a time, put the family over in the little boat, then all the effects belonging to that wagon, then unhook the team from the wagon and swim them over, then fasten a long rope to the end of the pole or tongue of the wagon, then take the rope across in the boat and pull the wagon over by hand. In order to carry out this program, one half the men were on either side.

Just as the sun was setting the terrible job was completed, and no life was lost, neither man nor beast.

The next point of any note was Fort Stockton.[9] The boy Russel Holman Slover got his left arm broken just as the Train was getting into camp, but the doctor being on hand, it was soon set and patiently he lay in the wagon until it was well again. He fell from the front end of the wagon down under the feet of the team going down hill, and the wagon run over him before he could be rescued.

East and west of Fort Stockton is the country where the wood, what little there is, has to be extracted from the ground or hauled for miles and miles, especially by emigrants; how far the soldiers had to haul theirs is hard for an emigrant to tell, and yet the nicest ricks [stacks] of wood were here that the writer ever saw, and it all seemed to have come from the ground.

There was the finest spring water the Train found, and a few miles northwest of the Fort were the bottomless holes of water, and the ground around them was very springy as though it was resting on the water, yet it seemed to be safe to walk around pretty close to the edge of the water. Even animals would pass about over the ground with safety. After leaving this Fort all heads were set for the Rio Grande, but a long and dry road was yet to pass over, and but little grass for the already suffering stock.

When Eagle Springs was reached, it was found to be a little seep on a hill side that did not furnish half water for the animals. The Preacher's oxen, by the way, got all the water they wanted for that day, but the rest could not get half what they wanted, and it was thirty-five miles to the Rio Grande which was the next water. After camping at these springs all night, a very early start was made. At sundown the head of a fifteen-mile canyon was reached, and down that dark lonely canyon the Train must go before stopping. Already about sixty or seventy herd of the loose cattle had stampeded and got away from the herders, and turned back in search of water. The rest had scented the damp atmosphere and made their way down the canyon to the Rio Grande, and some of them drowned in the river, so said the Mexicans who were camped on the river with a band of horses.

About three o'clock in the morning a halt was made and the wagons corralled and oxen tied up until daylight within less than three miles of the river, but all the cattle did not stay tied until daylight. Some of the teams got loose and made their way to the river for water before daylight. On finding that a goodly number of the herd was missing, many conjectures were entertained as to their whereabouts. Some were satisfied that the Indians had made a break into the band and caused a stampede and got away with them. So four or five of the best young men were well armed and supplied with rations and put upon good horses, and sent in pursuit of the lost cattle. Late in the afternoon of the first day out, they came upon the lost stock; they had gone back beyond the Eagle Springs, and as it had fortunately rained the night before behind the Train, these cattle were found lying by a pond of fresh rain water all right and rested for the road. All were now on the bank of the Rio Grande some considerable distance below Fort Alexander.[10] Some of the loose cattle were lost in the river, but not many.

Now the road lay up the Rio Grande for one hundred miles to El Paso. The feed was a little better here than it had been for more than two hundred miles back. The settlers up the Rio Grande were mostly Mexicans, and had no fence for the most part. Consequently it took close watching to keep the loose stock off the gardens, and even then, in some of the little towns, damage would be to pay for. It was a matter of utter impossibility to keep them from committing depredations. The teams sometimes would take a shear on the driver and run over gardens. But amidst the hot weather of July the point of crossing was at last reached, which was up above El Paso in New Mexico, just a little north of west of Las Cruces. After fording the Rio Grande, there was a Mexican village called Mesilla.

On leaving the Rio Grande, water had to be taken, because another dry stretch was to cross before the San Pedro was reached.

Somewhere on this high dry region there was an artificial watering place. The country over which the road was located was high and rolling, and some man had ingeniously constructed a bulkhead or dam across a large hollow so as to form an artificial lake, and from the surrounding low hills he would conduct the rain water during the rainy season, by means of small ditches, into this pool or lake. A cavern was made in the dam where a filtering apparatus was constructed between the cavern and the lake, and from the cavern drinking and cooking water was taken, while the body of the lake was used for stock, promiscuously cattle. Oxen, mules, and horses could drink at five cents per head, and five cents was the cost for a common water bucket full of the filtered water for drinking and cooking.

Fort Cummings was situated somewhere on this road east of the Rio Grande and in New Mexico.[11] Here the Preacher excited a little ripple of anger in some of the Negro soldiers belonging to the Fort. The Train camped near by the Fort, and a little while before sundown the Preacher took a frying pan into the Government blacksmith shop to have the handle riveted on, and while in the shop, some of the soldiers came around and began talking about the Arkansas Train having with it a couple of Negroes, a boy and a girl, and in the course of their conversation, said they would overhaul the Train and take them away. The Preacher unthoughtfully said (although he meant just what he said), "You will have a happy or sweet time of it." The blacksmith told he could not rivet the handle on in time for him to get back to camp that night but that he would have it ready by the time the Train would pass next morning.

Morning came and the Train rolled on and as it neared the Fort, the Preacher left his team in charge of another, and went into the blacksmith shop inside the walls of the garrison, paid the blacksmith for the work done on the frying pan. By this time his Train was over a little eminence above the Spring and out of sight. He walked out at the gate where he met two large Negroes with clubs. They wanted to know what he had said about the soldiers taking the colored boy and girl from the Train the previous afternoon. He repeated the same to them and told them that was all. They looked ugly and talked about hitting him; he was perfectly in their power for he was alone and the Train not in sight, and he had no sort of a weapon but the little old frying pan, but from some cause or other they did not lay hands on him. The Preacher is inclined to think there were only twenty or thirty of the Black troops in the garrison, and they had reason to believe that there were at least fifty armed men in the Train, and if they (the soldiers) were to hurt the Preacher, the black skins would have to suffer for it or whip the whole Train, and the emigrants were just in the humor to whip the whole garrison, but suffice it to say, there was no blood shed.

But the Train and the Preacher with the colored boy and girl passed on unmolested after the little insult at the gate.

Tucson in Arizona—After crossing the San Pedro River—or creek for to a Tennessean it would be only a large branch—and traveling slowly for several days, the Train pulled into Tucson. Here was seen a few of the Apache Indians, horrible looking creatures. Tucson at that time was filled with Mexicans. After buying a few things, the Train moved westward a short distance out of town and camped in a grove of mesquite trees. Sunday morning John E. Slover, the Preacher's oldest boy, got into a saddle on one of the horses used for driving up oxen &c, to go out and help drive up the oxen preparatory to a move. Just as he started, the horse began to kick up is heels, or as the boys say, "He bucked," down came the rider full length on his back, too badly hurt to try it again.

The Preacher Loses His Pony—The Train camped at the Blue Water Wells on Monday night after leaving Tucson on Saturday, and the pony was seen running as though he was frightened; that was the last seen of him by any one belonging to the Train.[12] The Train moved on the next day about twelve or fifteen miles. Then the Preacher took with him a man and rode back in search of the missing horse but could not find him, nor never did.

A Sad Event in the Preacher's Family—The oldest child bled to death at the nose. All the particulars known are here given; his name is John Ephraim; he was born the thirtieth day of March A.D. 1853 in Washington County, Ark., and was sixteen years five months and one day old when the sad event of his death occurred, which was on the first of September A.D. 1869. For some weeks prior to his death he had dumb chills and part of the time could not drive his team, but Doctor Taylor was in the Train and give him some medicine and he got apparently well before reaching Tucson, and as before stated, he got a hard fall from a horse on Sunday morning.

On Monday night while at the Blue Water Wells his nose bled profusely, but was finally stopped. Tuesday morning the Train moved twelve or fifteen miles, having made an early start and stopping about noon. From this point his father went back immediately after dinner to search for his saddle pony, and about three o'clock in the afternoon the hemorrhage of the boy's nose began again, grew worse and worse, and the Doctor was fifty miles away. His father was sent for, but got to camp only to see him breathe his last few times, yet the son recognized his father as he approached him in the tent. Sad it was indeed to have to bury the lovely son among a wild tribe of Indians, but such is the fate of emigrants who cross the Plains with ox teams.

It was ten miles from the point where he died to the next stage stand, and there was a white man keeping this stand by the name of Thompson. The dead boy was put in the wagon with his father to set and hold his head on his lap until the stand was reached where the father found enough pine boards or plank at fifty cents per square foot to make a coffin, put him in it best they could under the circumstances, and took the casket in a southwesterly direction about one quarter of a mile from the stand and by a lone little tree buried it. This stand was called Pima Village after a tribe of Indians of this name.[13]

There the Preacher had to bury his boy and never more see the spot. From this village the route was down the Gila River to the Colorado at Fort Yumah.[14]

There were two other tribes of Indians in that part of Arizona, but separated at considerable distance from each other, to wit, the Maricopa and Yumah Indians.

A Son is Born to the Preacher—Just twenty-five days from the death of his son John Ephraim, his wife gave birth to a fine boy, and everything considered, this was a happy event. The weather was hot and dry, no doctor was near enough to be called, and none was needed, nevertheless. Mother and baby got along all right, and nothing else would do for a name but that of the baby's father, hence his name is James Anderson Slover.

Crossing the Colorado River—On reaching the mouth of the Gila River, it was advisable to go thirty miles down the Colorado before crossing it; this led through the Territory of the Yumah Indians, and they called on the Train for a little pay or damage, which was paid, and the Indians were well pleased. After crossing the Colorado, the Train pitched tents in a mesquite thicket for three weeks to recruit the stock, for there was a ninety-mile desert to cross.[15]

There was plenty of good feed at this camp. The time drew nigh for making this crossing of the desert. Many suggestions as to routes were made by different parties. One strange man said he would pilot the Train across for one hundred and fifty dollars, but they did not give it nor nothing else, for there happened to be a man in the company that had been there before and said he knew how to follow the meanderings of New River. This was a stream that was formed by the overflowing of the Colorado, and it flowed in a circuitous route and wasted itself on the desert, but it, in drying up, would leave lagoons or holes of water. As the weather would continue to be dry, the water in these lagoons would recede and then a fine grass would come up in the early fall and make good feed. So one day about noon the guide made a start, and the Train followed suit.

The first night there was not a blade of anything green or dry for the teams except what was in the wagons. The next day about eleven o'clock the Train came to a lone careless field of perhaps one hundred acres which had been irrigated by the waters of New River. This was fine feed for the seed was just getting ripe and the stalks were still green and the leaves were green also. Here every team was unyoked and turned into this large weed patch until they were filled up.

About one o'clock the teams were rounded up and a start was made. About sundown the large sandhills were encountered, and in the midst of these, dark came upon the Train and the tracks of the guide could no longer be seen, but after wandering on by star light for an hour or two, fortunately his light was espied by the wandering Train. Then all heads and herds cheered up and soon camp was pitched for the night, and as there were water and some grass, the Train lay by one day and a half. The Train then traveled all the next night to get to the Deep Water Well where the stage road was struck, which the Train left about one month before.[16] Here someone met the Train with the fattest beef that was met by that Train while crossing the Plains.

After considerable wandering through cactus thickets, a lovely spring known as Mountain Spring was reached. Then a day's drive over the mountain brought the Train into Milkatye [Milquatay] Valley [Campo district] where there were some pretty good vegetables and tolerable good grass. Here the Train scattered. They were in San Diego County, California, about sixty miles east of the City of San Diego [early November, six months after leaving Arkansas]. The Preacher here left the balance of the Train and rolled on to Sweetwater Creek or Valley, and pitched his tent at a public well, and began work that opportunity would offer, sometimes cleaning up around a new fine house built by the Kimble Bros.[17] at one dollar per day, sometimes hauling wood to San Diego at ten dollars per cord. Here he camped and hauled &c until sometime in February 1870. He was on this creek from the first days of November 1869 to sometime in February, when another start was made for Tulare County. In Anaheim the first California grape wine was seen. In Los Angeles City was seen ripe oranges on the trees; this was sometime in early March.

About the twenty-second of March Beals Ranch was reached in the northern part of Los Angeles County, where the equinoctial storm laid up the few families that were together for three or four days. After the storm was over, the travel was resumed, and two days drive brought them to Bakersfield, Kern County. From Bakersfield, following the foothills around through Plano, Porterville, Farmersville, and finally on the eighth day of April 1870 they reached Visalia, tired and dusty. The Preacher secured a house about one and a half miles out of the town of Visalia and lived there until November, then located on the Tule River.[18]

While stopping near Visalia he was employed by G. F. Pennebaker to make hay, and was introduced to a Buckeye Mower as a starter, and the first wheat he ever saw cut for hay he cut with that mower. After the cutting was done, the hay was to be hauled to the barn, a distance of about two miles. He and Pennebaker had to pitch the hay on to the wagon while the driver would load; the pitchers used four-tined forks. The Preacher observed after the hauling had been going on for a day or two that his employer stuck up his fork and left the field and went home.

Sometime after the job was done, the Preacher learned that Pennebaker said that Baptist preacher was the first man that ever made him stick up his fork and leave the field. In the latter part of August, he was attacked with erysipelas in his face, and was bad off with it for several days.[19] This was the first case he had ever seen.

The marks of the caustic applied to prevent its spreading are still visible and no doubt will be as long as he lives.

12

The Preacher locates a Preemption on the Tule River—Joins the Baptist church in Visalia—Is appointed by the American Baptist Home Mission Society to preach in Visalia and vicinity—His first attempt at farming in California—Dry season—Irrigating wheat—Crop short—Stage stand and Post Office at his residence—Another new comer in his family—His daughter Fannie narrowly escapes being burned to death—He is elected School Trustee and clerk of the Board—Is elected to the Office of Justice of the Peace—Another severe attack of erysipelas—The Doctor's bill—His daughter Rachel Jane marries Hugh W. Riggs—The last babe is born and dies—Borrows money at two per cent per month to pay for land—Gets United States Patent for the Preemption—Attends a South Methodist protracted meeting for six weeks—The Grange—Mutual Aid Society of Los Angeles, California

Having spent the summer near Visalia, Tulare County, California, he began casting around for a home, and in his ramblings found an old woman with her son-in-law whose names were Mrs. Monroe and Beasley. They each had claims on eighty acres of government land and were ready to sell their claims.

 A trade was soon consummated between the claimants and the home-seeker at a stipulated price, securing in the deal about four thousand feet of fencing lumber, and a quantity of split-out pickets of sugar pine. In November of 1870 he located with his family on this 160 acres of land and in about three months filed a Preemption Claim upon the same.

 This land was on the south side of the Tule River about twenty miles south of Visalia and fifty north of Bakersfield, Kern County, and on a line between the two towns.

He and wife gave their church letters to and united with the Baptist church in Visalia, and for the year 1871 he was employed by the American Baptist Home Mission Society to labor with this church and surrounding country at a salary of six hundred dollars from the Board and four hundred from the church. The Board paid its pro rata but the church failed, and only eleven months work was done.

The year 1871 was his first attempt at farming in the Golden State. He rented land that year as there were none fenced in his claim, nor no irrigating ditch and that being one of California's dry years, it was necessary to irrigate everything that was planted. He sowed one thousand lbs. of wheat and a ton of barley and reaped about ninety bushels of wheat and got about two tons of barley hay. This was a very short crop and was a great discouragement to the newcomer.

During the fall of this (1871) year, there was a stage road opened from Visalia to Bakersfield, which passed directly by his house and the proprietor of the line established a stand at his residence and kept two horses in his little barn erected for the purpose.

He now thought the opening good to have a Post Office established in his residence. A blank application was secured and a few of his neighbors signed the petition, and the office was established. He was appointed postmaster, which position he held for several years. He called the name of the office Woodville.[1] In September of this year another newcomer put in an appearance in the family. And it became necessary to give to him a name, so it was agreed among those concerned to call his name George Henderson. This was the fourth of the second crop of children, as Davey Crockett used to say about his second marriage.

In March 1872 his daughter Fannie Isadora had a narrow escape from being burned to death. It seemed that she had got hold of some matches, and gone outside of the yard and into the vineyard, and was striking the matches to see them burn, and her outer skirt got afire and she started for the house. As she entered the porch her father met her and attempted to tear the skirt off her, but failing to do this, her flaxen hair was soon in a blaze and her father rubbed the fire off her head with the palms of his hands which burned his hands badly, and at this juncture her mother came with a bucket full of water and dashed it on the burning child, and so the fire was conquered, but with a badly burned child. She was four years old at the time. She will carry the marks of that memorable day to her grave.

About the time he moved to his new home, the few settlers were forming a school district, and he was soon identified with the enterprise by being elected Trustee and Clerk of the board, which position he held for about eight years. When the District was divided, he resigned.

The crop of 1872 was quite different from the previous year. Rain came early and the earth soon dressed herself in living green. Alfileree [alfilaria, or pin clover] covered the plains early in January and was fine feed in February. Farming was better for five successive years, or in other words, for five years crops were good, plenty of rain, and everything in the agricultural line did very well.

At the general election in the fall of 1873 he was chosen by the people of Tule River Judicial Township as one of the Justices of the Peace, which office, with an appointment as Notary Public from the Governor of the State, he held for two years.

Pretty soon after this election he had another severe attack of erysipelas in his face, attended with the bilious fever. On the morning of the seventh day after the attack, his eyes were closed from the severe swelling in the nose and face, and he never saw light for eight days. Doctor Henrahan of Porterville was his physician who made at least seventeen trips, and his bill, together with the drugs he furnished, was two hundred and twenty-five dollars.[2]

In January of the year 1874 his daughter Elizabeth Jane was married to Hugh M. Riggs of San Joaquin County, California.

On the seventh day of January 1874 the last child was born, and died on the eleventh day of the same month. A very brief stay the little boy made in this world of trouble, sorrow, pain, and death; the little remains quietly sleep in Pleasant Grove graveyard, Tulare County, California.

The time soon came to make payment on the preemption. It, being within the limits of the railroad grant for the line of the Southern Pacific, was double minimum land; therefore he had to pay two dollars and fifty cents per acre.[3]

Now began financial trouble, because he had to borrow four hundred dollars and give his note and a mortgage on the land, and pay two per cent per month for the use of the money. This was a heavy tax on a small farmer, but so it had to be in order to secure the land and get a United States Patent, which, however, was obtained.

Early in March of this year, the M. E. Church South began a quarterly meeting at the Pleasant Grove Schoolhouse, which was continued for six weeks, and every night or evening for forty-two evenings he and his family were in attendance.[4]

This was the time of the Granger Movement in Tulare County. In the summer a Mr. Jolly came into the neighborhood and organized a grange in the Pleasant Grove Schoolhouse, and the subject of this autobiography was elected master. Having no other means of learning the unwritten work but from Mr. Jolly, he stuck close to him until ten o'clock at night after the organization, following with him from Woodville to Tipton in order to get posted in the work. He held connection with the institution until he was satisfied that there was no good to come to him as a farmer from the order, so he gave it up convinced that instead of its making less monopolies and less middle men, it only created more of these plutocrats.[5]

Also during this year, he met an agent of the "Mutual Aid Society of Los Angeles, California," who presented the claims of that institution to him and insisted on his taking out a policy. He was led to believe that perhaps it would be profitable to his family, so he paid the forty dollars and became a life member. No dues were to pay except death assessments which was three dollars within twenty days from the receipt of the notice of the death of any member, and as an annual benefit derived from the Society, there was a dividend declared every October. Suffice it to say that deaths were frequent, but dividends were small; about twenty-five or fifty cents per year.[6]

He stayed with this Society until he was out about eighty dollars all told, and the last he heard of it was that the Society had changed localities, and located at San Bernardino. Believing that this was another scheme to get his money without any equivalent in return, he failed to pay or rather refused to answer the notices that were sent to him, so his life membership was canceled. Whatever became of the Society he knows not.

13

With his farming in Tulare County, California, a failure—Two years in three total failures—Mortgage increases—The fifth crop is very cheap—No fence law passed for Tulare—His last year in California—Makes a desperate effort to make a good crop—Contemplates a move to Jackson County, Oregon—Mortgage foreclosed on his farm—Land redeemed by his two sons and son-in-law—He moves to Oregon in September 1881—Incidents of his trip.

Owing to the dry years in Tulare County, California, he could not succeed in the business of farming. Too many "drawbacks." Fencing material was very expensive.

In 1875, the no-fence law was enacted for that and other adjoining counties.[1] Then every animal he turned out of the corral had to be herded or fastened to the end of a stake rope, and the other end securely tied to a stake-pin and that well driven into the ground. This mode of farming was very inconvenient to him; poor as he was, he could not fence, and only having one hundred sixty acres of land, everything was consumed in feeding horses, cows, and hogs for the use of the farm. Even when a good crop was made, there were but a few tons of wheat and barley to spare to put on the market.

And then it was very expensive living there; he could raise but little garden for the want of a supply of water to irrigate. The river from which the water for irrigating purposes was taken was insufficient for the neighborhood, and this was annoying; it was no use to talk about ditch laws in a dry country, for in spite of all law or rule, the man or company who could tap the river the highest up or nearest to the foothills took the water, and those lower down the stream might suck their fingers for water.[2] There were plenty of men, and women, too, for that matter, who cared but little who sank so that they swam. "Money made the mare go," in that respect.

The crop of 1876 was pretty good, but was not worth very much. Wheat opened at one dollar per cental and before the crop was disposed of it was worth only ninety cents per cental or one hundred pounds. Barley was worth eighty cents per cental delivered on board the cars.

Of the next three years, 1877, 1878, and 1879, the first and last were total failures on his farm, and everywhere else, except where there was plenty of water to irrigate. But 1878 was a fine crop year and wheat was a very good price, about one dollar and twenty-five cents per hundred pounds, and it got up to one dollar and fifty cents per cental before the crop was all disposed of.

But when the time came to plant for the crop of 1879, there was no rain, and this Scribe told his family that no chances would be taken this season as were in 1877 to the time of putting the seed in for the crop that year, for it proved a loss of the seed sown. He would wait until it rained, and if it did not rain, no wheat nor barley would be put in on his farm. Time rolled on and the month of March came and no rain had fallen, and it was well understood that now the time for rain had gone by for that season, unless it be perhaps a few April showers, but these failed to come in that April.[3]

Therefore he resolved to leave his family and go to San Joaquin County to spend the summer, thinking perhaps he would find employment in some way, either in preaching or laboring in the harvest, for crops were good in that part of the state. All of the crop of 1878 except his seed was already stored in the depot at Tulare City, and one cent per pound had been advanced, and storage and insurance and interest paid; so he arranged for the trip to ride with a friend who was going north to Colusa County in his spring wagon, and they were soon off. Arriving at Woodbridge, he having his saddle horse led behind the wagon, they separated and pretty soon he rode down the river to a Mr. Ray's house who said he was a Baptist, but the Preacher could not find much Baptist comfort there with that professed Baptist. Nevertheless, he treated him kindly and commended him to the hospitable kindness of old father [Amasa Allen] Guernsey near Lodi in the same county, to whose house the Preacher soon repaired, having spent one night only with Ray.[4]

Father Guernsey was an aged Baptist minister and knew how to sympathize with a brother in adversity. So his house was kindly tendered him as a home. He and his loving wife lived alone on the farm; they were indeed kind and hospitable to the stranger they had never seen prior to this.

The old man was the owner of a threshing outfit and had all his men engaged to fill every position except one—fork team driver—and the newcomer applied for the vacancy. The old Minister looked at the gray hairs of the applicant with a look of surprise (for the applicant was in his fifty-fifth year) and said, "You are too old to fill that place." The stranger replied that he was willing to try it, and if he saw he could not fill the bill, he could get somebody in his place, suggesting at the same time that there would be plenty of men around about that season wanting work. This proved true, but it never became necessary to change, and for three months or more he run with that machine and grew in favor with the old Minister and all the crew, and returned to his family in the last of October. Having sold his horse, he boarded the emigrant train at Stockton and soon was home again.

Now some of the incidents of this absence will be of interest to young people.

A trip to the Calaveras River in April while stopping with Guernsey— He was recommended to a Brother Baldwin by his host, and accordingly he mounted his saddle horse and rode over the low hills by the way of the town of Linden and in the afternoon of the first day found himself on the premises of Brother Baldwin whom he found in a potato patch hoeing the potato vines. A formal introduction was made by the preacher, giving Baldwin his name as a Baptist minister. After the compliments of the hour, Baldwin asked the stranger if he had his credentials, who at once took in the situation and replied, "No," stating that they were in Tulare County where he lived when at home. Baldwin was pretty sure he had found an imposter, and said to the new Preacher, "There are a great many imposters around these days." The Preacher told him, yes, that was very true.

By this time Baldwin was ready to invite him to get off his horse and stay until morning. He did so. Next morning Baldwin had to make a trip to Stockton to take a school ma'am home, and invited the strange preacher to abide with his family until he returned. He was home in the evening of the same day and told the Preacher he could stop with him as long as he saw fit and preach at the schoolhouse. Doubtless he learned from the Baptist pastor in Stockton who his guest was, and the Preacher was not interrogated any more about credentials nor suspected as a imposter while in that county. He found a pleasant home with Baldwin and his family as long as he abided there.

A visit in the interest of a Sabbath school—He had not been with the old veteran minister (Guernsey) but a few days until Sabbath school was talked up for the Brick church, a Baptist house in the country and located on the big road known in that county as Cherokee Lane. Now suffice it to say that the lane was named for a family of people by the name of Post who claimed to be part Cherokee, but they were evidently part African of American descent and but little or no Cherokee blood in them. Be this as it may, the old Baptist minister requested the new preacher to visit three or four families and notify them that there would be Sabbath School and preaching at the Brickhouse the following Sabbath. For this visit the old man's buggy was forthcoming with his own gentle horse for a team, and receiving instructions as to road and the names of the parties to be visited he was soon on the go. The first family was a very nice widow woman (name forgotten) but the other two were sisters of Tom Post and had great thick lips just like an Arkansas Negro, and these were both widows. After making this visit he returned satisfied to let Guernsey do his own drumming among those would-be Cherokees about the Brick house.

He met an old Tennessee friend and acquaintance, James Henry by name, whom he had not seen in about twenty-six years.[5] The Preacher had stopped for the night with a man by the name of Owens, and from his house could be seen quite a number of farm houses scattered over the plains. On inquiry he found that James Henry occupied one of these residences. Learning from Owens all he could about Henry, he concluded that it must be his old friend with whom he was a boy in the Forties. On further inquiry, he learned that Henry would be by Owens' next morning going to Stockton. Sure enough, early next morning Henry was seen coming, and the Preacher told Owens not to introduce Henry to him, that he might see if he would recognize him.

Pretty soon Henry rode up in the presence of Owens and the Preacher. The morning compliments were passed. The Preacher was not long in recognizing his old friend and said to him, "You do not look quite so young as you did twenty-six years ago." Hearing this familiar voice, he turned his eyes into the Preacher's face and said, "Is not this Jim Slover?" He replied yes; then there was mutual joy for they were sure enough old friends, and with Henry, the Preacher spent many days of pleasure. They went to Stockton together and heard Judge Terry speak in favor of the new

Constitution which was then before the people of the State for adoption or rejection.[6]

Henry had come from Tennessee during the gold excitement and got quite a good lot of the precious metal, and went to Philadelphia and had it coined, and on his way back to California, he stopped in Washington County, Ark., to see his friend Slover. This was the spring of 1853, and from that time up to this meeting in 1879, they had not so much as known where each other was.

During this stay in San Joaquin County, the state election came on in September, and his friends in Tulare County desired to again run him for Justice of the Peace. For that purpose he was interviewed by letter as to whether he would serve or not. He answered that if they would elect him, he would serve. Some parties in the Judicial Township wanted another man, so his friends thought they must rally on his behalf, and there one of his friends was met by a man who had heard that Slover was a Minister of the Gospel, and was opposed to electing him. His friend replied that Slover was a hard-working man on a farm, and attended to his own business. The man said in reply, "Go home, sir, go home; we will elect him," and sure enough he was elected, and held that office until September 1881.

14

He emigrates to Oregon—Preparations for the trip—The move and incidents of travel—Is unloaded at the residence of his friend, G. F. Pennebaker—Soon locates in a rented house belonging to Wm. Erbe of Ashland, Jackson County, Oregon—The terms rather hard—Makes the best crop perhaps ever made on the farm—Gains the confidence of the Oregonians around him—Nine months on the Erbe farm—Buys hotel property in Jacksonville, Oregon—Moves and takes charge of the hotel—Changes places in the same town—Daughter marries A. F. Eddy—His son James A. goes into the employ of Dr. Roberson to learn the drug business—Has a cash sale—Moves to Roseburg—Nine months in the Hotel business there—The business there—The business closes on him—Attempts another cash sale—Emigrates south of Grants Pass.

During the spring and summer of 1881 a correspondence was conducted between the subject of this sketch and his friend, G. F. Pennebaker (who had some years previous emigrated from Tulare County, Calif., and located in Jackson County, Ore.), relative to the advantages and disadvantages of the Rogue River Valley and Baptists' interests. From this interview he received more or less encouragement to attempt a move.

Therefore he set about to dispose of the little personal property in his possession, his land having been sold under a mortgage in favor of Jeff Hunsaker in March of this year, and was subject to redemption. So his two sons by his first wife, and Hugh M. Riggs, his son-in-law, concluded with his consent to redeem the land which would cost them fifteen hundred dollars. They also bought all the personal property belonging to their father. After settlement he had about eleven hundred dollars in coin left, with which he started to Oregon about the fourth day of September

A.D. 1881. He, his wife and four children were brought on a wagon to Tulare City, where tickets were bought for Redding, Calif., with layover privileges.

At Goshen, an arrangement had been made to meet relatives and spend Sunday with them there. A brother and two sisters of his wife met them at the house of their Aunt Ann Williams, and a very pleasant day was spent, but the peace and pleasure of the family were broken by the drunkenness of the landlord, so that the Preacher and his family concluded that the better thing for them to do was to go, even at a late hour of the night, to the depot and spend the time there the best they could until the train came along—about three hours late. When his family boarded the train, they bid adieu to Goshen and the drunken landlord.

Now the way that delayed train sped over the plains to Lathrop was a caution. It seemed that it made in certain places a mile a minute. About nine P.M. of the first day, she pulled into Redding. Into the hotel he and his family went and found lodging for the night. He had to pay fifty cents per meal all the while he stopped at that hotel.

On going to the Post Office, he found a postal card from his friend Pennebaker stating that Mr. Elliot, whom he had engaged to come to Redding to take his family across the mountains to Ashland, had failed to start as soon as he was to, by five days. Supposing that he would have to lay by there until he arrived, he went out and procured a place where he with his family could board themselves. This house consisted of a workshop with a floor, and a stove in the yard. A supply of provisions was laid in, but he had not been in this house long when he was called upon by one Wagner of Cow Creek in Oregon. A proposition to haul him and family to Ashland was soon made by this man Wagner, and a contract was made between them for the sum of twenty dollars.

Wagner came around the next morning with a narrow track wagon, and the little effects of the Preacher and his family were soon loaded into the small wagon box. He had sent most of his goods by a freighter, by the name of True, some days previous. He fancied to himself a nice trip across the mountains, but to begin with, Wagner the teamster drove up to the hotel and took in another man and wife destined to Yreka. So they left Redding with eight persons in the wagon besides the Preacher, as well as a huge trunk of the Noah's ark build.

The road lay in the Scotts Mountain route, over which that wagon with its treasure started.[1] On reaching Scotts Valley, it was discovered by the emigrants that Wagner's wife and grown daughter were waiting for the wagon. The little narrow track could not take any more passengers, so a two-horse wagon was improvised and the living freight divided to suit, so that the peace and harmony of the emigrants were maintained. At Yreka the extra wagon turned back.

From this point Wagner and wife and daughter desired to take a trip to Butte Creek Valley about forty miles east and over the worst road imaginable. Obtaining the consent of the Preacher and family, the trip was undertaken, and after traveling one day and a half, the point was reached in the above mentioned valley, and the whole party rested for two days.

When the travel began again—setting out on Sunday morning en route for Klamath River—they finally camped at Shovel Creek Springs, a health resort in Siskiyou County, Calif. Leaving these Springs early on Tuesday morning, at noon the road from Yreka to Ashland was reached fifteen miles north of Yreka—that is to say, seven days had been spent and only fifteen miles gained, but such is life.

Cottonwood was the next camping place, a village on the north side of the Klamath River. From Cottonwood, the Siskiyou Mountain was crossed and the Preacher and his family were unloaded at the house of his friend, G. F. Pennebaker, on the afternoon of the twenty-first of September A.D. 1881.[2]

The next thing was to find a farm to rent. A horse and saddle were secured for a few days and a search made, and in about one week's time a small farm belonging to Wm. Erbe of Ashland was found and rented for twelve months, consideration one hundred and fifty dollars cash rent.

This farm was about two and one half miles south east of Ashland. With only about fifty acres in cultivation and rather poor land, upon the whole it was rather a hard bargain. This was the first time the Preacher ever lived on a rented place where he was not allowed to cut firewood. Nevertheless, there was plenty of timber growing on the farm. Near the road and in one corner of the wheat field stood two large pine trees which Erbe wanted taken down and out; he proposed to give them to the Preacher if he would take them off the land.

Suffice it to say, the trees did not stand in the field long, but were soon taken out and the ground plowed and sowed to wheat, and a good crop was made. It was said by those who knew the farm that that was the best crop they had seen for twenty years on that land. The Preacher got forty dollars worth of wood out of the two trees he cut and took off the land. The work he did and the way he did it showed the Oregonians that there was at least one Baptist preacher who knew something about work. He thereby soon gained the confidence of his neighbors.

An incident or two during this trip is proper to leave on record for those who may read this biography.

When Wagner proposed to bring the Preacher and family across the mountains, he asked the Preacher what he would give. The Preacher said fifteen dollars. Wagner looked at the children and examined into the amount of baggage there would be for him to haul, and then told the Preacher that he could not do it for that amount, but if he would give twenty dollars, he would drive around and load them in. This was agreed to on the part of the Preacher, thinking that he and his family would have the little narrow track all to themselves.

Alas, how that Oregonian teamster had deceived him. When the wagon came around the next day to load up, he said there was more to haul than he thought, and he wanted the Preacher to give him three or four dollars extra to help pay toll. O, said the Preacher, he would not mind to give him two dollars and fifty cents extra. This satisfied the teamster so far as a start was concerned, but when he finally reached the summit of the Siskiyou Mountain, while the team was resting and the emigrants were eating dinner, Wagner walked down to Dollarhide's to pay toll on the road. There he found that Elliot had made the trip to Redding with two wagons and had just passed there that morning on his way back, mad at Slover and Pennebaker. He (Elliot) had told Dollarhide that Pennebaker had agreed to give him twenty-five dollars to bring this man Slover from Redding to Ashland.

This was more than Wagner could stand, so when the Preacher was unloaded four miles south of Ashland, he pleaded with the preacher for two dollars and fifty cents more, and the Preacher just simply paid it, so it cost twenty-five dollars, over and above board bills, to get from Redding to Ashland.

After the crop on the Erbe farm developed enough to satisfy the Preacher that he could not cut it for grain, but must use it in the shape of hay, his garden was all destroyed, together with the fruit, by a snow and freeze which came about the fourth and fifth days of May. On the morning of the fourth day of May the snow measured just four inches, and although the snow did not stay long, on the morning of the fifth everything was frozen that was liable to freeze.

A new home had to be sought and a move made by the first of the coming October. Therefore he rode around looking for a farm to rent, and was directed to Jacksonville to interview Gen. Thomas G. Reames, a merchant in that town, but failed to find him.

Then in the same place he found a Baptist minister by the name of A. D. Manion who was running a rented hotel known as the Savage property. Manion was very anxious to sell his hotel fixtures and his lease of the house for the unexpired eleven months of the year. After some days to consider the matter, a deal was made, and seven hundred and fifty dollars was the price for the hotel fixtures belonging to Manion. By borrowing two hundred and forty dollars, the trade was closed.

On the twenty-first day of June, a move was made and the hotel taken charge of on the morning of the twenty-second. So about nine months was all the time spent on the little fifty-acre farm. When the Manion lease was out on the hotel, it was necessary to change localities. In May 1883 a location was rented from Patrick Ryan on California Street, and a move made. Here in this house in Jacksonville, four years and a half were spent in the flurry and worry of the unthankful business of hotel keeping.[3]

In the month of March 1885 his daughter Mary E. became the wife of Adolphus F. Eddy, and in May 1885, his son James Anderson went into the employ of D. Roberson to learn the drug business. Now there were but two children left with him.

As the year 1887 began to wear away, he discovered that his business in the hotel was growing so little that he would have to give it up. So in December he advertised to sell the hotel furniture, which by the way had been materially increased. During the Christmas holly days the sale came off—but lo and behold, he could not sell anything at near its value, so that it came about as near being a give away as a sale of the effects.[4]

In January 1888 he moved to Roseburg and took charge of the Cosmopolitan Hotel owned by Champayne and Hains. About nine months time there taught him that he could not make the business pay there. He run so far behind in that time that the business closed down upon him. Another cash sale was attempted, but he could not sell much to any advantage.

In October 1888 he emigrated south to Grants Pass. Soon after his arrival, his daughter Fannie, who had been in Pendleton [in eastern Oregon] for sometime learning to set type in a printing office, came home and began setting type in the Courier office, and arrangements were pretty soon made for her brother George H. and her mother to work in the Pass. The Preacher located a homestead in Sam's Valley, Jackson County, Ore., in the spring of 1890.[5] However, while residing in Roseburg, he corresponded with certain parties in Josephine County relative to returning to Grants Pass and giving himself to the work of the ministry, and whether or not he could be supported by the Baptists of that county. He obtained encouragement sufficient to induce his location in that town. And from October to the end of the year, he gave his time to preaching, but the support did not come to meet current expenses.

Then he received a call from New Hope Church in Sam's Valley, Jackson County, Ore., or was chosen as pastor. A short correspondence was conducted between himself and Deacon Nathaniel Fitzgerald. It was agreed that the Preacher would go up and hold a meeting beginning on the Saturday preceding the fourth Sunday in January 1889, and continue until the first Sunday in February which was the time of their regular business meeting, and at which conference meeting he would answer the church's call. At the appointed time he was present at Antioch Schoolhouse. At the close of the first service on Saturday, the meeting became so intensely interesting that it was continued from day to day for two weeks instead of one. The church was greatly revived.

The fact was known to the Preacher that some time prior to the church's calling him, she had received certain parties into membership from other denominations without baptizing them (they having been immersed by United Brethren and Campbellite preachers). Consequently, his answer when given was this: If you will undo that act that admitted without immersion, and give him [Slover] one hundred and twenty-five dollars per annum, he would be their Pastor; he would not pastor any church that practiced the reception of alien immersion. They took the matter up and at the March or April meeting a motion was submitted to rescind the act of the church that admitted those two aliens and unanimously carried. Suffice it to say, from year to year the church called him, agreeing to pay the stipulated salary, until he declined to accept the position because they failed to pay as agreed.

During his first year's pastorate, his attention was called to a tract of government land by Deacon Fitzgerald & family, and urged to take it up as a homestead. The Deacon's son, Walter D., conducted the Preacher over the land and showed him about where the lines were, the land being directly south of the Fitzgerald farm and west of the John Cardwell farm.[6] On returning from prospecting the locality of the tract, it occurred to the

Preacher that if the Deacon would sell him a certain small piece of his land known as a wild plum and whiteoak thicket, bounded on the north by a little creek known as Cardwell creek and on the south by the tract above mentioned and on the west by the end of the plum thicket and running to a point at the east, containing perhaps two acres more or less, he would be willing to file a Homestead entry on the government tract, provided it was subject to such entry.[7]

The Deacon responded and said, "Why I will give it to you and make you a deed to it without you paying anything, only what the law requires, which consideration would be at least one dollar." Then and there the Preacher concluded to try to make a home for himself and family.

The first thing after concluding to secure the land was to ascertain whether it was subject to Homestead entry or not. A letter was sent to the local Land Office at Roseburg, Ore., making inquiry as to the facts in the case. The Register replied that it was, one half of the land being in an odd section which he thought might be listed as railroad land, but it had a homestead filing at the time the grant was made to the railroad, and afterward abandoned. On receiving this information, the next thing was to get material to build a house. Without any money he had to resort to his own labor, so he borrowed a broadaxe, and got the same W. D. Fitzgerald and went up on the mountain and hewed the sills for a dwelling house twenty-four by sixteen feet, with a kitchen attached, sixteen by twelve feet, constructed in the shape of the letter T. This was done in the early spring of 1889.

It was a long way to where there was timber that would make boards or shakes for a roof, but one of Deacon Fitzgerald's boys had a claim on government land some twenty-odd miles northeast of their home at a place known as Chicago, so-called because a Mr. Hall first settled the claim of young Fitzgerald and he emigrated from Chicago to Jackson County, Ore. So in the month of May the two young Fitzgerald boys took their wagon and a team of two horses, and loaded in the Preacher, and his wife to cook for the party, and rolled away for Chicago to make shakes, the Preacher to have one third of the quantity riven. In about two weeks they had fifteen thousand two-foot shakes riven and nicely stacked, but in the next month they all burned up, supposed to have been caused by lightning setting an old dead pine tree on fire. In August the same three men returned to the same place and made twenty-five thousand more, two-thirds of which were three feet long, but the Preacher's were all two-foot shakes. But to get them drawn to the building place cost nearly half the shakes. Nevertheless, the fifty-five hundred answered his immediate purpose. About the month of November he had a sufficient quantity of material to build a comfortable dwelling.

At the January 1890 meeting of the New Hope church, the Preacher concluded to carry on a traveling prayer meeting, but a snow storm closed the prayer meeting at the expiration of one week. So great was the protracted snow storm that the Preacher was snowbound in the vicinity of Antioch Schoolhouse for about twenty days, after which he made his way to Gold Hill with the Rev. George E. Jones and boarded the train for the Pass where he rested until the snow was gone.

During his stay in Grants Pass, the county bridge across Rogue River went down, which event happened on the second day of March 1890. He with a neighbor walked down to see the river and look at the creeling bridge, and walked out some twenty-five feet to get a better view of the river. Fortunately for them they started home, and just a few minutes after leaving the bridge, down went the half next to the Pass, and about nine o'clock P.M. the same evening the other half fell.

On returning to Sam's Valley, his first work was to grub the plum thicket to plant fruit trees and garden. In the month of April a young man told him if he left any gaps down, meaning if he did not comply with the law in filing on the land selected for homestead, that a certain young man or party would jump the land.[8] Whether this was intended to hurry the Preacher up with his filing was a question.

So he arranged to file as soon as possible, and on the twenty-eighth of April 1890 his filing was recorded in the Land Office at Roseburg.

15

Homestead—His first improvised cabin—Builds a house ten by twelve feet as a homestead residence—Erects a good dwelling house, wood and poultry house—Clears and fences several acres of land—Plants an orchard—Miners desire to prospect for gold quartz—Harbin's placer—The Miners' contest—Homesteader loses forty acres of his Homestead—He submits his final proof—Riley Morrison enters a protest—He conceives a plan to build a house for New Hope Baptist church—Building erected under the supervision of a building committee—Dedication of the new church house—Incidents.

On hearing that there was a probability of someone looking for a gap in his proceedings by which he might enter and defeat the object of the Preacher, and being ignorant of the law governing homestead entries, and depending upon private information as to how to proceed, he was therefore told that he must have some sort of a tenement answering the purpose of a house. Seeing then that the material was about all on the ground for building purposes, he immediately proceeded to improvise a structure which he could occupy temporarily.

The next step was the money, which required twenty-five dollars, and not having it on hand, it occurred to his mind that probably his son James could get the amount necessary, and writing to him of the seeming necessity, the money was furnished. Then to Jacksonville he went and made the filing of his declaratory statement.

This little tenement was indeed an improvised structure, made by planting posts about eight feet from a pile of building material consisting of hewn and sawed timber. This material answered for one end of the structure, then planting two more posts hard by the side of this pile of lumber about six feet apart, the sides were closed with twelve-foot boards. The open end answered as an entrance and fireplace. He ate and slept in this house (which was covered with like material as the sides) at least one night before he made his way to Jacksonville to file, which was on Saturday, April the 19th, 1890. In due time he built a house ten by twelve feet with the design to use it as a homestead residence until such time as he could build a better house, and then use the small one as a store or smoke house.

    In the Spring of 1891 he raised and covered the body of a residence twenty-four by sixteen feet with a kitchen attached so as to form what is known as a T-shaped house. It was sixteen feet by twelve with a six-foot porch on each side. The building was sixteen feet high, a box-house made of surfaced boards, with three rooms below and three above, with a hall-way at the head of the stairs. The house required ten doors and thirteen windows. He had to suspend work on the residence for more than twelve months on account of clearing about five acres of land and assisting in the building of a Baptist church, but suffice it to say he continued the buildings from time to time until the residence, wood and poultry houses were all up and nearly finished, doing nearly all the work himself, and enclosed about eight acres principally with posts and eight-inch fencing boards.

    He also planted about sixty-five or seventy fruit trees; some of these were planted on the plum thicket land obtained from Fitzgerald's farm.

About the first of 1894, gold prospectors were unusually plenty, so Walter Fitzgerald came to the Preacher and told him that certain parties desired to prospect on his Homestead for gold quartz. He replied that he was unwilling on the grounds that they might find a "bonanza," that would prevent his getting a patent.[1] He said the miners would contest the final proof. He then told young Fitzgerald to tell them to dig the whole surface up because the Preacher did not believe there was any gold-bearing quartz anywhere on the Homestead. The same young Fitzgerald had told him that the land had been pretty thoroughly prospected and no quartz had been found, and so it proved to be a failure with these prospectors.

    But among them there was a certain Jackson Harbin, who in the absence and without the consent of the Homesteader, opened a placer mine in a small ravine, and blowed it around that he had found a good placer mine, and before long sold it to Thomas Pankey of Moonville, or Sam's Valley, for a cheap cow, valued by Pankey at twenty-five dollars. The cow was sold by Harbin for the enormous sum of eighteen dollars to liquidate his board and horse feed bills to one Wm. H. Beidler who at that time lived on the

Cardwell farm, located adjoining due east of the homestead in question. The first the Homesteader knew of all this underground chicanery, he was passing south of his house en route to Gold Hill on foot, and his attention was attracted by a notice describing the location of a mineral claim purporting to be a placer mine. It claimed twenty acres near or a little north of the center of the east eighty acres of the homestead, and was signed by Martin Perry as locator and witnessed by Thomas Pankey and William Selph. This claim was described by metes and bounds, and not by Government parallel lines as the law requires all placer claims to be bounded.

The Homesteader, after carefully reading the notice, passed on, thinking of the presumption of the locator of this claim in presuming to claim of a portion of the land which he had bought from the Government and had paid all that was required by the Government to entitle him to the peaceable possession of the land as a homestead.

Time passed on with more or less rumors afloat that there had been two placer mining claims located on the Homestead of the Rev. Slover. Finally, in November 1896, in front of the Sam's Valley Post Office, Thomas Pankey said to the homesteader, "Can't there be some arrangement between us, whereby we (meaning himself and William Selph) can mine out that little streak of land and then we will be your witnesses when you go to prove up?" To this proposal the Homesteader emphatically declared no, that he did not want that soil washed away, and that he would prosecute the man that mined there.

He heard no more of the subject until February 1897 when a certain Lindsey Sizemore appeared in his dooryard on horseback and presented him with a notice or summons from the local United States Land Office at Roseburg, notifying him that Thomas Pankey and William Selph had entered in that Office a contest for two mining claims on his Homestead, describing the same. This was new trouble to him; he had thirty days to prepare for the hearing before the County Judge.

On going to Jacksonville to secure the services of a lawyer, he went into the Clerk's Office to see if these claims were recorded as required by the mining laws, whereupon he found no record of such claims on the homestead. Mr. Selph had put upon record a twenty-acre claim on land that was on the Cardwell farm three-quarters of a mile east of said homestead. He showed this fact to a certain ex–county judge and asked what effect this record would have upon the contest. The judge replied that it would kill it.

Securing the services of William M. Colvig, he returned home to secure witnesses to prove that the land in question as per the summons was more valuable for farming than for mining.

The day of the hearing soon rolled around, and the parties met in the office of the County Judge, W. S. Crowell. Contestants produced Martin Perry (then County Commissioner–elect), Lafayette Row, Samuel Hodges, and Lindsey Sizemore as their witnesses, all of whom testified that the land was in their opinion more valuable for mining than for agricultural purposes. Some of them, after being examined as to their knowledge of mining and the extent of the prospecting the land in question, testified that the mining claims named in the contest would pay from two and a half to four dollars per day to the man who was ground sluicing.

The Homesteader introduced W. H. Beidler, Joseph Douden, and J. Dungan, who testified that in their opinion the land in question was more valuable for agricultural purposes than for mining.

When the case was reported to the Land Office at Roseburg, the Register and Receiver decided in favor of the miners. The Homesteader appealed to the General Land Office at Washington City, but Binger Herman, the Commissioner, sustained the ruling of the local office. The Homesteader then appealed from the Commissioner's ruling to the Secretary of the Interior where he was again defeated and the forty acres were canceled.

By this time the Homesteader had learned enough about the mining laws and miners in Oregon to reach a conclusion—that if he had known that after he bought and paid for a homestead it was subject to be prospected by miners at any time before the final proof is submitted, he never would have spent a dollar fighting a contest for mining claims on his homestead. When men would swear that from their knowledge of mining and prospecting the land in question that it would pay from two and a half to four dollars per day to the man ground sluicing, and that the bed rock was from nothing to seven feet deep, it would be vain to try to find agricultural land in southern Oregon that would be more valuable than such mining land.

Seeing that the time provided by the Homestead Law for proving up or submitting final proof of settlement and cultivating the land would in all probability expire before the contest would be ended, he therefore took the necessary steps, and on the twenty-sixth day of April 1898 made final proof as required by law, Frank Fitzgerald and Jeff Linvill being his witnesses.[2] After advertising that such proof would be submitted before Judge Crowell, as directed by the local Land Office authority at the time above stated, Madam Rumor said someone was going to enter a protest against his having a Patent to any of the land. About two weeks before the expiration of the notice, he was wending his way to Gold Hill on a trail across the homestead when suddenly he espied a paper tacked on a tree just south of the mining claims in contest, giving notice that another mining claim of twenty acres was located on his homestead and signed by Riley Morrison, as locator and properly witnessed by two witnesses, names forgotten. When he was returning from Ashland to get ready for the day of final proof, at Medford Atty. Solis boarded the train and said to the Homesteader, "I see you are going to prove up on your homestead." "Yes," was the reply, but said he to the lawyer, "I see another notice on the land for another mining claim. Do you know anything about it?" He said, "No. It will do him no good; it's too late."

But on the morning of the twenty-sixth of April, as the Homesteader and his two witnesses boarded a hack driven by Thomas Wyat, at Moonville for Jacksonville—behold! Mr. Morrison and Thomas Pankey and another were loading themselves into a like hack as though they were going to give the Homesteader and party a race to see whether or not they could get to Judge Crowell's office first. The Homesteader, however, was there first and immediately told the Judge his business. Just as he was finishing the evidence, Riley Morrison and Thomas Pankey came into the office.

Morrison called the attention of the Judge to a document he wished to file in his office. The Judge filed the paper and then said to the Homesteader, "You are entitled to see this." He replied that he would read it, but did not think it would do him any good. On reading he found that the document was a protest against his having a Patent for any of the land embraced in the homestead and attested by his (Morrison's) oath that the Homesteader had not complied with the law, neither in residing on the homestead nor cultivating the land.

He folded the paper and returned it to the Judge and said, "Judge, they will send me to the penitentiary." The Judge answered, "O, I think not in this world, and I don't think there is any in the next world," to which the Homesteader replied, "Well, if they do not, they should send the other man there, for one or the other of us has sworn a positive lie."

Adolphus Eddy [daughter Mary Ellen's husband] had come down from Ashland to be present and was in the Judge's office and saw what had been started and heard the remarks of the Homesteader. They together passed out into the hallway when he (Eddy) said to him, "You had better let Morrison mine in that little gulch, where you say he told you that he wanted to mine, if he will withdraw that protest, because he may give you trouble." Directly Morrison appeared in the hall, and the Homesteader called him and told him if he would withdraw that document he might mine as he had requested. Morrison answered, "If you will cancel that thirty acres south of Pankey's mining claim, I will withdraw it." The Homesteader emphatically replied that he would do nothing of the kind. Then for the first time, he saw the object of the protest, namely, to bluff the Homesteader, have him cancel the thirty acres, so that there would be nothing in the way of Morrison's brother-in-law (Thomas Pankey) turning a certain water in a gulch south of the Homestead, through said thirty acres, and onto his mine.

The Homesteader did not tarry to hear what Morrison would attempt to prove, nor did he ever hear or see any more of the shameful document.

While the Preacher/Homesteader was preparing to build his own dwelling house, the subject of erecting a house of worship for New Hope church of which he was Pastor engrossed his mind and culminated in the following plan. He first ascertained the wish of the church. It manifested a willingness not only to consent to have a house, but that all hands would assist in the work. Secondly, he consulted with Jacob Bowman who was a pretty good workman with carpenter's tools, especially in framing timbers together. He was not at the time a member of the church, but his wife and daughter and son-in-law were. The Pastor told him his plan to raise two hundred and fifty dollars from the Baptist churches of the United States, or as many of them as might see the two Baptist papers which at that time were published on the Pacific Coast, and had a will and the means to voluntarily make an offering, or from any other party who was disposed to assist with their money to raise the required two hundred and fifty dollars. The request was published for about six weeks in the *Pacific Baptist* and *Baptist Sentinel*.

Some of the church members had no confidence in the plan, but the Pastor did, and in due time the money began to come from Baptists of California, Oregon, and Washington, ranging from twenty-five cents up to five dollars. One kind brother and wife at The Dalles [Oregon] sent twenty dollars each. From time to time the Pastor would report to the same papers the amount raised. In the latter part of the Summer 1891, it was thought advisable for the Pastor to make a tour to the principal towns on the south side of the Rogue River to see what could be collected in the home field or Jackson County. He was gone ten or twelve days and returned with ninety dollars. This, with what came from a distance, and a subscription paper or two, footed up considerable over two hundred and fifty dollars. This gave the church encouragement when definite arrangements were entered into by electing a building committee and fixing the price of labor among themselves.

Thus by the first of July 1892, the building was finished and painted, except the seats. Services were held in it at the regular meeting embracing the first Sunday in that month. It was then suggested by the Pastor that the sisters or female members of the church undertake and collect thirty-six dollars to pay for seat ends or legs, which they did with a box social, less two dollars and fifty cents which a brother in Grants Pass supplied, inasmuch as the ends were made in the sash and door factory of that city where he worked. The male membership secured the lumber consisting of the broad boards to construct the body of the seats; the Pastor made the seats and had them ready for use at the meeting of the Rogue River Association in this church in September of that year. Suffice it to say, the house was completed and dedicated at said associational meeting clear of debt.

An incident occurred about this time or the year before, viz., the marriage of the Pastor's son James A. with Iva Parker of Jacksonville, Ore., which event happened on the thirtieth of June 1891.

In August 1892, the Pastor was called to the bedside of his old friend and co-laborer in building the above-mentioned church house, where he remained for two weeks or more. The name of this friend and co-worker in the planning and erecting said house was Jacob Bowman. He had, sometime before sending for the Pastor, been suddenly paralyzed on his left side, rendering useless his arm and leg. In fact the whole of the left side of his body was badly affected by the stroke, which finally killed him. He made a profession of his faith in Christ about ten days before the end came and desired membership in New Hope church, and asked that the Pastor baptize him, which was done by making a tank sufficiently large and filling it two-thirds full of warm water. Then on Sunday after the eleven o'clock service, being the first Sunday in September 1892, the pastor, with a committee of seven male members of the church, immersed him just in front of his own door. As he was raised out of the water, an expression of joy was manifested on his countenance.

In the fall of 1896, another incident occurred. The Pastor's daughter Fannie I. became the wife of Philander W. Ellis, a depot agent of the Southern Pacific Railroad, located at Grants Pass for several years, but at the time of their marriage he was at Separ, New Mexico. They were married at the residence of William G. Pennebaker, near the city of Visalia, Tulare County, Calif.[3] In April 1898 Mr. Ellis died while filling the office of depot agent at Separ, N.M. The bereaved wife accompanied his remains to Dallas, Ore., where his father's family resided, where the mortal remains were buried.

But heart-rending incident to the Preacher was the death of his own loving companion on the twenty-ninth of July 1898, who at time of her very sudden death was on a visit with her sisters in Tulare County, Calif. Heart trouble was the cause of her death, with which she had for several years previous to her demise been afflicted. Her body was brought and interred in the Ashland Cemetery on the first day of August 1898.[4] This affliction and death led the Preacher to break up housekeeping and make his home with his son-in-law, Adolphus F. Eddy in Ashland.

16

His move from his Homestead—Works on Deacon Glass' house—Is sick with pneumonia—Telephones to Ashland for medicine—All winter in Ashland—Holds a protracted meeting with New Hope church in May 1899—Again prostrated with pneumonia—Daughter Mrs. Eddy goes to San Francisco to attend the Baptist anniversaries—Three years labor on his son-in-law's Ashland farm—Homestead trouble renewed—Surveying had to be done before Patent could issue—Personal interview with the Commissioner, Binger Herman, at Medford—Homestead trouble ended after the lapse of 14 years.

The sad death of his wife necessitated his removal from his homestead in Sam's Valley to Ashland to make his home with his son-in-law's family. Household goods had to be packed and hauled six miles to Gold Hill, the nearest R.R. depot, and put aboard a car and sent to Ashland, this being done after several articles were sold and delivered.

He then sought employment in the capacity of a carpenter to work on Deacon [H. S.] Glass' unfinished dwelling house. He only did ten days' labor on the house when he was suddenly taken ill with pneumonia. The trouble seemed to be a deep-seated pain in the right lung. After trying what simple remedies were known to the Deacon's wife and himself with no avail, he sent a telephone message to his physician in Ashland for medicine, which came in due time with directions how to use it. Taking the medicine as directed, in a week's time he was able to be taken to Gold Hill, where he boarded the train for Ashland. Safely reaching his place of abode, he was soon as well as usual. And he remained in Ashland quietly during the winter of 1898 and 1899.

On the Friday night before the first Sunday in May 1899, he began a protracted meeting at New Hope Baptist church. This meeting continued for ten days and closed. Then on reaching Ashland, he was again prostrated with pneumonia fever, and had to be taken through a course of medicine as before. His doctor was closer to him this time and visited and prescribed for him in person.

Suffice it to say that in a few days he was well and up and pretty soon able to work again, and for about three years the little eight-acre farm of his son-in-law was where he spent his time in building fence, barn, and out-houses, together with making a garden &c.

In June 1898 the Homesteader was notified by the Commissioner of the General Land Office at Roseburg that the contest had been decided in favor of the miners, and forty acres of his homestead canceled as mining land. But before a Patent could issue, surveying would have to be done to segregate the mineral land from the agricultural.

Not knowing whose duty it was to do the surveying and supposing the miners or the United States would have it done and a Patent sent him for the one hundred and twenty acres, he rested quietly until the summer of 1900, when he began to enquire at headquarters about the balance of the homestead. He learned that in November 1898 the miners had, without notifying him, secured the County Surveyor, Carl T. Jones, whose residence was at Medford, and had the lines run around the two mining claims.

But this, being contrary to the rules of the Department at Washington City, could not be approved. He sought the Surveyor's office and found that the papers and plat of the claims had been to Washington and returned for want of legal proceedings. In the meantime he had secured from the office of the United States Land Commissioner a copy of the rules governing such surveys.

In September 1900 the Homesteader met and had a personal interview with the Commissioner as he was canvassing the state on behalf of McKinley for reelection to the Presidency of the United States. They met in Medford. After a hearty handshake of leading Republicans and others, and dinner in the Hotel Nash, the homestead matter was kindly interviewed briefly, without any definite benefit to the Homesteader. The Commissioner, however, instructed him to write and ask the United States Deputy Surveyor General the status of the survey &c, and saying at the same time, "I will be in Washington City by the time you get his answer and if you forward it to me, marked personal, and then I will give instructions what for you to do." The Homesteader immediately wrote to the Deputy Surveyor General at Portland, and as soon as his answer was received, he forwarded the same to the Commissioner.

The Homesteader was instructed to have the survey made, and have the same properly approved and sent up through the local Land Office at Roseburg, Ore. In the rules governing such surveys he saw that either the contestants or the Homesteader could have the survey made and the contestants having begun the survey, the Homesteader thought they ought to complete the work. Accordingly he interviewed Mr. Thomas Pankey upon the matter and solicited him to finish the survey so that a Patent could issue. Pankey replied, "I will not have anything more to do with it."

Then but one alternative was left to the Homesteader, and that was to undergo the expense of having the survey made according to the regulations of the General Land Office, which cost him even sixteen dollars cash. Even then, it was not until that Deputy Surveyor General was removed from the office and his successor was appointed and qualified that the County Surveyor's work was approved.

In February 1902, the Homesteader was called upon to forward to the local Land Office at Roseburg, Ore., the final Office fees of nine dollars. He being in Tulare County, Calif., at the time, he went to Tulare City and procured a Post Office Money Order for the nine dollars and forwarded the same to the Receiver at Roseburg. After the whittling [of] some more "red tape," the receipt came, which was virtually as good as a Patent for the one hundred and twenty acres.

17

A long desire gratified—Visits relatives and preaches in Tulare County, California—Receives fifty dollars from his (New Hope) church—Notifies his daughter at Ashland, Ore., to go east to the Southern Baptist Convention—Preparations for the long journey—Sends letter to Manly J. Breaker, D.D., to meet him at train in St. Louis—Visits old-time friend at Farmington, San Joaquin County, California—Four weeks in Stockton—Boards the train the second day of May at eleven P.M. for St. Louis—Reaches the city one day behind time—All night in City—Boards the train at eight A.M. Wednesday the 7th for Asheville, N.C.—Two and a half days at Convention—Left Asheville for East Tennessee—A week with friends at Mossy Creek—Reaches his sister's at Sandy Ridge on May 19th—Many places of his boyhood days visited in Jefferson and Sevier counties—On the 8th day of August leaves his sister Katherine via Mossy Creek, Cleveland, Chattanooga, Tenn., and Bridgeport, Ala., for Elmyra, Mo., arriving on the 12th of Sept.—On the 15th celebrates his 78th birthday there—Visits relatives in St. Joseph, Clinton and other places in Missouri—On the 23rd of October boards the Santa Fe train for his brother, Thomas Slover's, at Henderson, Okla.—Spends four months with relatives in Oklahoma and Indian Territory—March the 12th boarded the Santa Fe train at Purcell, Indian Territory, for Visalia, Calif.—Incidents of the journey—Visits in Visalia, Calif.—March the 27th boards the Southern Pacific train for home in Ashland, Ore.

After more than a half century absence from his native land, he was blessed with the opportunity to gratify a long cherished desire to see his native (Tennessee) State.

With health impaired for about three years, he concluded to try to go to Tulare County, Calif., to visit relatives, as well as to try a change of localities for the bettering of his health, accordingly getting ready. On the 27th day of December 1901, he boarded the Southern Pacific train at Ashland about one o'clock P.M., reached Sacramento at five o'clock A.M. the next day, and had to lay over there for five hours, during which time he visited the State Capitol building and grounds. There for the first time in his life he saw the palm trees growing and many other species of trees new to him.

Ten o'clock A.M. found him aboard the train for the completion of his journey and at seven P.M. he arrived at Visalia and at the residence of his brother-in-law, Thomas W. Holder, and had a few minutes visit pleasantly with W. G. Pennebaker and Miss Lou Jones, an old maid sister-in-law.

The next day being Sunday, he went to the Christian Campbellite church and heard their Minister preach also in the evening. On Wednesday, the first day of the new year 1902, in company with his brother-in-law, T. W. Holder, he walked to the cemetery and looked at the grave of his mother-in-law, Mrs. Sarah Jones. Thursday, the second day of January, he strolled westward for a mile and a half, and found the residence of an old friend, Abraham Murry, and had a short visit with him and talked of other days. Friday he met Mr. Murry in town, who introduced a Dr. Johnston to him, on telling him the object, or one of the objects, of his visit in Visalia—the bettering of his health. The Doctor volunteered his services and said he thought he could effect a restoration of health to the Preacher in three months.

A prescription was given with instructions how to use the medicine, but at noon that very day he was attacked with something in the nature of an approaching chill and fever; others thought it was La grippe [influenza], and gave some medicine which had the desired effect and in a week he was over the trouble.

Thursday the ninth at five o'clock P.M., he made a start for Woodville where he had lived for eleven years before going to Oregon, expecting to meet his grandson-in-law at Tulare City with a buggy to take him to Woodville, a distance of sixteen miles. The grandson, failing to get the notice, did not come, and the Preacher had to put up for the night at a hotel. Next morning a dollar was handed over by the Preacher to the hotel clerk, and the stage boarded at an early hour for Tule River near Woodville. About ten A.M. the stage stopped at the residence of his grandson-in-law, where he found his daughter, Mrs. Jennie Frye, who had been called from her home in Stockton to look after her daughter, Mrs. Minnie LaMarsna, who was expecting to be confined soon, which event happened on Friday the 17th day of January 1902.

Woodville being the place where he had lived, farmed, and preached for eleven years, he was in the midst of many of his old neighbors, notwithstanding quite a few had been called to their long home and strangers had taken their places. He visited and preached in Tulare County among kinfolks and old acquaintances until the tenth day of April, then boarded the Santa Fe train for the city of Stockton to visit with his daughter, Mrs. Jennie Frye, and family.

In the meantime he was notified by D. W. Fitzgerald of Sam's Valley that New Hope church, for which he had labored as Pastor for several years, had collected some money for him and desired to know whether to send it to him or to his home in Ashland, Ore.

He answered by telling him to send the money to him. On receipt of the same, he wrote to his daughter, Mrs. Eddy, that he was going to Tennessee—in case he never returned. The amount of money collected and sent was only fifty dollars, but nearly every place he preached he was remunerated in a lesser or greater degree, together with small donations from relatives and acquaintances.

When he saw money enough to purchase tickets to make the trip, together with the aid of his Clergy Certificate, he learned that the Southern Baptist Convention would convene in May in Asheville, N.C.[1] This enhanced his desire to make the desired trip east. Therefore, committing his keeping to his heavenly Father, he purchased a ticket on May the second for St. Louis, Mo., and boarded a train on the Santa Fe overland road at or about midnight of the same day. In the afternoon of the fourth day's travel over valleys, mountains and deserts, brooks and rivers, the train pulled into St. Louis, Mo. Here he was met by the Rev. Manly J. Breaker and lodged for the night in a sanitarium kept by Dr. Mayfield of that city.

But before leaving the city of Stockton, it occurred to him that it would be well to visit his old Tennessee friend James R. Henry at Farmington, fifteen miles from Stockton, having made arrangements with his son Albert to meet him at the depot at Farmington; on the fifteenth day of April he boarded the train and soon was in a buggy wending his way to the farm house of his friend, driven by the son, Albert.

It was indeed sad to find his old friend severely afflicted in the last stages of that terrible disease, consumption [usually tuberculosis], from which he never recovered but succumbed to it in June following. Nevertheless the visit was made pleasant by the kindness of the son and his amiable wife for four or five days. On his bidding the sick man farewell for the last in life, his friend put two five-dollar pieces of gold in Slover's hand as an expression of his friendship, and good wishes for his friend's safe travel across the Rockies and return to the Coast again. On the nineteenth Slover returned to his daughter's in Stockton, and spent ten or eleven days more with her and family.

On the second day of May, fortunately for his trip, he received from his sister, Mrs. Elizabeth Langford, of Elmyra, Mo., a Post Office Money Order for the sum of fifteen dollars, which he barely had time to have cashed before four o'clock P.M. of the afternoon of the day of his departure from Stockton.

As before stated, the train pulled out of Stockton about midnight of the second day of May, with the Preacher seated with his lunch basket at the front end of the coach which he occupied until the train pulled into Kansas City on the forenoon of Tuesday the sixth of May. Here a change of cars was made, and the Wabash train boarded for St. Louis.

Suffice it to say that no mishaps occurred except, having lost the right of way, the train failed to make proper passing side tracks on time and was just twenty-four hours behind schedule time at St. Louis.

At the Mayfield Sanitarium, several ministers en route to the Southern Baptist Convention were lodged for the night and quite an interesting prayer meeting was held in the sitting room. Then a night's good rest was very refreshing, especially to the "Hero" of these pages.

Very early in the morning of Wednesday the seventh day of May, all hands were at the Union Depot for breakfast, and an eight o'clock start was made for Asheville, N.C., where the Southern Baptist Convention was to convene on the ninth of the same month. The agent of the Southern Railroad was on hand to secure cut-rates to the delegates and visitors to the convention. At the hour of eight, all hands were aboard the train and it pulled out on time and across the Mississippi River into Illinois glided.

At sundown it pulled in Louisville, Ky., where a few hours stop was made, then on through the State of Kentucky all night, reaching Knoxville, East Tennessee, for breakfast and another resting spell of three hours. Then the train ran fifty miles in one hour, without stopping, to Morristown, where a change of cars was made. From there on the railroad was located up the valley of the French Broad River to Asheville, which station was reached at three o'clock P.M. Here the train was met by a committee who secured lodging and boarding houses for all. This Preacher was very pleasantly housed with a Baptist family named Buckhanan, who was keeping a boarding and lodging house, where he was royally entertained for two days and a half at one dollar per day.

Realizing that his finances would not permit him to remain longer at the meeting, he settled the hotel bill and boarded the train early Sunday morning, the eleventh day of May, for Jefferson City, Tenn., and at eleven o'clock A.M. disembarked at that depot or station. Leaving trunk, valise, and lunch basket in charge of ticket agent, he wended his way up the meandering county road up Mossy Creek to W. L. Dotson's, a Baptist and the grandson of Wm. Dotson with whom he was acquainted in his boy days in the "Forties."

After a rest and refreshing and hearing the Rev. Phillipps, the pastor of Mossy Creek Baptist church, preach, he boarded a mail hack for Dandridge, a distance of ten miles. There he met young Jake Wilkinson, who had been sent by Dr. B. Rainwater to take him from Dandridge to the doctor's house.[2] Soon getting bag and baggage aboard a double buggy, and crossing the French Broad River, then through the hills four or five miles, late in the afternoon he pulled up to Sandy Ridge to the doctor's residence, where he met his aged sister and her son's family with whom she lived. He said, "I am going to kiss you." She said, "What are you going to kiss me for?" He replied, "Because it has been 56 years since I saw you." She said, "No, I saw you in Dandridge the fall of 1849 when that Negro, John, was hung." He told her that he was there but had no recollection of meeting her or her husband. She called up some events of the hanging which he remembered distinctly. He thought how remarkable her memory at the age of eighty-four.

He, while on a visit in Dandridge, made it a special point to find the locality where the above-named criminal was executed, but thinking it further than it was from town, he passed the place. He soon met an oldish-looking man and inquired of him. He directed the Preacher to the sink-hole (as such sinks in that country are called) where John was hung, and also told him how his son was broken of a bad habit of going by the place to spend the evenings in town. A neighbor had told the young boy how, that many years ago, a Negro John had been hung and buried in that sinkhole near the present road, and if the young man would turn aside to that place and call "John," he would answer, "I am down here." This stopped the youth's walks after dark by that place.

He left Dandridge with his nephew, I. B. Slover, and soon returned to Dr. B. Rainwater's and spent some time writing letters to friends and relatives in Oregon and California. During this month (June) he preached at Hills Chapel where his Mother held at one time her membership in the Methodist Episcopal Church. He also preached in Antioch Baptist church where his Grandfather Slover held his church membership.

In his rambling conducted by one Harrison Burchfield, he found his Grandfather Slover's old mill, which, however, had been rebuilt and changed from an undershot to an overshot waterwheel. This necessitated a change of the locality of the dam in the creek and a change in the millrace or ditch which convened water to the wheel. But the dwelling house was still standing, with its hewed log walls and stone chimney and fireplace. A new frame building had long since been constructed at the west end of the old hewed-log residence, making a kitchen and dining room, so that the whole is an L-shaped residence now.

He found the property has passed out of his nephew's, into the hands of a William Moore who happened to be on the place, to whom he was introduced by his conductor Burchfield. In their conversation about former days, the drowning of the little Negro owned by Old Man Slover was called to the attention of the present owner. Moore replied very readily and said, "Yes, I am taking care of that grave up there in that field on the hillside."

The old hewed-log dwelling, the lay of the land, the locality of the county road, and the old, ever-flowing spring were perfectly familiar. He more than once sought the old plantation upon which he was born, but every building had been removed; nothing but the natural lay of the land and the deep spring, walled up with natural rocks, were natural to him.

On the twenty-eighth day of the same month [June] he was present at the celebration of his sister's eighty-fourth birthday; four generations sat at the dinner table on that day—aged Mother and Brother, children, grandchildren, and great-grandchildren.

From the birthday celebration until the eighth day of August was spent in traveling from place to place in Jefferson and Sevier Counties, the land of his nativity, visiting relatives and friends or old acquaintances, and preaching more or less among them. He had the pleasure of preaching one sermon in the large church-house at Dumplin Creek where he united with the Baptist church at the age of eighteen and was baptized in the waters of the large cave spring near where the old house then stood, which had been long since torn down and a new one erected a short distance from the old structure. Quite a number of memorable old localities were seen in his meanderings, as well as a few old men and women of his boy day's knowing.

Time admonished him that he must turn his head toward the Far West again, and on the eighth of August 1902 he bid his aged sister, Katherine Rainwater, and her sons a final farewell. His nephew, I. B. Slover, brought him on his way to Dandridge. From there he made a visit with George W. Cate and other old acquaintances in Sevier County, returning to Dandridge on Friday the fifteenth, and spent Saturday and Sunday with his niece, Mrs. Robert Swan, attended Sabbath School in the Baptist church. As he was arranging his toilet for Sunday School, he discovered that he had left his cuffs with the gold buttons in them at his friend Cate's house. He immediately wrote for them to be sent to the railroad station at Jefferson City, but after waiting there for three days for them, they had not come. He then arranged with the postmaster to forward them to Cleveland, Bradley County, Tenn., where he was going to spend a few days with relatives.

On Thursday the twenty-first he boarded the train for Cleveland, and as his letter of notification had failed to reach his niece's family, he found himself at the depot without a guide. Fortunately on inquiry he found a delivery man there with his wagon who offered a free conveyance for him and his baggage to his niece's house. Accepting this offer he was soon unloaded at the front gate of John Thomas' dwelling where he met his niece and children, none of whom had he ever met.

On inquiry for his brother [Abraham] (the father and grandfather of this Thomas family), someone of the family, looking up the sidewalk, answered, "Yonder he comes." The newly arriven uncle said he would go out and meet him and see whether he would know him. They met and after salutations, the newcomer inquired of his brother, "Do you know me?" "No," was the quick reply, unless it be "old man" so and so, meaning some old man of the town whose appearance on the street called forth remarks not of the highest quality. The new brother said, "Not much. My name is Slover." The older brother, realizing his mistake, said quickly, "That's my name. Let's go back to the house." Suffice it to say, this was indeed a reunion of two brothers who had not met for fifty-three years.

After fourteen days pleasantly spent with relatives in the city of Cleveland, the two brothers, bidding all adieu, left for Bridgeport, Ala., where the older lived with his daughter, Mrs. Williams, stopping one day with his grandson at East Chattanooga where the Preacher brother was invited to preach at a prayer meeting service, which he did to an attentive congregation. On reaching Bridgeport he found another niece and three grown-up children. Indeed, this was a week of pleasure with his older brother and his daughter's family.

While visiting with these dear ones, he procured a Clergy Certificate over the line of Southern Railroad from Bridgeport to Nashville, and from there over the Illinois Central to St. Louis, Mo.

Having written to his sister, Mrs. Elizabeth Langford, that he would be at her home in Elmyra, Mo., on the twelfth of September to celebrate his seventy-eighth birthday at her residence on the fifteenth of that month, all things being ready, he bid farewell to his brother and his niece's family. He boarded the train for Nashville, arriving just in time to get a ticket for St. Louis over the Illinois Central, leaving Nashville at dark, then traveling all night over a strange country by the way of Cairo. He reached St. Louis at seven o'clock A.M. the next morning, then went by the Wabash line to Kansas City, then on the St. Paul, Milwaukee and Chicago Railroad to Elmyra, arriving at nine P.M. where he was met by relatives at the station and conducted to the residence of his sister. He had a joyful meeting with her whom he had not seen for more than half a century.

After spending about ten days with her and her daughters and grandchildren, in the meantime celebrating his seventy-eighth birthday at her house and attending the Modern Woodman's Picknick, where the assembled people of Ray County, Mo., listened to a fifteen-minute lecture from him on the natural scenery of the Pacific Coast, he made his way to St. Joseph in Buchanan County to visit another older sister, Mrs. Sallie S. Bettis.

He also had the pleasure of spending a few hours with his brother Thomas' oldest daughter and children, Mrs. Pauline Hackney, and attended Wyatte Park Baptist church where Rev. Custer was pastor on Sunday, and preaching for him in the evening. He then with his sister Sallie boarded the train for Elmyra on Wednesday, the first day of October, in order to be with his sister Elizabeth at the celebration of her seventy-sixth birthday on the fourth day of October. A delightful day this was to all present. The next day being Sunday, he preached both morning and evening in the M. E. church South.

On Friday the tenth he bid farewell to his two sisters and other relatives in Elmyra, and in company with his nephew James Langford boarded a train for Clinton in south Missouri, arriving in the afternoon. At the depot he was met by a nephew and a Rev. Lenard whom he had once met at a Baptist convention in Pendleton, Ore., but did not know him at sight. From Clinton he was taken eleven miles in a northerly direction to the residence of James Langford, where he met his great nephews and niece, and for thirteen days was royally entertained by the families of his nephews and substantially aided by them and the members of the Quarles Baptist church, at which he preached and attended the Pastor's service.

On Thursday, twenty-third day of October, he gave relatives the parting hand and boarded the train for Oklahoma, by the way of Kansas City, to Purcell, Indian Territory, thence on two-horse wagon to his brother's place in Cleveland County. He had a joyful meeting with him [Rev. Thomas H. Slover] and wife whom he had not met for forty-two years.

During the month of November he, in company with his brother T. H. and wife, made a visit with their children at Davis, Mill Creek, and Tiehamingo, Indian Territory, also at Sulphur with a Dr. George Slover, a grandson of an older brother. Suffice it to say that all these relatives were very kind and made the visitors comfortable, and indeed it was very pleasant to find so many young Slovers that the old Preacher from Oregon had never met before.

On the thirtieth day of January he was taken in a buggy by his nephew John Slover to Shawnee, to visit a nephew and family (a son of his brother Abraham) whom he had not seen since he was a little babe in the arms of his mother in the Summer of 1849; Oliver Henry Slover is his name.

Then on Friday the thirteenth, he bid farewell to nephew, niece, and a young woman whom they had raised, and boarded the train for Romulus where the same young man, John Slover, met him with team and buggy to convey him to the home of his brother, Thomas, in Cleveland County, where he remained for another month, during which time the weather was quite cold and stormy.

On the eighth of March he gave this dear brother and wife and son the final parting hand, and came to the home of their son-in-law, Thornton Wilson, where he had a pleasant stay for three days and nights, and by the kindness of his niece, Sallie Wilson, had his lunch basket well stored with eatables for his long journey to Visalia, Calif. On Thursday the twelfth of March, her husband brought him and his baggage to Purcell, across the South Canadian River into the Indian Territory.

At the ticket office of the Santa Fe Railroad he requested to be sent over the quickest and cheapest road to Visalia, Calif. The agent quickly replied, "Well, we'll send you over the Santa Fe, and twenty-five dollars." The preacher knew that meant by the way of Newton, Kansas, and asked whether or not he would have to lay over there. "O, no," replied the agent, "the train will be there ready," but unfortunately the train was four hours or more late at Purcell, and then a short stop on account of a small wreck to the southbound train detained it until one-thirty A.M. reaching Newton, Kansas, where he was to change cars for the West. On interviewing the agent, he learned that no train would go West until 8:30 P.M. except the limited. Here he found he had to stay about nineteen hours, and being unacquainted, he sought lodging in the Depot Hotel, being conducted into its office by a stranger. He asked the clerk what a bed would cost. He replied, "A bed alone is a dollar." Paying the dollar, he was conducted upstairs to a finely furnished room where he slept until nearly eight o'clock. He then arose and arranged his toilet, and appeared pretty soon before the same clerk and said to him, "You are up, I see." "Yes," the clerk responded, saying, "Breakfast is ready." The Preacher said, "You will not charge me for my breakfast after charging me one dollar for the bed?" "Yes, sir," was his ready answer. "I will not eat then," replied the Preacher and walked out and soon found a lunch counter where he got all the breakfast he wanted for ten cents, and then spent the day walking around on the sidewalks and seeing the city, and resting in the waiting room until the overland west-bound train pulled in. At 8:30 P.M. he was aboard and rolling westward for Visalia, Calif. Reaching the city of Visalia on Monday the 16th of March, he was again among relatives and old friends.

On Friday the twenty-seventh day of March at 9:35 o'clock A.M. he boarded the train for Ashland, Ore. After a layover in Sacramento, he boarded the train around midnight and was brought on his way up the Sacramento River with no stops except midway up the south side of the Siskiyou Mountain, on the side track where the trains generally pass, the southbound further north had a little mishap by the dining car jumping the track which took about four or five hours time to get it back and run down to the waiting Northbound. The way being all clear, the train pulled into Ashland about midnight. Mrs. Eddy having changed houses, the Preacher had to go to the hotel for the want of someone to pilot him to his new one, which he found in the early morning and had breakfast at home after an absence of fifteen months.

18

He takes charge of rented garden—A trip to Grants Pass and his (New Hope) Church in Sam's Valley—A cart for conveyance—The cart and horse for sale—A sudden attack of cholera morbus while en route for home—The kindness of a good brother and wife—Reaches home safely—Has grippe—Weeds grow all the same—Berries to take to packing house—He is notified that a purchaser for his Homestead is ready to conclude the deal—They meet at the Real Estate office of Dan Richards in Gold Hill—Visit to Homestead—A deed is made and four hundred dollars received as the consideration—Then the Preacher boarded the train for Grants Pass to meet with the Rogue River Association—Returns to Ashland—Places his money in First National Bank of Ashland, Ore.—Stores wood for the winter—The family moves to another house—Pleasant winter passes—Three hundred dollars invested in the Story Cotton Company of Philadelphia, Pa.

Shortly after his return from his eastern visit with relatives, he took charge of the garden connected with the berries already rented by his daughter, and planted potatoes and other vegetable seeds.

Now having a few leisure days, he concluded to visit his two sons in Grants Pass, and return by the way of his church (New Hope in Sam's Valley).[1] As the latter place is not on the railroad, he arranged with his daughter to drive Ed, the horse, and try to sell him, inasmuch as she desired to dispose of him, so a cart was secured from T. K. Bolton, the druggist, but this needed painting and other repairs, all of which the Preacher did for the use of the vehicle for the trip. He had a very pleasant time at the Pass with the two boys, the little granddaughter, and her mother. Leaving the Pass early in the morning of Friday before the first Sunday in May, he drove to Sam's Valley Post Office and lodged with the late

N. D. Fitzgerald family. Saturday he drove to Deacon H. S. Glass's, and met the Associational Missionary, Rev. Holcroft, and heard him preach on the Sabbath.

Having been instructed by Bolton to sell the cart along with the horse, he concluded to leave the meeting at New Hope and drive over to Medford on Monday morning and try to sell the property. Arriving at the livery stable in the city of Medford in the early forenoon, he told the stableman the outfit he drove was for sale, separate or together, horse and cart, but made no sale. He spent the noon with his nephew and family, Alonzo Slover. After spending the greater part of the afternoon in endeavoring to sell the horse and cart without any success, he paid the stable bill and left Medford for Ashland. As he approached the little village of Phoenix or Cassburg, as it was familiarly called, and stopping at the yard gate of an old friend and brother Baptist, he was suddenly attacked with choleramorbus, and had to alight and have a dose of ginger tea, and was kindly treated by this good brother and wife. Having obtained relief and spending an hour or more with them, he drove to Ashland, the greater portion of the way in the darkness of the night; he reached home safely, however. To his surprise he had not been long in Ashland after returning from this visit, when he was for the second time in life attacked with La grippe, which disabled him to work in that garden.

But the weeds grew all the same. They would not wait for the Preacher to get over his suffering, so a boy or young man had to be employed to kill them. This held them in check until such time as the Preacher was able to do the work himself.

Before he was thoroughly over La grippe, the berries were ready for the picking and wheeling to the packing house, which had to be done by the means of a hand cart. This berry gathering and wheeling was a new business to him and a tiresome one to an already fatigued man.

About the first of September of this (1903) year, he was notified by his real estate agent [Daniel Richards] of Gold Hill that a purchaser for his homestead had been found, and he was requested to come down that the deal might be closed. After the elapse of a few days, he boarded the train at Ashland for Gold Hill and found the party in waiting.

A trip to the homestead had to be made for the purpose of a better understanding where the boundary lines were located. A livery rig was secured and the drive of six or seven miles was made, and the premises soon shown, together with the dwelling house and other buildings, also a view of the two mining claims which had been taken in the year 1898. Then returning to Gold Hill and to the office of Daniel Richards, where a deed was drawn up for the remaining one hundred and twenty acres of the original homestead, and signed and acknowledged, the purchaser paid four hundred dollars in gold coin of the United States of America, on receipt of same the deed was passed to his possession.

Then for about eight months, he contended with the officials of the U.S. Land Office for a rebate of the fourth part of the original filing fee of $20, which the District Office at Roseburg had told him he was entitled to have. True it was but five dollars, and this was denied; he was informed officially that he was not entitled to the money. Thus ended a struggle of more than fourteen years for a government homestead. In the contest he learned that a miner could prove anything he wanted to prove, and that all that was proven to the contrary did not amount to anything with the Register and Receiver of the local office. All of which is passed and to a finish, and the Homesteader still lives, to admonish all homesteaders to look out for miners.

Then the Preacher boarded the train for the Baptist Association, which held its annual session of 1903 in Grants Pass in September. During his stay at this meeting he met his two boys and several other of his acquaintances.

At the close of this association, he returned to Ashland. Not many days after his return from the meeting of the association, he placed his money, three hundred and eight dollars, in the First National Bank of Ashland, Ore., for safe keeping.

Winter was now approaching. He assisted his daughter in storing wood for the winter months, her husband being absent in the employ of E. J. Bowen Seed Company of San Francisco and had been the preceding spring and summer. About the first of November it became necessary for the family to remove to another house, inasmuch as the one then occupied was sold. This gave the Preacher, as well as his daughter, more hard work, but they pulled through it all the same. He had been for two months casting about for some enterprise in which he could invest what little money he had, and finally the Story Cotton Company of Philadelphia, Pa., was by two of its investors so highly recommended to him that he concluded to invest, and so deciding he first and last invested three hundred dollars. The company agreed to use the money in buying cotton for future delivery, and from month to month give the investor seventy-five percent of the nett proceeds, they retaining the other twenty-five percent for their trouble and expense of doing the business. This proved a losing enterprise to the "investors," or at any rate to the Preacher. He at one time drew out seventy-two dollars and ninety-five cents, and that was all he ever got of the amount invested in the long chain of "financial" mistakes of his life.

He has long since learned that all things work together "for the good to them that love God," and he still thinks so, although this case is wrapped in much mystery. Nevertheless, the doctrine is true. The pathway of all good people is beset with thieves, robbers, and villains.

19

He leaves Ashland, Ore., for San Francisco, Calif.—Work for Book and Bible House—Also for Royal Manufacturing Company, Detroit, Mich.—In April 1905, he goes to Tulare County to spend the summer with daughter and granddaughter—He preaches to Woodville church and baptizes two—Then accompanies his daughter to Sanger, the town of her residence and church membership under Pastor Williams—A move to Rosedale, Kern County—Attends Baptist Association at Orosa—Death of daughter and funeral services conducted by her Pastor, Rev. Williams—Interment in Tulare Cemetery—He with granddaughter returns to her home at Woodville—The Preacher sorely afflicted with an ingrown toenail and boils—Two weeks rusticating at the Deer Creek Hot Springs—His return to Porterville—Thence to Woodville—In the latter part of October he makes his way to Dinuba and Fresno to visit grandchildren and acquaintances—And thence to San Francisco, his home.

Sometime in May of the year 1904, Mrs. Eddy, the Preacher's daughter, was notified by her husband that it would be necessary for her and children, with her father, to change her place of residence for a place in San Francisco, Calif. [where he had rented a cottage in the Sunset District]. This meant another hard job for the Preacher, as well as his daughter, to dispose of such things of a household nature that were inconvenient to ship and that the family could spare, consisting of furniture, cook-stove, heating or parlor stove, washing apparatus, &c &c. Some things were sold or given away; others were burned, consisting of bedsteads, books, and papers. The articles retained had to be boxed and put in shape for shipping, all of which required time and labor.

About the tenth or eleventh day of June, the train was boarded in Ashland for San Francisco. With little trouble the rented cottage in Sunset

District was found, and as soon as the baggage was brought from the depot and new furniture could be secured, the family were in living quarters again, relieved of the labor and worry, and all together again.

But the Preacher had no employment.[1] He pretty soon had an opportunity to canvass for a Book and Bible House in Denver, Colo., which he did for several months, but he soon found that the house required him to sell more books than was possible in order to secure a District Manager's appointment at a salary; therefore he ceased to canvass for that house.

Seeing an advertisement in a newspaper from the Royal Manufacturing Company of Detroit, Mich., for agents to canvass and take orders for Brazil silverware, he applied for an agency, soon had the outfit in hand, and began early in the year 1905 with this new business. It had plenty of traveling for house to house, and from neighborhood to neighborhood, but little remuneration for the Preacher. In fact, about all the benefit he derived was the physical exercise, which he has always considered necessary to a healthy body.

In March of this year, his oldest daughter [Elizabeth Jane Slover Riggs Hicks Frye] by his first wife requested him to come to Woodville in Tulare County and preach, also stating that her daughter, Mrs. Minnie [Riggs] LaMarsna, had been converted and desired to unite with the Baptist church at that place, further stating that she desired her Father to spend the summer with her and family. Early in the month of April he packed his valise and boarded the Santa Fe train for Tulare City, the nearest or most convenient depot to Woodville, where he was met by his granddaughter with buggy, and conveyed to her own cottage near the village of Woodville.

And on Sunday following his arrival on Friday, he had the pleasure of hearing the Rev. Fisk, the pastor, preach an excellent sermon and seeing his granddaughter unite with the church for baptism. By request, he was delighted to meet with the church and congregation at a certain water tank near a neighbor's barn, and there lead the willing subject into the water and bury her living body in the liquid grave of baptism into the name of the Father, the Son, and the Holy Spirit, and raise her up out of the water grave to walk in newness of life with that church.

In the evening he preached and the services were protracted during the following week. After the protracted meeting at Woodville closed, he accompanied his daughter to the town of Sanger in Fresno County, where she then resided in the residence of Mrs. Hudgepath. His daughter's husband, Burrell J. Frye, for several years an employee of the Santa Fe Railroad, was about this time put in charge of the section hands at Rosedale, near Bakersfield, Kern County, and on the sixth day of May, had his wife with her father transferred by train to this station. This flag station was a lonely locality for the Preacher and his daughter because there was no one lived there but Mexicans and they could not talk to them.

Now the San Joaquin Valley Baptist Association had arranged to hold its annual session for 1905 at Crosie Baptist church in Tulare County beginning May 19. So in the early morning of that day, Mrs. Frye and the Preacher boarded the Santa Fe train for Cutler, the nearest station to Crosie. He had a pleasant time with the Association and several old acquaintances, returning on Monday following the third Sunday in May to Rosedale, where on the fifteenth day of June following the Association, Mrs. Frye was attacked with a paroxysm with which she had for several years been afflicted, and never could rally, although two physicians were in attendance and did all they could. She suffered until about eight o'clock Sunday morning, the eighteenth day of June 1905, when she peacefully breathed her last time.

Now Mrs. Minnie LaMarsna, with her family sorrowing, took the Preacher, her grandfather, to her home at Woodville where he remained until the latter part of October of that year. Pretty soon after the funeral of his daughter, he was afflicted with an in-grown toe-nail and a tormenting boil on the back of his neck, which rendered him unfit for visits or labor or preaching. A doctor was visited, a prescription and medicine secured for the swollen foot, and later on a plaster of honey and flour was made by the granddaughter and applied to the painful boil, and the foot soon got all right and the boil gradually became less painful.

Finally a trip to Deer Creek Hot Springs was discussed by the family and neighbors, and decided in favor of going. After a two-days long, hot and weary drive with a big wagon and rather light team, or rather one light weight and a heavy weight horse, the place of camping at the Springs was reached, admission fee paid, and tent stretched. The party was at ease where two weeks time were spent, and the hot baths proved a decided benefit to all the family, as well as the Preacher.

In the latter part of October, he made his way to Dinuba, Tulare County, travelling on the Santa Fe to Sultana, where he was met by his granddaughter, Miss Edna Riggs, with buggy and conveyed to the residence of Virgil Grimsley, where she was employed as a housekeeper and to care for the little son of Mr. and Mrs. Grimsley, both being teachers in the Dinuba public school.[2] Here the Preacher had a pleasant stay for several days, in meantime calling on old friends and acquaintances, until the first day of November.

In the early morning of the first day of November he took the train (Southern Pacific) to Fresno City where he had two grandsons and a granddaughter living. With these children and other friends he remained until midnight of Sunday, the fifth day of November, then boarded the Santa Fe train for his home in San Francisco, reaching his home in the forenoon of Monday, the sixth day of the same month.

There are two incidents belonging to this chapter, namely, first the Preacher had a Clergyman's Certificate for the year 1904, and in packing his small trunk in Ashland for the move to San Francisco, he had placed the document in a small paper box which was carefully placed in the trunk, thinking all the time that the valuable certificate was in the breast pocket of his dress coat. On applying at the ticket window for his ticket, Lo and behold! to his surprise he was minus that ever-precious little document, but the train being late, he told the agent to give him time to see if he could produce it. All right, the agent replied, so the Preacher hastened to his little trunk already on the truck for shipment, unloosed the rope and examined all the coat pockets, but no certificate could be found. Never thinking once that he had placed it in the little paper box, consequently he never opened it to look, so rebinding the trunk went back to the agent and paid full fare. The financial fun of this incident was about five dollars and fifty cents loss to the Preacher.

Second incident—Misplaced Confidence. This grew out of a natural inclination of the Preacher's mind, viz., he always did think that other men were like himself—honest, until they proved to the contrary. This is indeed a pleasant state of mind, until tested. He had in nearly every instance found that he was the loser. Nevertheless in the following incident, he misplaced his confidence again.

While at the Deer Creek Hot Springs, there was the son of an old-time friend, who was intending to go down to the city of Porterville alone with his team and two-horse wagon, and the Preacher's granddaughter, knowing that her grandfather wanted to go, spoke to the young man about a ride with him. He replied, "Of course, I had rather have him as not." This reply led the granddaughter to conclude that her grandfather would get a free ride. Now it so happened that the young man was delayed one day longer than at first he thought he would start, and finding that he could get two other passengers with a little baggage, during the day he said to the Preacher, "I will call for you tomorrow morning pretty early." He came as stated and called for the Preacher, who was all packed for the ride and boarded the wagon; nothing said, nor demanded. About three o'clock P.M. the Preacher was unloaded at his Aunt Billingsley's, and as matter of courtesy he asked the teamster what he charged him. The young man said, "One dollar and fifty cents, just what I charged each of the other two." It was instantly paid, and the old lesson repeated or tested, viz., "Thinking that all men are as strictly honest as yourself."

20

Change of houses—The new residence—The Preacher again killing time with Brazil silverware—Granddaughter Edna Riggs' letter relative to her marriage—The great Earthquake and fire of San Francisco, April 18th, 1906—Works six days for Uncle Sam on refugee camps—Another visit with grandchildren—Visits one week in Visalia—The marriage of granddaughter Edna and Elbert S. Hicks at San Diego—He remains there until the third day of September—Meets his niece in Los Angeles, whom he never had seen—Arrives in Tulare City at ten A.M. Sept. 4th and is taken to his granddaughter's, Mrs. J. W. LaMarsna, at Woodville—A carpenter's job—Death of Carrie Jenks at San Diego—In March 1907 begins canvassing for Royal Manufacturing Co.—His equipage and success—Changed localities—At Dinuba with his granddaughter, Edna Hicks—Begins canvassing July 6th—Edna Hicks' first child—Starts for San Francisco about the 20th of November—Parlier and Fresno City and whom he meets at those places—Leaves Fresno City in the night of 29th of November for San Francisco—Arrives there in forenoon of 30th.

A change of houses does not occur as often in San Francisco as S. P. Henson said they did in Chicago—once a month. Nevertheless, the Preacher's daughter had to find a new location the month of November 1905 for her family. Fortunately it was only across one block. The new residence was located on Ninth Avenue near L Street in Sunset District, a two-story house with a basement located on a hillside. Approached from the north it looked rather tall, about twenty-four feet wide by forty long, susceptible of housing three families. After getting settled in the new location, he again took up the work of canvassing for the Royal Manufacturing Co. with Brazil silverware, more to kill time for exercise than the profit in the business.

About the beginning of 1906, he was surprised to receive a letter from Edna Riggs, making inquiry about a certain young man near Dinuba, E. S. Hicks by name, whom she afterward married. She said in that letter, "It seems that you are the only one to whom I can look for advice now (meaning since the death of her mother six months before). I am alone and have to work, and liable to have to go from place to place. I have concluded that I had better get married, and I want you to tell me what you know about Elbert S. Hicks. He is a son of your old friend Hicks where you went while at Dinuba last fall."[1] This letter somewhat puzzled her grandfather, as his acquaintance with this Hicks family dated prior to the birth of the young man in question. So to throw the responsibility of her choice upon her own judgment, he replied that he knew absolutely nothing about the young man, and she must be her own judge. She had stated in the letter referred to that she was satisfied that he loved her. Therefore he give her to understand that if the young man was like his parents, he thought her choice was well taken, for the people are nice folks.

At about five fifteen o'clock A.M. of April the 18th, 1906, there was decidedly the severest shaking of the earth that this Preacher had ever experienced. Houses trembled like a leaf in a gale of wind, tops of chimneys were shaken off, hotels crushed like egg shells under the tread of elephants, brick walls tumbled, steel rails and waterpipes severed like icicles in the hands of children, and in less time than it takes to write it, the city was on fire in more places than one. Firemen, powerless for the want of water to check the raging, resorted to dynamiting the houses.

The flames swept on until 450 blocks of the great city went to ashes and smoke, covering about five square miles, with a few brick and stone walls, with some steel frames left standing. Men, women, and children fled before the raging flames, with little or nothing of their household goods, to any and every kind of refuge. Then untold deprivation and suffering of an appalling character followed in the wake of the fire.[2] But the good people of the United States and elsewhere come with supplies and money to relieve as far as possible the wants of the suffering. Barracks were constructed somewhat after the plan of the United States soldiers' quarters. The Preacher got employment on these for one week's time at four dollars per day.

About the first of June of this year, he was requested to officiate at the wedding of his granddaughter Edna Riggs and Elbert S. Hicks, which was to be on the twenty-seventh of the same month in the city of San Diego, Calif., at the residence of her sister, Carrie Jenks. So fitting himself up for another visit with his grandchildren and other relatives and friends, he left San Francisco on the fourteenth day of June for Visalia, where he made a stay of about a week with the families of Wm. G. Pennebaker and Judge Thomas W. Holder, brothers-in-law of his. He found Visalia partially under water from the immense quantity of snow in the mountains.

Then he went to Tulare by rail where he met his granddaughter Minnie LaMarsna, who conveyed him to her home at Woodville, where he remained for a few days, then returned to Tulare and boarded the Southern Pacific train of Los Angeles, thence aboard the Santa Fe to San Diego, thence on a streetcar to George E. Jenks' home, where he met the Bride with two of her lady friends from Los Angeles, Miss Maggie Dennis and Miss Dill Spence. On the 27th of June, the Bridegroom appeared with the Bride before the Preacher with a license from the County Clerk's Office of San Diego, Calif., and the rights of matrimony were solemnized by the Preacher in the presence of George E. Jenks and Carrie Jenks, and Maggie Dennis and Dill Spence. The happy couple left for their home in Dinuba, visiting some relatives on their way.

The Preacher remained with his granddaughter, Carrie Jenks, and had a pleasant time until the third day of September. During his stay in this city, he would visit the Baptist church on Sunday and occasionally hear the pastor, Rev. Hinson, preach, but his pulpit was principally supplied by someone else.

Sometimes during the week he would try to catch fish in the Bay, but the only fish he ever got was caught with a silver hook; this, however, never failed to catch the fish in abundance and at a low price. He made one trip across the Bay to see the Coronado Hotel, and saw what money could do in the way of beautifying nature.[3] This is a grand place.

Also he made one trip south to National City where in 1869 he saw the first dwelling house ever erected in that place, built by a Mr. Kimbal who was still living in National City, but he said the house and all his other property had left him, and he was conducting a real estate business for a living for his family.[4] But there are more than one house there now, not only houses, but railroad, streetcars, and other enterprises.

Returning to Tulare city, he was taken to his granddaughter's, Mrs. J. W. [Minnie] LaMarsna, at Woodville. Here during the remaining days of September he did nothing but loaf around and go to church on Sundays.

His granddaughter's house was badly in need of a porch, and a new roof on dining room and kitchen. Finally about the first of October, he began work, taking an old header apart to see how much material could be obtained for repairs on the dwelling. Nothing, however, was found that would answer for the new porch or roof, but some fine Oregon pine was secured from the old header, which came in handy in making cupboard, cooler, table, door and window screens, gate, and other out-buildings.

On the sixth day of November 1906 his granddaughter, Mrs. Carrie Jenks, died in San Diego of typhoid pneumonia, which shocked her sisters as soon as they heard of it and not little surprised their grandfather. To think that only two months had passed since she was apparently so lively and in good health. But such is death that none can tell how nor when the Monster is going to come.

This sad event frustrated for a time the carpenter's job on the dwelling, but he finally resumed work and continued during the winter when the weather would permit him to be out of the house, until about the first of March.

One incident of note occurred as he was painting the roof of the house and porch. He had finished all the roof except two courses of shingles (only 10 inches wide) at the lower side of the porch. Consequently he had taken all his brackets off, intending to paint the two courses from a ladder which was placed against the eave of the porch about the center. He took his paint bucket in one hand and his brush in the other and started for the ladder. He unthoughtedly placed his foot on the fresh-painted shingles and it slipped. Instantly he saw he must go one way or the other, so to save a precipitation, he threw himself backward on the roof with his body from hips upward on the roof, but lower limbs jutting over the eaves and on his back. If he had of made the least effort to relieve the situation, he would have fallen to the ground, a distance of about nine feet. Fortunately his grandson-in-law was close to the ladder and soon relieved him by placing the ladder close enough for him to lay hold of it and save himself from a fall.

Having his canvassing outfit with him, he secured a rig from his grandson-in-law, and thus equipped he began travelling over the county, taking orders for table ware, and continued in Woodville and surrounding country until the latter part of June with fairly good success and with improved health. The first day of July he boarded the local train for Dinuba in the northern part of Tulare County where his granddaughter Edna Hicks lived; her husband Elbert S. Hicks was running a livery business.

Here again he was furnished with horse and buggy the greater part of the time, until the latter part of November 1907, for canvassing, and he had better success here than about Woodville. On Wednesday the twenty-seventh, he boarded the Santa Fe train for Fresno City where he had three grandchildren, two sons and a daughter of Russel H. Slover, who had died more than ten years previous.[5] But on reaching Fresno City, none of the children could be found. The older boy was a fireman on the Santa Fe freight train, the other boy was in some sort of financial difficulty with his employer, and the married granddaughter had gone to San Francisco to visit with her sick mother, who died about three weeks later at her home in San Francisco. However, he was fortunate enough to meet all three of them before he left the city of Fresno. Parting with each one with a farewell shake of hands, he boarded the Santa Fe train in the night time of the twenty-ninth of November for San Francisco, reaching his home in the early forenoon of the next day, after an absence of about eighteen months.

The foregoing pages embrace the eventful incidents of the writer's life from the time he was two years old until he became eighty-three, inclusive.

Some other hand will have to write the events of the few remaining years or days of his eventful life.

The end.

Editor's note: James Anderson Slover died from pneumonia on November 13, 1913, at the home of his daughter Mary Ellen (Mrs. Adolphus F. Eddy), in Berkeley, California. He was eighty-nine. Burial was in the Ashland, Oregon, pioneer cemetery.[6]

NOTES

ACKNOWLEDGMENTS

1. See, for example, Barbara Cloud, *The Business of Newspapers on the Western Frontier* (Reno: University of Nevada Press, 1992).

INTRODUCTION

1. For a discussion of the role of the individual who has, for a brief moment, some impact on the world see Gordon Wright, *Insiders and Outliers: A Procession of Frenchmen* (Stanford: Stanford Alumni Association, 1980).
2. William Warren Sweet, *Revivalism in America: Its Origin, Growth, and Decline* (Gloucester MA: Peter Smith, 1965), 129.
3. Charles A. Johnson, *The Frontier Camp Meeting: Religion's Harvest Time* (Dallas: Southern Methodist University Press, 1955), 52–64, 79–80.
4. Sweet, *Revivalism in America*, 133. See also, for example, Minutes of the Dumplin Creek Baptist Church, 6 October 1847, in which members preferred charges against A. M. Bryan for "imprudent conduct" toward several women in the church. Microfilmed records, Dumplin Creek Baptist Church, 1797–1938, Southern Baptist Historical Library and Archives, Nashville.
5. Sweet, *Revivalism in America*, 129.
6. William O. Lynch, "Westward Flow of Southern Colonists," *Journal of Southern History* 9 (1943): 315; Tommy W. Rogers, "Migration from Tennessee during the Nineteenth Century I: Origin and Destination of Tennessee Migrants, 1850–1860," *Tennessee Historical Quarterly* 27 (summer 1968): 122.
7. John Slover died in November 1852, after his son left Tennessee, according to a notebook of family births, marriages, and deaths that Slover compiled about the same time he wrote his memoir. The notebook is in the possession of the editor and is hereafter cited as JAS.
8. The French Broad River joins the Holston River to form the Tennessee River just east of Knoxville. It then heads south into Alabama before making a horseshoe turn to flow north to the Ohio River. By the time it reaches the Ohio at Paducah, Kentucky, it has covered some 650 miles. Water travel was common in the mid-nineteenth century. As a guide for their trip, Slover and his

companions may have referred to Zadok Cramer, *The Navigator,* 8th ed. (1814; reprint, Ann Arbor: University Microfilms, 1966), which gives an almost mile-by-mile description of the Ohio and Mississippi Rivers.

9. Lynch, "Westward Flow of Southern Colonists," 317; Rogers, "Migration from Tennessee," 121.

10. Lynch, "Westward Flow of Southern Colonists," 317.

11. For background on the split see, for example, John Lee Eighmy, *Churches in Cultural Captivity; A History of the Social Attitudes of Southern Baptists* (Knoxville: University of Tennessee Press, 1972), as well as E. Luther Copeland, *The Southern Baptist Convention and the Judgement of History: The Taint of an Original Sin* (Lanham MD: University Press of America, 1995).

12. See E. C. Routh, "Henry Frieland Buckner," *Chronicles of Oklahoma* 14 (1936): 456–66.

13. For more about the Cherokee removal see John Ehle, *Trail of Tears: The Rise and Fall of the Cherokee Nation* (New York: Doubleday, 1989), or any history of the Cherokee Nation for the period prior to 1840.

14. William G. McLoughlin, *The Cherokees and Christianity, 1794–1870: Essays on Acculturation and Cultural Persistence,* ed. Walter H. Conser Jr. (Athens: University of Georgia Press, 1994), 198–99.

15. McLoughlin, *The Cherokees and Christianity,* 198. The white Southern Baptist preachers made little effort to learn the language of their congregations because they thought learning English would have a civilizing effect on the Indians. Lexie O. Wiggins Jr., "A Critical History of the Southern Baptist Indian Mission Movement, 1855–1861" (Ph.D. diss., University of Alabama, 1980), 154–55.

16. Cramer, *The Navigator,* 277.

17. Mary French Caldwell, *Tennessee: The Dangerous Example; Watauga to 1849* (Nashville: Aurora, 1974), 162.

18. Major Ridge had, at various times, been co-chief with John Ross, member of the executive council, and businessman. He generally favored white civilization. His son John was educated at the Cornwall Mission School in Connecticut and was a lawyer and businessman. Boudinot, also a former Cornwall student, was editor of the *Cherokee Phoenix,* the first Native American newspaper. *The Papers of Chief John Ross,* ed. Gary E. Moulton, 2 vols. (Norman: University of Oklahoma Press, 1985), 2:717, 730–31. See also William G. McLoughlin, *After the Trail of Tears: The Cherokees' Struggle for Sovereignty, 1839–1880* (Chapel Hill: University of North Carolina Press, 1993), 4.

19. The two factions are often described as mixed- or half-bloods (Treaty Party) and full-bloods (Ross Party), but they did not divide so neatly. For example, the leader of the "full-bloods," John Ross, was only one-eighth Cherokee (McLoughlin, *After the Trail of Tears,* 3). "Full-blood" became the label for anyone who primarily spoke Cherokee and favored traditional ways. William G. McLoughlin,

Champions of the Cherokees: Evan and John B. Jones (Princeton: Princeton University Press, 1990), 345.

20. See Principal Chief John Ross's letter to Confederate Brigadier General Benjamin McCulloch, 17 June 1861, in *The War of the Rebellion: A Compilation of the Official Records of the Union and Confederate Armies*, series 1 (1881; reprint, Pasadena: Historical Times, 1985), 3:596–97.

21. Ross to McCulloch, 24 August 1861, *War of the Rebellion*, series 1, 3:673–76.

22. W. Craig Gaines, *The Confederate Cherokees: John Drew's Regiment of Mounted Rifles* (Baton Rouge: Louisiana State University Press, 1989), 54, 81–91.

23. Some of Ross's sympathies for the North no doubt reflect the fact that his second wife, Mary Brian Stapler (1825–65), was the daughter of a Quaker merchant from Wilmington, Delaware. Ross's first wife, Quatie (Elizabeth Brown Henley, 1791–1839), died on the Trail of Tears. Gary E. Moulton, *John Ross: Cherokee Chief* (Athens: University of Georgia Press, 1978), 12–13, 100–101; McLoughlin, *After the Trail of Tears*, 46, and *The Cherokees and Christianity*, 274.

24. McLoughlin, *Champions of the Cherokees*, 403–27 passim. Laurence M. Hauptman has observed that "no other Native American community was more disastrously affected by the Civil War than the Cherokee Nation of Indian Territory." *Between Two Fires: American Indians in the Civil War* (New York: Free Press, 1995), 42.

25. McLoughlin, *Champions of the Cherokees*, 344–47. Abolition was not a specified objective of the Keetoowah Society, but was representative of the differences between the full-bloods and the half-bloods. "Keetoowah" is a variation on the ancient name for the Cherokee people. Georgia Rae Leeds, *The United Keetoowah Band of Cherokee Indians in Oklahoma* (New York: Peter Lang, 1996), 1. See also Patrick Minges, "The Keetoowah Society and the Avocation of Religious Nationalism in the Cherokee Nation, 1855–1867" (Ph.D. diss., Union Theological Seminary, Columbia University 1999): *http://www.users.rcn.com/wovoka/Pmchap2.htm#*.

26. McLoughlin, *After the Trail of Tears*, 158, 211–12.

27. McLoughlin, *Champions of the Cherokees*, 355–56.

28. Thomas Perkins Abernethy, *From Frontier to Plantation in Tennessee: A Study in Frontier Democracy* (University: University of Alabama Press, 1967), 327. In his handwritten family record, Slover notes that John Brabson, a brother of his wife's mother, "owned a good farm on French broad River, a flouring mill, a ferry, and a tanyard and lots of Negroes." JAS.

29. *Arkansas Baptist*, 8 August 1860, 1.

30. Orville W. Taylor, "Baptists and Slavery in Arkansas: Relationship and

Attitudes," *Arkansas Historical Quarterly* 38 (autumn 1979): 220; *Papers of Chief John Ross*, for example, 2:397, 450, 465.

31. In 1839 a vigilante group presumably supporting the Ross Party murdered the two Ridges and Boudinot. Stand Watie was away when the killers reached his home and thus survived. McLoughlin, *After the Trail of Tears*, 16.

32. Kenny A. Franks, *Stand Watie and the Agony of the Cherokee Nation* (Memphis: Memphis State University Press, 1979), 114; McLoughlin, *After the Trail of Tears*, 155.

33. Franks, *Stand Watie*, 117.

34. See Gaines, *The Confederate Cherokees*, 11–15.

35. In her *The Life of General Stand Watie: The Only Indian Brigadier General of the Confederate Army and the Last to Surrender* (Pryor OK: privately published, 1931), 69, Mabel Washbourne Anderson lists a Rev. J. N. Stover as chaplain of Watie's Regiment. This is apparently a reference to Slover.

36. E. L. Compere more than once traveled to Alabama and elsewhere in the South to obtain supplies for Watie's Regiment and for Cherokee refugees. See, for example, Franks, *Stand Watie*, 175, and Edward E. Dale, ed., "Additional Letters of General Stand Watie," *Chronicles of Oklahoma* 1 (1921): 136.

37. James Anderson Slover to E. L. Compere, 26 June 1861, E. L. Compere Papers, Southern Baptist Historical Library and Archives.

38. McLoughlin, *Champions of the Cherokees*, 392–97.

39. See also Wiggins, "A Critical History," 178.

40. Generally, bushwhackers were Confederate guerrillas, but Slover seems to apply the term to any of the armed groups that were taking whatever they wanted from noncombatants. Mark Mayo Boatner III, *The Civil War Dictionary*, rev. ed. (New York: David McKay, 1988), 109.

41. See, for example, Rev. Worcester Willey, *A Tale of Home and War*, ed. E. P. Howland (1888; New Haven CT: Research Publications, 1975, Western Americana Series, reel 604, no. 6219.1); William Monks, *A History of Southern Missouri and Northern Arkansas: Being an Account of the Early Settlements, the Civil War, the Ku-Klux, and Times of Peace* (1907; New Haven CT: Research Publications, 1975, Western Americana Series, reel 377, no. 3701); Hannah W. Hicks, "The Diary of Hannah Hicks," intro. Mary Elizabeth Good, *American Scene* 13, no. 3 (1972): 3–24; and Carl H. Moneyhon, *The Impact of the Civil War and Reconstruction on Arkansas: Persistence in the Midst of Ruin* (Baton Rouge: Louisiana State University Press, 1994).

42. Moneyhon, *The Impact of the Civil War*, 104.

43. David M. Chalmers, *Hooded Americanism: The History of the Ku Klux Klan*, 2nd ed. (New York: New Viewpoints, 1981), 8–19.

44. See Ralph Moody, *The Old Trails West* (New York: Thomas Y. Crowell, 1963), ch. 2; Waterman Lilly Ormsby, *The Butterfield Overland Mail by Waterman L. Ormsby, Only Through Passenger on the First Westbound Stage*, ed.

Lyle H. Wright and Josephine M. Bynum (San Marino CA: Huntington Library, 1962); and Roscoe Conkling and Margaret B. Conkling, *The Butterfield Overland Mail, 1857–1869; Its Organization and Operation over the Southern Route to 1861; Subsequently over the Central Route to 1866; and under Wells, Fargo and Company in 1869*, 3 vols. (Glendale CA: Arthur H. Clark, 1947).

45. Moody, *The Old Trails West*, 93.

46. Roy M. Robbins, *Our Landed Heritage: The Public Domain, 1776–1936* (Lincoln: University of Nebraska Press, 1942), 240. Given that the purpose of the Homestead Act was to distribute land for agricultural purposes, some of these land deals were clearly questionable.

47. Some five hundred miles of principal irrigation ditches were built in Tulare County by companies and cooperatives. *Memorial and Biographical History of the Counties of Fresno, Tulare, and Kern, California* (1892; Americana Unlimited, 1974, pt. 1, CA, reel 9, no. 30, p. 189).

48. Paul W. Gates, *Land and Law in California: Essays on Land Policies* (Ames: Iowa State University Press, 1991), 266.

49. Minges, "The Keetoowah Society," 7–14.

50. See Solon Justus Buck, *The Granger Movement; A Study of Agricultural Organization and Its Political, Economic, and Social Manifestations, 1870–1880* (1913; reprint, Lincoln: University of Nebraska Press, 1963); also Earl Pomeroy, *The Pacific Slope* (1965; reprint, Seattle: University of Washington Press, 1973), 174–75.

51. Dennis Nordin argues that Buck's classic work put too much emphasis on reform, ignoring the educational and social thrust of the movement, but Slover seems most interested in the reform activities of the Grange, giving support to Buck's position. Nordin, "A Revisionist Interpretation of the Patrons of Husbandry, 1867–1900," *Historian* 32, no. 4 (1970): 630–43.

52. Eleventh U.S. Census, 1890.

53. Federal land law invariably exempted mineral lands from settlement. Robbins, *Our Landed Heritage*, 151.

54. C. H. Mattoon, *Baptist Annals of Oregon, 1844 to 1900* (McMinnville OR: Telephone Register, 1905), 411.

55. Mattoon calls Slover a "Landmark" Baptist and explains that Landmarkers were adamant in their refusal to accept alien or infant baptism. The less strict Anti-Landmarkers would accept alien immersion if they were convinced that the applicant had had a true conversion before immersion. Pacific Northwest Baptists were about equally divided between the two views. *Baptist Annals of Oregon*, xxi. Gregory A. Wills, in *Democratic Religion: Freedom, Authority, and Church Discipline in the Baptist South, 1785–1900* (New York: Oxford University Press, 1997), says Landmark Baptists would not share their pulpits with non-Baptists (8). Slover, however, seems to have been willing to share his pulpit and even eager to debate with other Protestant ministers. Copeland notes that Landmarkism was

especially influential in Tennessee, Kentucky, Alabama, the Southwest, and in westward expansion, essentially Slover's trail across the country. *The Southern Baptist Convention*, 61–63.

56. Slover to E. L. Compere, 26 June 1861.

1. JAMES ANDERSON SLOVER

1. The story of this massacre was related by Abraham's brother, John Slover, in his account of his second capture by Indians. The latter occurred in 1782. Slover, who was illiterate, told his story to Henry Hugh Brackenridge, a Pittsburgh publisher, judge, novelist, legislator, and a leader of the Whiskey Rebellion, who published it in *Narratives of a Late Expedition Against the Indians; with An Account of the Barbarous Execution of Col. Crawford; and the Wonderful Escape of Dr. Knight and John Slover from Captivity, in 1782* (1783; New York: Readex Microprints, 1985, Early American Imprints, microfiche no. 1793). The narrative was reprinted as "Private Slover's Escape," *Susquehanna Monthly Magazine*, February 1986, 22–27. See also Parker B. Brown, "The Historical Accuracy of the Captivity Narrative of the Doctor John Knight," *Western Pennsylvania Historical Magazine* 70 (January 1987): 53–67.

2. Slover descendants have traced their family to French Huguenots who fled to the Netherlands, in particular Zeeland, to escape persecution. The French name was Seloivre, which became Seloover in the Netherlands. It had a variety of other mutations, including Slover, after the family moved to the American colonies. James Anderson Slover's branch of the family is believed to descend from Isack Seloover, who settled in Delaware around 1683. JAS.

3. The Indians were Miamis. "Private Slover's Escape," 23.

4. John spent twelve years with the Indians and was twenty years old when he returned to his parents' community. "Private Slover's Escape," 23.

5. Col. William Crawford, a militia leader in the Revolutionary War and friend of George Washington, became an Indian fighter in the 1770s and 1780s. In 1782 he led an expedition against Indians in Ohio, and John Slover, who as a result of his earlier captivity spoke several Algonquian dialects, was hired as a guide. Crawford was known for taking no prisoners and scalping Indian women and children. This reputation was in part responsible for the subsequent torture and death he suffered at the hands of the Delaware Indians, who captured him and Slover. The latter reported that Crawford was scalped alive on his second day of captivity and that he died on the third day. "Private Slover's Escape," 22–23.

6. John Slover's account to Brackenridge suggests he was captive about eighteen days before the Indians decided to burn him, but he is not precise. "Private Slover's Escape," 25–26.

7. The Muskingum flows into the Ohio River at modern Marietta, Ohio. In his

narrative John Slover says he had a good start on the Indians by the time he swam the river and had not heard any of them for a day or two. He eventually reached the white settlement at Wheeling, Ohio. An editor's note to "Private Slover's Escape" says that John Slover settled on Canoe Creek in Henderson, Kentucky, had a large family, and lived a long life (27). Henderson County, Kentucky, tax rolls for 1799 show a John Slover with two hundred acres on Canue Creek. http://www.members.aol.com/patander73/h1799tax.html.

8. The sons were Aaron, Abraham, Isaac, Jacob, and John. Rachel Taffe (b. 10 June 1790, d. 22 May 1848) was the sixth of seven children of George Taffe. According to Slover, the others were James, Jessee, Wiley, George, Isaac, and Sallie. JAS.

9. Water turns the wheel by passing underneath it, instead of dropping from a height. Various kinds of waterwheels are illustrated in Eric Sloane, *Sketches of America Past* (New York: Promontory Press, 1986), 36.

10. Isaac W. Slover (b. 10 June 1812, d. August 1839), "Not a professor of religion." JAS. His siblings' religious preferences were of considerable interest to James Anderson Slover.

11. Later in the memoir, Slover says the property was sold to a William Moore.

12. Also known as a bar share. Leo Rogin, *The Introduction of Farm Machinery in Its Relation to the Productivity of Labor in the Agriculture of the United States during the Nineteenth Century* (1931; reprint, New York: Johnson Reprint, 1966), 8.

13. The Cary plow, more commonly spelled Carey but also known as the Deagan, Dagan, Dagen, or Connecticut plow, was a wooden implement developed in the early 1800s particularly for use on land with few stumps or roots. It was well received in the South. Rogin, *Introduction of Farm Machinery*, 8–9.

14. Mary (b. 20 March 1814, d. 1837 or 1838) was a member of the Methodist Episcopal Church. JAS.

15. Construction materials, tools, and techniques described in Sloane's *Sketches of America Past* are probably similar to those with which Slover was familiar. Sloane used a diary written in New England in 1805, together with his collection of early American tools, as starting points for his book. Author's note, n.p.

16. In *Southern Cross: The Beginnings of the Bible Belt* (Chapel Hill: University of North Carolina Press, 1997), Christine Leigh Heyrman discusses the evangelicals' success in reaching young people and their role-playing (see, especially, 86).

17. Elsewhere Slover says the marriage occurred in the winter of 1832–33. JAS.

18. The great Leonid meteor shower of 13 November 1833. Periodically these showers are particularly close to earth, as they were in 1833. See Gary W. Kronk, *Meteor Showers: A Descriptive Catalog* (Hillside NJ: Enslow, 1988).

19. George W. Slover (b. 27 March 1816, d. 1863) became a Baptist minister.

2. Death of Grandfather Slover

1. The dates Slover provides do not correspond to those in "Private Slover's Escape" (24). John Slover's narrative says he returned to white settlements in 1773 at the age of twenty, which would mean he was born in 1753. If Abraham was eighty-five in 1835, he was born in 1750, yet James Anderson Slover says Abraham was the younger brother.
2. Thomas H. Slover was still living when Slover wrote his memoir. JAS.
3. Katherine Slover (b. 28 June 1818) was still living when Slover wrote his memoir. Slover visited her when he returned to Tennessee. JAS. See ch. 17.
4. Dumplin Creek flows into the French Broad River, which, together with the Holston River, creates the Tennessee River.
5. This is the same James Henry that Slover encounters in California some thirty-five years later. Nicolas Pike published what is generally considered the first American arithmetic text, *A New and Complete System of Arithmetic: Composed for the Use of the Citizens of the United States* (1788; New York: Readex Microprint, 1985, Early American Imprints, First Series, microfiche, no. 21394). He followed his original 512-page volume with a much-reduced version, *Abridgement of the New and Complete System of Arithmetic,* in numerous editions. "Pike never seemed to run out of rules," wrote Charles H. Carpenter in *History of American Schoolbooks* (Philadelphia: University of Pennsylvania Press, 1963), 136.

3. His Religious Experience

1. The Dumplin Creek Baptist Church was organized in 1797. It is now a modern building on a ridge above Interstate 40. Its records from 1797 to 1938 are on microfilm at the Southern Baptist Historical Library and Archives.
2. Undoubtedly a reference to biblical descriptions of baptism by immersion, not practiced by the Methodists.
3. Abraham Slover was born 7 January 1822; he and John Slover were twins. JAS.
4. The Tennessee River flows south into Alabama before turning north and heading for the Ohio River, thence to the Mississippi River.
5. Muscle Shoals, probably a variant spelling of the mussels that were once plentiful there, was a relatively shallow stretch of the Tennessee River with flinty, jagged rocks near the surface that made it a notorious major hazard to steamboats and other watercraft. The construction of Wilson Dam in 1916 eliminated the hazards.
6. Gunter's Landing, now Guntersville, east of Huntsville in northeastern Alabama, is the southernmost point of the Tennessee River and a transfer point for shipping. Slover left the flatboat here and did not complete the full trip to New Orleans.
7. A narrow passage of the Tennessee River through Lookout Mountain near

Chattanooga. Slover gives more details about the region around the "Suck" in chapter 4 when he describes immigrating to Arkansas on a flatboat.

8. John died in 1863–64 and may have been one of the brothers Slover says was killed in Texas in the Civil War. JAS.

9. In 1846 the United States went to war with Mexico when the latter refused to accept U.S. annexation of Texas. At war's end, Mexico ceded what became the states of New Mexico, Arizona, California, Nevada, and Utah. It was during this war that Davy Crockett, Slover's fellow Tennessean, lost his life at the Alamo.

10. Congress authorized President Polk to call up fifty thousand volunteers for the war with Mexico in order to supplement the poorly manned and poorly trained militia companies mandated by federal law since 1792. It was common for local militia leaders to parade their men in a community to inspire volunteers in the manner Slover describes. Despite the youthfulness of some leaders, response was strong. Tennessee, for example, oversubscribed its quota ten to one, and lots were drawn to determine who would get to go to war. James M. McCaffrey, *Army of Manifest Destiny: The American Soldier in the Mexican War, 1846–1848* (New York: New York University Press, 1992), 16–19.

11. Slover's manuscript says he "taught" school, but other references suggest he was still getting his own education at this stage, so he probably attended the three-month school as a student. He typically attended—and subsequently taught—subscription schools for which several families would get together to hire the teacher.

4. His Call to the Ministry

1. Slover's dates do not add up. From 24 April 1848 to 1 November 1849 is about eighteen months, whereas three five-month sessions and one seven-month session equal twenty-two months.

2. Harriet Ingram was the daughter of John Ingram; her mother's surname was Scruggs. She had three brothers and a sister. JAS.

3. Some of his and his wife's relatives apparently preceded them in the journey westward. This may account for his choice of Washington County, which is in the northwest corner of Arkansas.

4. Rachel Jane Slover (b. 21 December 1831, d. 1896 or 1897); "if religious, she was a Baptist." JAS.

5. As early as 1832 the U.S. Army Engineers attempted to make the Suck and other treacherous passages on the Tennessee River safer for navigation. They built canals and dams, but these efforts were described as largely "worthless." Leland R. Johnson, "Army Engineers on the Cumberland and Tennessee, 1824–1854," *Tennessee Historical Quarterly* 31 (summer 1972): 152-54.

6. This is an often-repeated story. See, for example, Donald Davidson, *The Tennessee*, vol. 1, *The Old River: Frontier to Secession* (New York: Rinehart, 1946), 205-7.

7. Tennessee had three steam sawmills by 1851, but they were in the Cumberland and western parts of the state, not in Slover's territory. Steven A. Schulman, "The Lumber Industry of the Upper Cumberland River Valley," *Tennessee Historical Quarterly* 32 (fall 1973): 259.

8. Cramer locates Island Number 10 near the left shore of the Mississippi River, fifty-seven miles from the mouth of the Ohio. The best channel is to the right of the island. "This island and the right bank opposite it, shew the first evident marks of the effects of the earthquake which commenced December 16, 1811." *The Navigator,* 177.

5. HIS FIRST SCHOOL IN ARKANSAS

1. Slover subsequently identifies the location of his first subscription school in Arkansas as Mount Comfort, which was the site of several early schools, including the Far West Seminary and the Mount Comfort Female Seminary. Dean G. Carter, "Some Historical Notes on Far West Seminary," *Arkansas Historical Quarterly* 29 (winter 1970): 348, 360.

2. Baptists could transfer membership from one church to another by providing a letter from their former church. See Slover's letter from the Dumplin Creek Baptist Church, 4 January 1850, microfilmed records of the Dumplin Creek Baptist Church.

3. Cumberland Presbyterians split from the main church in 1810, primarily because they thought that educating their ministers inhibited their effectiveness in revivals. Heyrman, *Southern Cross,* 284, n. 7.

4. Southern Baptists first licensed potential preachers, then ordained them after they had lived up to expectations as men of good character who understood the principles of Southern Baptist theology and practiced their lives according to those principles. Ordination came when a man was called to be pastor of a church; it allowed him to perform the two principal ordinances of the church, baptism and the Lord's Supper. Decisions on whether to license and/or ordain were up to individual congregations. Heyrman, *Southern Cross,* 83; also telephone interview with C. O. Jackson, minister of the Southern Baptist Church at The Lakes, Las Vegas, Nevada, 10 March 1998.

5. Baptist churches, each of which operated quite independently, formed themselves into associations.

6. Slover seems to include even baptism by other Baptists as "alien immersion" if the candidate does not submit a formal letter of transfer from another Baptist church.

6. HE ACCEPTS AN APPOINTMENT

1. Henry Frieland Buckner, from Tennessee, was appointed Southern Baptist missionary to the Creeks in 1846. Routh, "Henry Frieland Buckner," 457.

Buckner was described as "our earnest, laborious and indefatigable missionary." *Proceedings of the Sixth Biennial Session of the Southern Baptist Convention, Louisville, Kentucky, May 1857* (Richmond VA: H. K. Ellyson, 1857), 30.

2. His friend and colleague E. L. Compere, son of Lee Compere, longtime missionary to the Cherokees, also received $500 when he became a missionary at in 1859. Compere's assignment was split between missionary work with the Cherokees and the white church in Fort Smith, Arkansas. Baptist missionaries were often supported by individual congregations; the Cherokee Baptist Convention of North Georgia supported Compere. Slover was paid by the Southern Baptist Domestic and Indian Mission Board, which had its headquarters in Marion, Alabama. Inventory to E. L. Compere Papers, Southern Baptist Historical Library and Archives, June 1992, 1; Wiggins, "A Critical History," 69.

3. Slover's hiring is recorded in the Domestic Mission Board report of the *Proceedings*, 1857, 30.

4. John Ross was principal chief of the Cherokees from 1828 until his death in 1866. His supporters constituted the Ross Party, basically traditionalists who opposed the Treaty Party, which had negotiated the sale of ancestral lands to the Americans.

5. McLoughlin notes that there were five evangelical Protestant denominations ministering to the Cherokees—northern Baptist, Southern Baptist, Methodist Episcopal, Congregational, and Presbyterian—and by 1860 about 12 percent of the Cherokees in Indian Territory belonged to one of them. *The Cherokees and Christianity*, 198–99.

6. Tahlequah is now the headquarters community for the Cherokee Nation; it is near Ross's old Park Hill home.

7. The extended Foreman family was prominent in the Cherokee Nation. Johnson Foreman attended the Brainerd Mission School, operated by Presbyterian minister Thomas Brainerd in the East; Stephen Foreman studied at Princeton Theological Seminary, among other schools, and helped translate the Bible into Cherokee. In the 1830s David Foreman was an interpreter for northern Baptist missionary Evan Jones; later he apparently interpreted for the Southern Baptists. *Papers of Chief John Ross*, 2:723; McLoughlin, *Champions of the Cherokees*, 162; *Proceedings of the Eighth Biennial Session of the Southern Baptist Convention* (Richmond VA: MacFarlane & Ferguson, 1861), 41.

8. The Cherokees had a long association with English-speaking settlers. In the East they published a bilingual newspaper, the *Cherokee Phoenix*, the first Native American newspaper. When they moved west, the Cherokees established the *Cherokee Advocate*, but it was not published during the period Slover was in Indian Territory. Althea Bass, *Cherokee Messenger* (Norman: University of Oklahoma Press, 1936), 69–89, 293–95; McLoughlin, *After the Trail of Tears*, 52, 333–34.

9. Evan Jones was one of the most influential of the northern Baptist missionaries in Indian Territory. See McLoughlin, *Champions of the Cherokees*.

10. Wiggins suggests the Southern Baptists were successful because their position on slavery protected the southern way of life. "A Critical History," 170.

11. Rev. Samuel Austin Worcester (1798–1859) was a Congregational missionary to the Cherokees from 1825 until his death. He was arrested and jailed when he protested the treatment of the Cherokees in the 1830s; his case was appealed to the U.S. Supreme Court, *Worcester v. The State of Georgia*, 6 U.S. 515 (1832). He was deeply involved with the *Cherokee Phoenix*, and after he moved with the Cherokees to Indian Territory he set up a printing press and with Cherokee assistants translated and published the Bible, pamphlets, and other materials. McLoughlin, *After the Trail of Tears*, 84. See also Bass, *Cherokee Messenger*.

12. See McLoughlin, *Champions of the Cherokees*, 278, for the views of other denominations on accepting slaveholders.

13. According to Southern Baptist records, "During the first year he labored under great disadvantages—was the subject of suspicion, opposition and persecution. No church was organized—no baptism of converts during the year." *Proceedings of the Seventh Biennial Session of the Southern Baptist Convention* (Richmond VA: H. K. Ellyson's Steam Presses, 1859), 76.

14. Slover accused other missionaries—Evan Jones and his son, in particular—of spreading rumors about him and linking him to "the Mormons of Salt Lake." See *Proceedings*, 1861, 41.

7. Encouraging Prospects

1. The Bushyheads were a prominent Cherokee family. Jesse Bushyhead was a Native preacher who had been converted by Evan Jones before the Cherokees were removed to Indian Territory. Jesse's son, Edward Wilkerson Bushyhead, was an editor who founded the *San Diego Union*. See Carolyn Thomas Foreman, "Edward W. Bushyhead and John Rollin Ridge: Cherokee Editors in California," *Chronicles of Oklahoma* 14 (1936): 295–311. Jacob Bushyhead was a Baptist preacher. The Baptist Foreign Mission Board was concerned that he owned slaves, and although Jones argued that the slaves had been inherited by Mrs. Bushyhead, the board insisted that Jacob withdraw from the church. Norbert R. Mahnken, "Old Baptist Mission and Evan Jones," *Chronicles of Oklahoma* 67 (summer 1989): 186.

2. Slover does not appear to have learned the language. Wiggins says that unlike missionaries from other denominations who learned the Cherokee language and/or translated religious materials into Cherokee, the Southern Baptists preached in English because they thought it would have a civilizing influence on the Indians. "A Critical History," 154–55. But see also *Proceedings*, 1861, 40, which reports that H. F. Buckner and his interpreter had translated the Gospel of John and a hymnbook, among other publications, for the Creeks.

3. Probably Thomas Fox Taylor (1818–62). Active in Cherokee politics,

Taylor became a lieutenant colonel in the Civil War and died at the Battle of Bayou Manard. *Papers of Chief John Ross*, 2:737.

4. In Slover's first year, 1857, he organized no churches and baptized no converts. In 1858 he organized two churches with twelve and sixteen members; in 1859 he organized a third church, for a total of fifty-three members. He also arranged for four Cherokee preachers. *Proceedings*, 1859, 76. By 1861 the Southern Baptists had eight Cherokee preachers: Thomas Wilkinson, John Foster, Jesse H. Owens, [first name not given] Walker, George Cochran, George Owen, James Fallen, and Saughat Mush (*Proceedings*, 1861, 41).

5. Slover reported to the Mission Board that Cherokee preachers were forced to oppose slavery in order to continue in their northern Baptist positions. He used this to recruit Cherokee preachers and claimed that four of them—including Thomas Wilkinson—had joined the Southern Baptists. Wiggins, "A Critical History," 165–68.

6. Isaac Reed was based in Maysville, Arkansas. He, too, claimed that the northern Baptists interfered with his meetings. *Proceedings*, 1861, 41; Wiggins, "A Critical History," 161.

7. The Methodist Episcopal Church is a U.S. form of Methodism that developed in the colonies in the 1760s. In the nineteenth century, Methodists divided over the slavery issue much as the Baptists did. In 1845 southern Methodists organized the Methodist Episcopal Church South, with sympathies for slavery. Slover's main quarrel with the Methodists, north and south, however, centered on their failure to insist on baptism by immersion.

8. The Coosa Association was a Baptist association in the Cherokees' former home of Georgia. McLoughlin, *Champions of the Cherokees*, 357.

9. Upon arrival in Indian Territory in 1839, the Cherokee Nation West divided into three districts for election purposes. Delaware was the northern section. McLoughlin, *Champions of the Cherokees*, 185.

10. In 1860, Robert J. Cowart, a native of Georgia, was Cherokee agent. Carol B. Broemeling, "Cherokee Indian Agents, 1830–1874," *Chronicles of Oklahoma* 50 (winter 1972–73): 451. Either this is one of the few times Slover remembers a name incorrectly or "Mr. Post" held a different position. None of the standard accounts of this period mention Post. In chapter 13, Slover refers to a man named Post in connection with some reported Cherokees in California; he may have confused the two men.

11. "Fire-eaters" commonly refers to Southern radicals who advocated secession. However, the term had earlier been applied in both the North and the South to extremists, and Slover seems to be using it in this broader sense. See Eric H. Walther, *The Fire-Eaters* (Baton Rouge: Louisiana State University Press, 1992), 2.

12. 1845. See, among others, Copeland, *The Southern Baptist Convention*, 8.

13. Stand Watie was a leader of the Treaty Party that opposed Chief John Ross. Biographers give Watie's Cherokee name as Degadoga, "he stands [on two

feet]." Franks, *Stand Watie*, 2; *Papers of Chief John Ross*, 2:738, 146. Benjamin McCulloch (1811–62) went from his native Tennessee to Texas, where he served in the War for Texas Independence and the Mexican War. When Texas seceded, McCulloch took up arms again and commanded Confederate forces in Indian Territory, Arkansas, and Missouri at various times. He was victorious at Wilson's Creek but was killed at the Battle of Pea Ridge. Stewart Sifakis, *Who Was Who in the Civil War* (New York: Facts on File Publications, 1988), 412.

14. The "Pin" Indians were militant members of the Keetoowah Society, a secret association with historic roots in the Cherokee Nation and identified with full-bloods, traditionalists, conservatives, and abolitionists. The Keetoowahs were influenced by northern Baptist missionary Evan Jones and his son, ardent abolitionists. McLoughlin, *Champions of the Cherokees*, 345. The history of the Keetoowah Society is detailed in Minges, "The Keetoowah Society," especially ch. 2; see also Leeds, *The United Keetoowah Band*. The Pins took their name from the straight pins they wore on their jackets. Slover appears to have been right to fear them. See also McLoughlin, *After the Trail of Tears*, 211–12.

15. Little Rock lawyer Albert Pike (1809–91) was also a writer, teacher, and newspaper editor who spoke several Indian languages and represented Native Americans in legal matters. The Confederacy named him commissioner to negotiate treaties with the Indian nations. Gaines, *The Confederate Cherokees*, 7; *Papers of Chief John Ross*, 2:744; Sifakis, *Who Was Who*, 507.

16. At this point, Ross was trying to remain neutral in the North-South conflict. Proclamation, Park Hill, 17 May 1861, in *Papers of Chief John Ross*, 2:470.

17. Chief Ross and other pro-Union leaders had expected that they would be able to remain neutral in the conflict and that the Union army would protect them, but when Confederate forces appeared to be the stronger, Ross had a change of heart and agreed to join the Confederacy.

18. General Pike wrote the Cherokee Nation's "Declaration of Independence," which was proclaimed 24 October 1861 and allied the Nation with the Confederacy. See McLoughlin, *Champions of the Cherokees*, 397.

19. The Treaty of New Echota, signed in 1835 by Cherokees who wanted to make accommodation with the federal government, resulted in the sale of eastern Cherokee lands for $5 million. This went into a trust fund, along with money paid to the Cherokees for earlier land sales, to create the annuity of which Slover writes. The turmoil of the Civil War period interrupted payment of the income from the trust fund. See Moulton, *John Ross*, 72–86; McLoughlin, *Champions of the Cherokees*, 135–40; Franks, *Stand Watie*, 25–26.

20. Part of the agreement prepared by General Pike required the Cherokees to create a mounted regiment under Colonel John Drew. Stand Watie had already formed a battalion, but Chief Ross wanted to prevent Watie from gaining additional stature or power. However, General McCulloch authorized Watie to

raise a regiment as well, and he apparently considered Watie's men better soldiers. Gaines, *The Confederate Cherokees*, 13.

21. John Drew (1796–1865), who was sixty-five at the time he was called into military service, was a businessman and lawyer in Webbers Falls in the Canadian district in the southern part of the Cherokee Nation. He was considered a rich man, had a number of slaves, and had led patrols to capture escaped slaves. His sympathies were generally with the Confederacy, but his troops were evidently less enthusiastic about the cause; in major battles such as Pea Ridge, they deserted in great numbers. Gaines, *The Confederate Cherokees*, 16–17; *Papers of Chief John Ross*, 2:721. Drew's Regiment, officially mustered in on 5 November 1861 for twelve months of service, totaled 1,214 men. Watie's Regiment was formed 12 July 1861 for two years. Both claimed the title of First Regiment. Jessie Randolph Moore, "The Five Great Indian Nations," *Chronicles of Oklahoma* 23 (autumn 1951): 324–36.

22. Douglas Hancock Cooper (1815–79) was named U.S. commissioner to the Choctaws and worked with Albert Pike to forge an alliance between the Indian nations and the Confederacy. An adopted member of the Chickasaw tribe, he was colonel of the First Choctaw and Chickasaw Mounted Rifles, among his military assignments. After the war he represented the Indians in claims against the U.S. government. Sifakis, *Who Was Who*, 141; *Papers of Chief John Ross*, 2:741.

23. The Battle of Pea Ridge, also called Elkhorn Tavern, on 7–8 March 1862 left the Confederate forces depleted and in disarray. Gaines gives the figures of Confederates killed and wounded at 185 and 525, respectively, although estimates ranged as high as a total of 1,000. The Union army reported 203 killed and 980 wounded. Most of the Indians returned to their homes after the battle. See Gaines, *The Confederate Cherokees*, 74–90.

24. James McQueen McIntosh (1828–62) was a West Point graduate who was commanding a mounted Arkansas regiment when he was killed at Pea Ridge. Sifakis, *Who Was Who*, 417. Sterling Price (1809–67) first commanded the Missouri State Guard, then was tapped to command the Army of the West for the Confederacy. Sifakis, *Who Was Who*, 522–24.

8. Union Troops on Cherokee Territory

1. Slover originally spelled it "Blount" throughout, probably confusing the name with William Blount, a well-known Tennessee leader. James G. Blunt (1826–81), a Kansas doctor, was brigadier general of the Kansas Volunteers and assigned to command various units in the Union Department of Kansas, which included Indian Territory. His headquarters was at Fort Leavenworth. The spelling has been corrected in the text. Sifakis, *Who Was Who*, 60.

2. Attorney William Penn Adair was one of the leaders of the Ridge or Treaty Party. He owned a large plantation with many slaves. He was killed in this raid

on Stand Watie's camp on Cowskin Prairie. Gaines, *The Confederate Cherokees*, 95; McLoughlin, *Champions of the Cherokees*, 365.

3. Dr. Rufus Gilpatrick, Chief Ross's physician, at this time served in the Union army. Gaines, *The Confederate Cherokees*, 105; see also *The War of the Rebellion*, series 1, 13:138. The council was actually sought by Colonel William Weer, commander of the Tenth Kansas Infantry Regiment, who sent the letter. Gaines gives the date as 7 July 1862. Gaines, *The Confederate Cherokees*, 105.

4. Fort Gibson is southwest of Tahlequah. Originally established in 1824 to end the fighting between the Osage and the Cherokees, among other purposes, Fort Gibson was turned over to the Cherokee Nation in 1857 and renamed Keetoowah. Some of the Cherokees wanted to make it their capital, but Ross vetoed the proposal. It was occupied by Union troops in 1863 and abandoned in 1890. Robert Walter Frazer, *Forts of the West: Military Forts and Presidios, and Posts Commonly Called Forts, West of the Mississippi River to 1898* (Norman: University of Oklahoma Press, 1965), 120–21; Leeds, *The United Keetoowah Band*, 6.

5. In April 1862 the mayor of New Orleans refused to lower the Louisiana state flag in surrender to Admiral David Farragut, even though the military situation was obviously hopeless. "We yield to physical force alone, and maintain our allegiance to the Government of the Confederate States. Beyond this a due respect for our dignity, our rights, and the flag of our country does not, I think, permit us to go." Quoted in Marion A. Baker, "Farragut's Demands for the Surrender of New Orleans," in *Battles and Leaders of the Civil War* (New York: Thomas Yoseloff, 1956), 2:95. Baker was the mayor's private secretary. The mayor's refusal was but a gesture; the city did not resist. Farragut was a bold and competent commander, probably best remembered for shouting "Damn the torpedoes! Go ahead!" during the Battle of Mobile on 5 August 1864. A. T. Mahan, *Admiral Farragut* (New York: University Society, 1905), 168–71. Or see also "Go On, Damn the Torpedo!" in George Cary Eggleston, *The History of the Confederate War: Its Causes and Its Conduct, a Narrative and Critical History*, 2 vols. (1910; reprint, New York: Negro Universities Press, 1970), 2:281, or the best-known version, "Damn the Torpedos: Full Speed Ahead," in *The Oxford Dictionary of Quotations*, 3rd ed (Oxford: Oxford University Press, 1980), 210, which also alerts readers to the Mahan version.

6. Confederate Cherokees were changing sides in great numbers in July 1862. An estimated eight hundred from Drew's Regiment joined Union forces 4–6 July. At this point Chief Ross, too, decided that the future of the Nation lay with the Union. Gaines, *The Confederate Cherokees*, 105–12.

7. General Blunt sent Colonel William F. Cloud to Park Hill on 27 July to take Chief Ross into protective custody, technically making him a prisoner of war. Cloud took Ross to Fort Leavenworth to see Blunt, who agreed to let him go to

Washington DC to meet with President Lincoln. McLoughlin, *Champions of the Cherokees*, 404–5.

8. Chief John Ross died 1 August 1866 in a hotel room in Washington DC, where he had gone to negotiate a postwar treaty with the U.S. government.

9. Whites had fears of a slave revolt. For the most part, slaves went to Union army camps. Gaines, *The Confederate Cherokees*, 104–5.

10. Tahlequah was officially occupied by Union forces on July 14. Gaines says only four men were in the town when the soldiers arrived, the others having fled as Slover did. *The Confederate Cherokees*, 108.

11. The Indians served in armies on both sides, and three regiments of Kansas Indian Home Guard occupied the Cherokee Nation after the main Union forces withdrew to Kansas. Gaines, *The Confederate Cherokees*, 113.

12. These kinds of raids were not uncommon. Hannah Hicks, the daughter of Rev. Samuel Austin Worcester and wife of a Cherokee, tells of similar experiences during the war. "The Diary of Hannah Hicks," 8.

13. On a flintlock rifle, the gunpowder is put in the pan and the frizzen strikes the flint, making the sparks that in turn ignite the gunpowder which fires the main charge.

14. Buck "fever," or the excitement of the hunt.

15. Thomas Carmichael Hindman (1828–68), an Arkansas lawyer and politician, was promoted to major general after service at Shiloh and transferred back to Arkansas where he was the Confederate commander at Prairie Grove. He was assassinated in Arkansas after the Civil War. Sifakis, *Who Was Who*, 310–11. Henry Wager Halleck (1815–72), a West Pointer who became a San Francisco lawyer, was in charge of all Union forces in the West when they won the Battle at Pea Ridge. Union general in chief from 1862 to 1864, he subsequently proved to be a better administrator than field commander, but was not popular with other military leaders. Sifakis, *Who Was Who*, 275–76.

16. The Battle of Prairie Grove, together with the Battle of Pea Ridge, both in northwestern Arkansas, were the major Civil War battles in this part of the country.

17. E. L. Compere more than once traveled to Alabama and elsewhere in the South to obtain supplies for Watie's Regiment and for Cherokee refugees. This may have been one of those trips. See, for example, Franks, *Stand Watie*, 175, and Dale, "Additional Letters of General Stand Watie," 136.

18. Frederick Steele (1819–68), a West Point graduate and career Army man, participated in a number of battles in Arkansas and Mississippi. He was promoted to brigadier general after the capture of Little Rock. Sifakis, *Who Was Who*, 619.

19. Slover had to take an oath of allegiance to the United States or risk being imprisoned or even shot.

20. Joseph Orville Shelby (1830–97), described as "one of the Confederacy's

most effective cavalry leaders," was a planter and rope manufacturer in Kentucky and Missouri. He rose from captain to brigadier general for the Confederacy and led troops in the key battles in the Trans-Mississippi campaign. Sifakis, *Who Was Who*, 585.

9. Another Skedaddling Necessary

1. Rev. Lee Compere began missionary work with the Creek Indians in South Carolina in 1819. See Carolyn Thomas Foreman, "Lee Compere and the Creek Indians," *Chronicles of Oklahoma* 42 (autumn 1964): 291–99.

2. Another Tennessee connection. John Sevier was governor of the short-lived state of Franklin. In 1784, after North Carolina ceded its western territory to the United States, settlers in the region formed a new state, naming it in honor of Benjamin Franklin. It was as a representative of the state of Franklin that Sevier and other settlers signed the Treaty of Dumplin Creek with the Cherokees. Congress ignored the settlers and never approved their new "state." Sevier later became the first governor of Tennessee, which entered the United States in 1796. Caldwell, *Tennessee*, 150, 154, 162.

10. The Missionary and Widow

1. In an 1863 report to the Domestic and Indian Mission Board, Russell Holman, then chairman, noted the unfortunate plight of both white and Native missionaries. The white missionaries who had withdrawn from Indian Territory were "laboring as opportunity affords, in the army or among destitute and feeble churches," and he urged his brethren to provide employment whenever possible. He also warned that when channels of communication reopened, missionaries would seek payment for their services, as Slover subsequently did. *Proceedings of the Ninth Biennial Session of the Southern Baptist Convention* (Macon GA: Burke, Boykin, 1863), 50.

2. Chief John Ross was a Master Mason, and many other Cherokees belonged to Masonic lodges. Minges suggests their experience as Masons influenced their formation of secret societies such as the Keetoowah. "The Keetoowah Society," ch. 2.

3. Slover's name continues to appear in the *Proceedings* through 1867, at which time the remark was made: "Rev. J. A. Slover, our former missionary to the Cherokees, has been laboring in Arkansas, upon Red river, as missionary of the Board for the past year, and will not return at present to the Nation." *Proceedings of the Southern Baptist Convention* (Baltimore: John F. Weishampel Jr., 1867), 43.

4. Buckner was the person who originally recommended Slover for the post of missionary to the Cherokee Nation.

5. Compere married Josephine I. Mullins of Copiah County, Mississippi, on

13 December 1863. Biographical note to Inventory of the E. L. Compere Papers, Southern Baptist Historical Library and Archives.

11. His Labor as Missionary Ceases

1. Isaac Murphy was named provisional governor of Arkansas in 1864 after Little Rock fell to the Union army and the Confederate government moved south. After the war ended, Murphy, although a Unionist, tried to get all Arkansas residents, including former Confederates such as Slover, working together. See Timothy P. Donovan, Willard B. Gatewood Jr., and Jeannie M. Whayne, eds., *The Governors of Arkansas: Essays in Political Biography* (Fayetteville: University of Arkansas Press, 1995), 42–45.

R. D. Sessions was the person elected county clerk. Fay Hempstead, *A Pictorial History of Arkansas from the Earliest Times to the Year 1890* (1890, Western Americana, reel 243, no. 2502, p. 1122). Slover subsequently explains that he had stood for the office of county clerk but lost the election. The winner of the election was unable to serve, so Governor Murphy appointed Slover. At the time, former Confederates controlled the state legislature and many other offices in the state. By the 1868 election, however, Congress had passed the Reconstruction Acts, disenfranchising ex-Confederates. Although Slover describes himself as a man of God rather than a political person, his associations with the Confederacy—as Stand Watie's chaplain, for example, however briefly—must have put him in an awkward position. Nevertheless, he apparently won over his fellow citizens enough to be elected justice of the peace. In the 1868 elections, Murphy was not a candidate. See also Hempstead, *A Pictorial History of Arkansas*, 1121–22.

2. These were but two of a number of killings in that part of the state in 1868. Slover blames "Texas bushwhackers," although one of the party is identified as a local man. Other accounts blame the "Knights of the White Camelia or Ku Klux Klan." See, for example, Thomas S. Staples, *Reconstruction in Arkansas, 1862–1874* (New York: Columbia University, 1923), 294.

3. Martial law was declared on 4 November 1868 and remained in effect for about four months. See Staples, *Reconstruction in Arkansas*, 294–95.

4. Located in north-central Texas, Fort Griffin was in service from 1867 to 1881. It served as a supply center for buffalo hunters and protected cattle trails and immigrants. Frazer, *Forts of the West*, 151.

5. Harriet Bunyard tells a similar story in her diary, published as "The Gila Trail: Texas to California, 1868," in *Covered Wagon Women: Diaries and Letters from the Western Trails 1840–1890*, ed. Kenneth L. Holmes (Spokane WA: Arthur H. Clark, 1990), 9:217. Except for the different years, hers could well have been the "Texas company" to which Slover refers.

6. Fort Concho dates from 1867 to 1889 and was located near modern San Angelo, Texas. Frazer, *Forts of the West*, 147.

7. The Staked Plains are part of the High Plains of Texas, a flat, dry area bounded on the east by the Cap Rock Escarpment and on the southwest by the Pecos River. The area is known for fierce sandstorms, flash floods, and, in winter, severe blizzards.

8. See also Bunyard's account of crossing the Pecos in Holmes, *Covered Wagon Women*, 222–23.

9. Fort Stockton, in service from 1859 to 1886, was established in western Texas to protect a stage route. Frazer, *Forts of the West*, 163. The migrants are generally following the route first blazed by Spanish priests and soldiers, also known as the Gila Trail. The Butterfield Overland Mail further developed it in 1857, and the Texas-Pacific Railroad line subsequently followed it. See Conkling and Conkling, *The Butterfield Overland Mail*.

10. Neither Frazer nor the Conklings record a Fort Alexander. Slover may be referring to Fort Quitman, about seventy miles below El Paso and not far from Eagle Springs. Fort Quitman was established in 1858 to protect the stage line and emigrants, and was garrisoned off and on until it was abandoned in 1877. Frazer, *Forts of the West*, 157–58.

11. Fort Cummings, in service from 1863 to 1891, was fifty-three miles west of the Rio Grande. Built to protect the Butterfield Trail, it was reportedly "the most dangerous point on the southern route to California" because of Apache hostility. Frazer, *Forts of the West*, 98. See also Andy Gregg, *Drums of Yesterday: The Forts of New Mexico* (Santa Fe: Press of the Territorian, 1968), 28–30.

12. Blue Water was an intermediate water station the Butterfield Stage Company established in the late 1850s.

13. If Slover is accurate in his mileage, this probably what the Butterfield Stage Company called Sacaton. The area is home to the Pima Indians. Conkling and Conkling, *The Butterfield Overland Mail*, 2:165–66.

14. Fort Yumah lay on the west side of the Colorado River, in California across from the site of modern Yuma, Arizona. The post was in operation from 1850 to 1884 and, like many other southern forts, was intended to protect travelers along the southern routes, in this case against the Yuma Indians. Frazer, *Forts of the West*, 34–35.

15. The desert, which the Conklings describe as 110 miles, would have included what is now California's Imperial Valley, a major fruit- and vegetable-producing area. Conkling and Conkling, *The Butterfield Overland Mail*, 2:216–17.

16. The wagon train appears to have rejoined the Butterfield route somewhere around Indian Wells. Conkling and Conkling, *The Butterfield Overland Mail*, 2:225. Past Mountain Spring, it generally followed what is now California Highway 94 into San Diego.

17. Slover is probably referring to the Kimball brothers—Frank A., Warren C., Levi W., George L., and Charles H.—who settled in San Diego County in 1868–69. They bought Rancho de la Nacion, an old Mexican land grant consisting of

forty-two square miles on San Diego Bay, and established National City. Frank and his wife built a "show place" home, perhaps the one where Slover did cleanup work. See Clarence A. McGrew, *History of the City of San Diego and San Diego County: The Birthplace of California* (1922), Americana Unlimited, pt. 1, CA, reel 26, no. 103, pp. 378–79; Richard F. Pourade, ed., *Historic Ranchos of San Diego* (San Diego: Union-Tribune, 1969), 90–94.

18. Slover was heading for Tulare County because friends and relatives, including a brother and two sisters of his wife, had already settled there.

19. A strep infection that can lead to blood poisoning; sometimes called St. Anthony's fire.

12. THE PREACHER LOCATES A PREEMPTION

1. Local history suggests the town was, for a period, called Sloverville, but in 1871 Slover renamed it Woodville. Rodney Prestage Homer, *The Pioneer Communities of Porterville, Vandalia, and Plano* (Porterville CA: Andiron, 1982), 99. In *History of California Post Offices, 1849–1990* (Lake Grove OR: The Depot, 1991), Harold E. Salley identifies Thomas B. Fuguay as the first postmaster (235), but Slover's obituary, undoubtedly supplied by the family, credits Slover. *Ashland Tidings*, 17 November 1913.

2. Dr. W. S. Henrahan was noted in 1892 for his new five-acre orange grove in Tulare County. *Memorial and Biographical History of the Counties of Fresno, Tulare, and Kern, California*, 205, 212.

3. To help finance western railroad building, the federal government gave railroads alternate sections of public land along their routes. The sections along the right-of-way reserved by the government for public sale were considered more valuable than other locations and were "double minimus" land because they had a price of $2.50 per acre, double that of other preemption land. Robbins, *Our Landed Heritage*, 89; see also Everett Dick, *The Lure of the Land: A Social History of the Public Lands from the Articles of Confederation to the New Deal* (Lincoln: University of Nebraska Press, 1970), 162.

4. Given the strictness of Landmark Baptists, with whom Slover has been identified (see introduction), Slover's attendance at an extended "alien" church meeting is surprising.

5. The National Grange, or Patrons of Husbandry, a secret order not unlike the Masons, was formed in 1867. California farmers welcomed the Grange following the Panic of 1873, which severely affected agriculture. The farmers hoped the Grange would help them economically and politically, but they were disappointed. The classic analysis is by Buck, *The Granger Movement*. Nordin holds that Buck minimizes the importance of the Grange as a social and educational influence in farmers' lives. See "A Revisionist Interpretation." Buck may indeed have unfairly neglected this aspect, but Slover's comments fit the interpretation that California

farmers, at least, looked to the Grange to solve their economic, not their social, problems.

6. In 1900 his daughter Elizabeth asked his advice about the "Fraternal Aid Association," an insurance/investment society. He wrote to her, "I got badly left by a Mutual Aid Association in California one time. I think I would have to understand pretty well what I was doing and How often I would have to repeat the money bills, and what assurance I had that I would be profited.... Look before you jump." Slover to Mrs. B. J. (Elizabeth Jane) Frye, 12 April 1900, possession of editor.

13. WITH HIS FARMING A FAILURE

1. Farmers and cattle ranchers argued over who was responsible for preventing grazing animals from straying and eating or damaging a farmer's crop. The California Trespass Act of 1850 said the farmer was responsible for fencing out the offending animals. With the cost of even a cheap fence as much as $700 a mile, farmers lobbied for a change in the law. Because the Trespass Act was known as the "Fence Law," farmers sought a "No Fence Law" under which they would not be responsible for building the fences. In the California legislature in 1874, they were successful in getting an added provision in the law that a landowner could claim any animals that strayed onto his property, either returning them in exchange for compensation or, if the owner could not be identified, keeping or selling them. See John Ludeke, "The No Fence Law of 1874: Victory for San Joaquin Valley Farmers," *California History* 59, no. 2 (1980): 98–115. Slover apparently was more worried about his liability if his own animals strayed than about damage to his crops from others.

2. Slover is referring to the doctrine of "prior appropriation," which was a first-come, first-served approach to allocating water. See Donald J. Pisani, *Water, Land, and Law in the West: The Limits of Public Policy, 1850–1920* (Lawrence: University of Kansas Press, 1996), 1–23.

3. For a discussion of the weather during this period see Eugene L. Menefee and Fred A. Dodge, *History of Tulare and Kings Counties, California* (1913), Americana Unlimited, pt. 1, CA, reel 36, no. 138, p. 75.

4. Amasa Allen Guernsey was born in Vermont in 1806. He was a minister in several states before moving to California in 1853. He taught school and preached until his eyesight failed; then he bought the small farm where Slover found him. *An Illustrated History of San Joaquin County, California* (1890), Western Americana, reel 279, no. 2765, p. 382.

5. Henry is mentioned at the end of chapter 2.

6. Judge David Terry is perhaps best remembered for threats he made against U.S. Supreme Court justice Stephen J. Field, which led to his own death in 1886 at the hands of Field's bodyguard. Terry and Field were on the California

Supreme Court together, and Terry called Field "the most corrupt judge ever on the bench." George H. Tinkham, *History of San Joaquin County, California* (1923), Americana Unlimited, pt. 1, CA, reel 30, no. 119, p. 289; also, A. E. Wagstaff, ed., *Life of David S. Terry* (1892), Western Americana, reel 586, no. 6041. In a reform spirit in 1879, California revised its constitution. The reforms were largely ineffective. See Pomeroy, *The Pacific Slope*, chs. 7 and 8.

14. He Emigrates to Oregon

1. On modern maps these are the Scott Mountains; they lie west of Mount Shasta and southwest of Yreka in northern California.
2. The Siskiyou Mountains lie along the border between California and Oregon, south of Ashland. Siskiyou Summit or Pass is 4,310 feet.
3. The *Ashland Daily Tidings* during this period carried a number of references to Slover's performing marriages in Ashland, sometimes at "Slover Hotel." See, for example, 8 June 1885.
4. *Ashland Daily Tidings*, 15 January 1888.
5. Sam's Valley is north of the Rogue River between Medford and Grants Pass.
6. John A. Cardwell was one of the founders of Ashland in 1852. Hubert Howe Bancroft, *History of the Pacific States*, vol. 30, *Oregon II, 1848–1888* (San Francisco: History Company, 1888), 712.
7. Slover was obviously concerned that there might be some other claim on the land, such as timber, mining, or railroad. Land also had to be surveyed before it was available for homesteading. Robbins, *Our Landed Heritage*, 238.
8. A homesteader who built and occupied a dwelling, dug a well, plowed at least 10 acres, and put up some fences could claim 160 acres at the end of five years. The five years did not start until he had filed his intent to homestead with a land office. Robbins, *Our Landed Heritage*, 238.

15. Homestead

1. This subsequently proved to be the case because mineral rights took precedence over ordinary occupancy. Robbins, *Our Landed Heritage*, 151.
2. If Slover's dates are accurate, he was beyond the five to seven years provided for in the Homestead Act, since he says he initially filed in 1890.
3. Fellow Baptist William G. Pennebaker arrived in Tulare County in 1868, settled southwest of Visalia, and raised peaches and prunes. J. M. Guinn, *History of the State of California and Biographical Record of the San Joaquin Valley, California* (1905), Americana Unlimited, pt. 1, CA, reel 1, no. 19, p. 409.
4. Mrs. Slover's death was noted in the *Ashland Tidings*, 1 August 1898.

17. A Long Desire Gratified

1. The railroads commonly gave discounts and passes to members of the clergy.

2. His sister Katherine (b. 1818) married Eli Rainwater in 1836; the doctor referred to was Slover's nephew.

18. He Takes Charge of Garden

1. James Anderson Slover Jr. (1869–1942) and George H. Slover (1871–1950). JAS.

19. He Leaves Ashland for San Francisco

1. Slover is eighty years old at this point but still worrying about gainful employment.

2. Another daughter of Elizabeth Jane by her first husband, Hugh M. Riggs. Lura Edna Riggs was the editor's paternal grandmother.

20. Change of Houses

1. Slover's first connection with Elbert Stephen Hicks's father, Stephen Hicks, is not recorded, but it apparently predates 1885 when the younger man was born. The elder Hicks moved to California in the gold rush in 1852 and subsequently settled on a ranch near Dinuba; the son ran a livery stable in the town. Guinn, *History of the State of California*, 729.

2. San Francisco burned for three days. The earthquake and fire destroyed some 28,000 buildings in the center of the city. Hundreds died and 250,000 people were left homeless.

3. The Hotel del Coronado, built in 1888 on Coronado Island in San Diego Harbor, has been host to many celebrities and the setting for films and television shows over the years. It is a National Historic Landmark.

4. Probably Frank Kimball, who lost much of his fortune after the Santa Fe Railroad decided not to develop National City as a terminus. McGrew, *City of San Diego and San Diego County*, 381.

5. Russel Holman Slover married Lucy A. Dennis in 1884 and farmed east of Woodville. He died in 1897. *Memorial and Biographical History of the Counties of Fresno, Tulare, and Kern, California*, 669.

6. *Ashland Tidings*, 13 and 17 November 1913.

SELECTED BIBLIOGRAPHY

The following listings by no means exhaust the available source material on any of the topics that intersect with James Anderson Slover's life. Rather, they represent specific sources for specific information that verifies, explains, and/or expands upon Slover's narrative.

Unpublished Material

Compere, E. L. Papers. Southern Baptist Historical Library and Archives, Nashville TN.
Dumplin Creek Baptist Church Minutes, 1797–1938. Microfilm. Southern Baptist Historical Library and Archives, Nashville TN.
Jackson, C. W., minister, Southern Baptist Church at The Lakes, Las Vegas NV. Telephone interview, 10 March 1998.
Kimball, Russell F. "Campo, California: A Brief History." *http://www.sdrm.org/ history/campo.html*
Minges, Patrick. "The Keetoowah Society and the Avocation of Religious Nationalism in the Cherokee Nation, 1855–1867." Ph.D. diss., Union Theological Seminary, Columbia University, 1999. *http://www.users.rcn.com/wovoka. dissertation.html.*
Slover, James Anderson. Family record notebook. Manuscript.
Wiggins, Lexie O., Jr. "A Critical History of the Southern Baptist Indian Mission Movement, 1855–1861." Ph.D. diss., University of Alabama, 1980.

Published Material

Abel, Annie Heloise. *The American Indian as Slaveholder and Secessionist.* 1915. Reprint, Lincoln: University of Nebraska Press, 1992.
Abernethy, Thomas Perkins. *From Frontier to Plantation in Tennessee: A Study in Frontier Democracy.* University: University of Alabama Press, 1967.
Anderson, Mabel Washbourne. *The Life of General Stand Watie: The Only Indian Brigadier General of the Confederate Army and the Last to Surrender.* Pryor OK: privately published, 1931.
Baker, Marion A. "Farragut's Demands for the Surrender of New Orleans." In

Battles and Leaders of the Civil War, 2:95–99. New York: Thomas Yoseloff, 1956.

Bancroft, Hubert Howe. *History of the Pacific States.* Vol. 30, *Oregon II, 1848–1888.* San Francisco: History Company, 1888.

Bass, Althea. *Cherokee Messenger.* Norman: University of Oklahoma Press, 1936.

Begaye, Russell. "The Story of the Indian Southern Baptists." *Baptist History and Heritage* 18, no. 3 (1983): 30–39.

Black, Samuel. *History of San Diego County.* Vol. 2. S. J. Clarke, 1913. Tucson: America Unlimited, 1974, pt. 1, CA, reels 25–27, nos. 99–102.

Boatner, Mark Mayo, III. *The Civil War Dictionary.* Rev. ed. New York: David McKay, 1988.

Bolton, S. Charles. *Territorial Ambition: Land and Society in Arkansas, 1800–1840.* Fayetteville: University of Arkansas Press, 1993.

Broemeling, Carol B. "Cherokee Indian Agents, 1830–1874." *Chronicles of Oklahoma* 50 (winter 1972–73): 437–57.

Brown, Parker B. "The Historical Accuracy of the Captivity Narrative of the Doctor John Knight." *Western Pennsylvania Historical Magazine* 70 (January 1987): 53–67.

Buck, Solon Justus. *The Granger Movement: A Study of Agricultural Organization and Its Political, Economic, and Social Manifestations, 1870–1880.* 1913. Reprint, Lincoln: University of Nebraska Press, 1963.

Caldwell, Mary French. *Tennessee: The Dangerous Example; Watauga to 1849.* Nashville: Aurora, 1974.

Carpenter, Charles H. *History of American Schoolbooks.* Philadelphia: University of Pennsylvania Press, 1963.

Carter, Dean G. "Some Historical Notes on Far West Seminary." *Arkansas Historical Quarterly* 29 (winter 1970): 345–60.

Chalmers, David M. *Hooded Americanism: The History of the Ku Klux Klan.* 2nd ed. New York: New Viewpoints, 1981.

Clayton, Powell. *The Aftermath of the Civil War in Arkansas.* 1915. Reprint, New York: Negro University Press, 1969.

Conkling, Roscoe P., and Margaret B. Conkling. *The Butterfield Overland Mail, 1857–1869, Its Organization and Operation over the Southern Route to 1861; Subsequently over the Central Route to 1866; and under Wells, Fargo and Company in 1869.* 3 vols. Glendale CA: Arthur H. Clark, 1947.

Copeland, E. Luther. *The Southern Baptist Convention and the Judgement of History: The Taint of Original Sin.* Lanham MD: University Press of America, 1995.

Cramer, Zadok. *The Navigator.* 8th ed. 1814. Reprint, Ann Arbor: University Microfilms, 1966.

Cunningham, Frank. *General Stand Watie's Confederate Indians.* San Antonio: Naylor Company, 1959.

Dale, Edward E., ed. "Additional Letters of General Stand Watie." *Chronicles of Oklahoma* 1 (1921): 131–49.
Dale, Edward Everett, and Gaston L. Litton, eds. *Cherokee Cavaliers*. Norman: University of Oklahoma Press, 1995.
Davidson, Donald. *The Tennessee*. Vol. 1, *The Old River: Frontier to Secession*. New York: Rinehart, 1946.
Dick, Everett. *The Lure of the Land: A Social History of the Public Lands from the Articles of Confederation to the New Deal*. Lincoln: University of Nebraska Press, 1970.
Donovan, Timothy P., Willard B. Gatewood Jr., and Jeannie M. Whayne, eds. *The Governors of Arkansas: Essays in Political Biography*. 2nd ed. Fayetteville: University of Arkansas Press, 1995.
Eggleston, George Cary. *The History of the Confederate War: Its Causes and Its Conduct, a Narrative and Critical History*. 2 vols. 1910. Reprint, New York: Negro Universities Press, 1970.
Ehle, John. *Trail of Tears: The Rise and Fall of the Cherokee Nation*. New York: Doubleday, 1989.
Eighmy, John Lee. *Churches in Cultural Captivity: A History of the Social Attitudes of Southern Baptists*. Knoxville: University of Tennessee Press, 1972.
Foreman, Carolyn Thomas. "An Early Account of the Cherokees." *Chronicles of Oklahoma* 34 (summer 1956): 141–58.
———. "Edward W. Bushyhead and John Rollin Ridge: Cherokee Editors in California." *Chronicles of Oklahoma* 14 (1936): 295–311.
———. "Lee Compere and the Creek Indians." *Chronicles of Oklahoma* 42 (autumn 1964): 291–99.
Foreman, Grant. *Marcy and the Gold Seekers: The Journal of Captain R. B. Marcy, with an Account of the Gold Rush over the Southern Route*. Norman: University of Oklahoma Press, 1968.
Franks, Kenny A. *Stand Watie and the Agony of the Cherokee Nation*. Memphis: Memphis State University Press, 1979.
Frazer, Robert Walter. *Forts of the West: Military Forts and Presidios, and Posts Commonly Called Forts, West of the Mississippi River to 1898*. Norman: University of Oklahoma Press, 1965.
Gaines, W. Craig. *The Confederate Cherokees: John Drew's Regiment of Mounted Rifles*. Baton Rouge: Louisiana State University Press, 1989.
Gates, Paul W. *Land and Law in California: Essays on Land Policies*. Ames: Iowa State University Press, 1991.
Goen, C. C. *Broken Churches, Broken Nation: Denominational Schisms and the Coming of the American Civil War*. Macon GA: Mercer University Press, 1985.
Gregg, Andy [Andrew K.]. *Drums of Yesterday: The Forts of New Mexico*. Santa Fe: Press of the Territorian, 1968.

Guinn, J. M. *History of the State of California and Biographical Record of the San Joaquin Valley, California*. 1905. Tucson: Americana Unlimited, 1974. Microfilm.

Halliburton, R., Jr. *Red over Black: Black Slavery among the Cherokee Indians*. Westport CT: Greenwood Press, 1977.

Hamilton, Robert. *The Gospel among the Red Men: The History of Southern Baptist Indian Missions*. Nashville: Sunday School Board of the Baptist Convention, 1930.

Hauptman, Laurence M. *Between Two Fires: American Indians in the Civil War*. New York: Free Press, 1995.

Hempstead, Fay. *A Pictorial History of Arkansas: From Earliest Times to the Year 1890*. 1890. Microfilm, Western Americana, reel 243, no. 2502.

Heyrman, Christine Leigh. *Southern Cross: The Beginnings of the Bible Belt*. Chapel Hill: University of North Carolina Press, 1997.

Hicks, Hannah. "The Diary of Hannah Hicks." Introduction by Mary Elizabeth Good. *American Scene* 13, no. 3 (1972): 3–24.

History of Southern Oregon. Portland: A. G. Walling, 1884.

Holmes, Kenneth L., ed. *Covered Wagon Women: Diaries and Letters from the Western Trails, 1840–1890*. Vol. 9. Spokane WA: Arthur H. Clark, 1990.

Homer, Rodney Prestage. *The Pioneer Communities of Porterville, Vandalia, and Plano*. Porterville CA: Andiron, 1982.

An Illustrated History of San Joaquin County, California. 1890. Microfilm, Western Americana.

Johnson, Charles A. *The Frontier Camp Meeting: Religion's Harvest Time*. Dallas: Southern Methodist University Press, 1955.

Johnson, Leland R. "Army Engineers on the Cumberland and Tennessee, 1824–1854." *Tennessee Historical Quarterly* 31 (summer 1972): 149–69.

Kronk, Gary W. *Meteor Showers: A Descriptive Catalog*. Hillside NJ: Enslow, 1988.

Leeds, Georgia Rae. *The United Keetoowah Band of Cherokee Indians in Oklahoma*. New York: Peter Lang, 1996

Lewis, Charles Lee. *David Glasgow Farragut: Our First Admiral*. Annapolis: U.S. Naval Institute, 1943.

Lewit, Robert T. "Indian Missions and Antislavery Sentiment: A Conflict of Evangelical and Humanitarian Ideals." *Mississippi Valley Historical Review* 50 (1963–64): 39–55.

Ludeke, John. "The No Fence Law of 1874: Victory for San Joaquin Valley Farmers." *California History* 59, no. 2 (1980): 98–115.

Lynch, William O. "Westward Flow of Southern Colonists." *Journal of Southern History* 9 (1943): 303–27.

Mahan, A. T. *Admiral Farragut*. New York: University Society, 1905.

Mahnken, Norbert R. "Old Baptist Mission and Evan Jones." *Chronicles of Oklahoma* 67 (summer 1989): 174–93.
Mattoon, C. H. *Baptist Annals of Oregon, 1844 to 1900*. McMinnville OR: Telephone Register, 1905.
May, Katja. *African Americans and Native Americans in the Creek and Cherokee Nations, 1830s to 1920s*. New York: Garland, 1996.
McCaffrey, James M. *Army of Manifest Destiny: The American Soldier in the Mexican War, 1846–1848*. New York: New York University Press, 1992.
McGrew, Clarence A. *History of the City of San Diego and San Diego County: the Birthplace of California*. 1922. Tucson: Americana Unlimited, 1974. Microfilm.
McLoughlin, William G. *After the Trail of Tears: The Cherokees' Struggle for Sovereignty, 1839–1880*. Chapel Hill: University of North Carolina Press, 1993.
———. *Champions of the Cherokees: Evan and John B. Jones*. Princeton: Princeton University Press, 1990.
———. *The Cherokees and Christianity, 1794–1870: Essays on Acculturation and Culture*. Ed. Walter H. Conser Jr. Athens: University of Georgia Press, 1994.
McPherson, James M. *Battle Cry of Freedom: The Civil War Era*. New York: Oxford University Press, 1988.
Memorial and Biographical History of the Counties of Fresno, Tulare, and Kern, California. 1892. Tucson: Americana Unlimited, 1974. Microfilm.
Menefee, Eugene L., and Fred A. Dodge. *History of Tulare and Kings Counties, California*. 1913. Tucson: Americana Unlimited, 1974. Microfilm.
Moneyhon, Carl H. *The Impact of the Civil War and Reconstruction on Arkansas: Persistence in the Midst of Ruin*. Baton Rouge: Louisiana State University Press, 1994.
Monks, William. *A History of Southern Missouri and Northern Arkansas: Being an Account of the Early Settlement, the Civil War, the Ku-Klux, and Times of Peace*. 1907. New Haven: Research Publications, 1975, Western Americana Series. Microfilm.
Moody, Ralph. *The Old Trails West*. New York: Thomas Y. Crowell, 1963.
Mooney, James. *Historical Sketch of the Cherokee*. Chicago: Aldine, 1975.
Moore, Jessie Randolph. "The Five Great Indian Nations." *Chronicles of Oklahoma* 23 (autumn 1951): 324–36.
Moulton, Gary E. *John Ross: Cherokee Chief*. Athens: University of Georgia Press, 1978.
Narratives of a Late Expedition Against the Indians; with An Account of the Barbarous Execution of Col. Crawford; and the Wonderful Escape of Dr. Knight and John Slover from Captivity, in 1782. As told to Henry Hugh

Brackenridge, 1783. New York: Readex Microprint, 1985, Early American Imprints.

Nordin, Dennis S. "A Revisionist Interpretation of the Patrons of Husbandry, 1867-1900." *Historian* 32, no. 4 (1970): 630-43.

"Oklahoma and the Cherokee Strip." Pamphlet. Chicago: Poole Bros., 1893.

Ormsby, Waterman Lilly. *The Butterfield Overland Mail by Waterman L. Ormsby, Only Through Passenger on the First Westbound Stage*. 1858. Ed. Lyle H. Wright and Josephine M. Bynum. San Marino CA: Huntington Library, 1962.

Perdue, Theda. *Slavery and the Evolution of Cherokee Society, 1540-1866*. Knoxville: University of Tennessee Press, 1979.

Phillips, Joyce B., and Paul Gary Phillips, eds. *The Brainerd Journal: A Mission to the Cherokees, 1817-1823*. Lincoln: University of Nebraska Press, 1998.

Pike, Nicholas. *A New and Complete System of Arithmetic: Composed for the Use of the Citizens of the United Statess*. 1788. New York: Readex Microprint, 1985, Early American Imprints.

Pisani, Donald J. *Water, Land, and Law in the West: The Limits of Public Policy, 1850-1920*. Lawrence: University of Kansas Press, 1996.

Pomeroy, Earl. *The Pacific Slope*. 1965. Reprint, Seattle: University of Washington Press, 1973.

Pourade, Richard F., ed. *Historic Ranchos of San Diego*. San Diego: Union-Tribune, 1969.

"Private Slover's Escape." *Susquehanna Monthly Magazine*, February 1986, 22-27.

Proceedings of the Southern Baptist Convention. Richmond VA: H. K. Ellyson 1857, 1859; Richmond: MacFarlan & Ferguson, 1861; Macon GA: Burke, Boykin, 1863; Richmond: Dispatch Steam Presses, 1866; Baltimore: John F. Weishampel Jr., 1867, 1868.

Robbins, Roy M. *Our Landed Heritage: The Public Domain, 1776-1936*. Lincoln: University of Nebraska Press, 1942.

Rogers, Tommy W. "Migration from Tennessee during the Nineteenth Century I: Origin and Destination of Tennessee Migrants, 1850-1860." *Tennessee Historical Quarterly* 27 (summer 1968): 118-22.

Rogin, Leo. *The Introduction of Farm Machinery in Its Relation to the Productivity of Labor in the Agriculture of the United States during the Nineteenth Century*. 1931. Reprint, New York: Johnson Reprint, 1966.

Ross, John. *The Papers of Chief John Ross*. Ed. Gary E. Moulton. 2 vols. Norman: University of Oklahoma Press, 1985.

Routh, E. C. "Henry Frieland Buckner." *Chronicles of Oklahoma* 14 (1936): 456-66.

Salley, Harold E. *History of California Post Offices, 1849-1990*. Lake Grove OR: The Depot, 1991.

Schulman, Steven A. "The Lumber Industry of the Upper Cumberland River Valley." *Tennessee Historical Quarterly* 32 (fall 1973): 255–64.
Sifakis, Stewart. *Who Was Who in the Civil War*. New York: Facts on File, 1988.
Sloane, Eric. *Sketches of America Past*. New York: Promontory Press, 1986.
Staples, Thomas S. *Reconstruction in Arkansas, 1862–1874*. New York: Columbia University, 1923.
Sweet, William Warren. *Revivalism in America: Its Origin, Growth, and Decline*. Gloucester MA: Peter Smith, 1965.
Taylor, Orville W. "Baptists and Slavery in Arkansas: Relationship and Attitudes." *Arkansas Historical Quarterly* 38 (autumn 1979): 199–226.
Tinkham, George H. *History of San Joaquin County, California*. 1923. Tucson: Americana Unlimited, 1974. Microfilm.
Toomery, Glen A. "The Romance of a Sesquicentennial. The Dumplin' Creek Baptist Church, Jefferson City TN, organized, 1797." (1947). Pamphlet.
Wagstaff, A. E., ed. *Life of David S. Terry*. 1892. New Haven: Research Publications, 1975, Western Americana Series. Microfilm.
Walther, Eric H. *The Fire-Eaters*. Baton Rouge: Louisiana State University Press, 1992.
The War of the Rebellion: A Compilation of the Official Records of the Union and Confederate Armies. Series 1, vols. 3 and 13. 1881. Reprint, Pasadena: Historical Times, 1985.
Weisberger, Bernard A. *They Gathered at the River: The Story of the Great Revivalists and Their Impact on Religion in America*. Boston: Little, Brown, 1958.
Willey, Rev. Worcester. *A Tale of Home and War*. Ed. E. P. Howland. 1888. New Haven: Research Publications, 1975, Western Americana Series. Microfilm.
Wills, Gregory A. *Democratic Religion: Freedom, Authority, and Church Discipline in the Baptist South, 1785–1900*. New York: Oxford University Press, 1997.
Wright, Gordon. *Insiders and Outliers: A Procession of Frenchmen*. Stanford: Stanford Alumni Association, 1980.

INDEX

Adair, Lafayette, 70
Adair, William Penn, 65
Adams, John, 92–93
alien immersion, xxxi, 42, 135
allegiance to United States, oath of, 87
American Baptist Home Mission Society, 122
American Baptist Missionary Society, 60
Anderson, James (Tennessee judge), 1
Antioch Baptist Church, 40, 135, 154
Apache Indians, 116
Arkansas, xxvii, 30; martial law in, 106. *See also under specific locales*
Arkansas Baptist, xxv, 39
Arkansas River, 30, 75

Bakersfield (CA), 120, 121, 165
baptism, 39, 58, 164; of slaveholders, 49–50; of Slover, 25. *See also* alien immersion
Baptists, xx, xxii, xxiv, 28, 41, 130; Antioch Baptist Church, 40, 135; building campaign, 143, 144, 147; Coosa Association (GA), 57; First Baptist Church of Dandridge (TN), 29; First Baptist Church of Fort Smith (AR), 61; Middle Oregon Association, xxxi; Mount Zion Association (AR), 41; New Hope Church (Sam's Valley OR), 137, 147, 159; Rogue River Valley Association, xxxi; San Joaquin Valley Association, 165; split into North and South, xxii. *See also* Southern Baptist Convention; Southern Baptists
Baptist Sentinel, 143
battalion muster (Mexican War), 24, 181 n.9 n.10
Bayou Manard, 56, 58
Beals Ranch, 119
Beidler, William H., 141
Benton County (AR), 40, 41
Bettis, John (brother-in-law), 15
Bettis, Sallie S. (sister), 15, 156
Bettis, William B., 32
Billingsley, John D., 110
Billingsley, William B., 110
Black Oak Grove Seminary, 26
Blue Springs Landing, 29, 32
Blue Water Wells (AZ), 117
Blunt, Gen. James G., 65, 66, 68, 69, 72–75
Boatright, C. H., 39
Boiling Pot (Tennessee River), 33
Bolton, T. K., 159–60
Boudinot, Elias, xxiii, xxiv, xxvi, 174 n.18 n.19
Boudinot, John, xxiii
Bowman, Jacob, 144
Bowen Seed Company, E. J., 161
Brabsone Ferry, 31
Breaker, Manly J., 151

Brown, Asaph, 41
Bryant, Allen, 32–38
Buckner, H. F., xxii, 47, 103, 104
Burchfield, Harrison, 154
Bushwhackers, xxvii, 91, 93, 176 n.40
Bushyhead, Jacob, 51, 184 n.1
Butterfield Overland Mail, xxviii

Cairo (IL), 34
Caldwell, Alexander, 24
California: drought in, 125–26; and gold rush, 129; land policies in, xxix, xxx; and no fence law (California Trespass Act of 1850), 125, 194 n.1
Calihan, Mary (step-grandmother), 19
camp meetings, xx, 18
Caney Creek Shoals, 22
Cardwell, John, 135
Cate, Henry, 26
Caughran, James, 110
Caughran, James Wesley, 110
Caving Banks, Battle of, xxiv
Chastain, Jehue, 42
Cherokee Nation, xxii, xxvii, 55, 58, 63, 70, 100, 101, 185 n.10; Pin Indians (see Keetoowah Society); Ross Party, xxii–xxiii, xxiv, 174 n.18 n.19; Treaty of New Echota, xxii, 62–63, 186 n.19; Treaty Party, xxiii, xxiv; Treaty Regiment (Drew's), 63, 66, 67; Treaty with the Confederacy, 62; Stand Watie Regiment, 61, 70
Cherokee Southern Baptist Association, 55
Cherokee steamer, 102
childhood activities, 9
Clergy Certificate, 151, 166
Cloud, (Col.) William F., 83
Colorado River (AZ), 118
Colusa County (CA), 126
Colvig, William M., 141

Compere, E. L., xxvi, 64, 68, 80–81, 103–104, 183 n.2
Compere, Lee, 95–96
Compere, Thomas H., xxv, 68, 80–81, 97
Confederate Army, xxiv; Texas Volunteers for Confederate service, 61
Confederate Cherokees, xxiv
Confederate States of America, Cherokee Treaty with, 62–63; formation of, 59; and military, 90; and money, 91; surrender to North of, 97
Cook, Alpha, 34
Cook, Samuel, 27–38
Cooper, Gen. Douglas, 69–70
Coosa Baptist Association (GA), 57
corn. See under farming practices
Cosmopolitan Hotel, Roseburg (OR), 134
Cox, Samuel, 30, 48
Crawford, Col. William, 2, 178 n.5
Creek Nation, 62, 103
Crosie Baptist Church, 165
Crowell, W. S., 141
Cumberland Presbyterian. See under religious denominations

Dale, Taylor, 110
Dandridge (TN), 7, 27; execution in, 17, 27, 153
Dardenelle (AR), 80–83, 87–91, 92, 94
Davis, Jefferson, 59
Davis, L. W., 104
Davis, Martin, 110
Dead Man's Creek (TX), 112–13
Deer Creek Hot Springs (CA), 166
Delaware soldiers, 58
Dennis, Maggie, 170
desert crossing, 117–18
Dillard, George, 110

Dinuba (CA), 165
Dittoes Landing (Tennessee River), 33
Domestic and Indian Mission Board, 100, 102
Dotson, W. L., 153
Douden, Joseph, 141
Drew, John, 63
Drew's Regiment. *See* Cherokee Nation: Treaty Regiment
drought, 125–26
Dumplin Creek, 15, 18, 29, 30, 180 n.4
Dumplin Creek Baptist Church, 18, 19, 39, 154, 180 n.3.1
Dungan, J., 141

Eagle Springs (TX), 114
East Tennessee. *See* Tennessee
Eddy, Adolphus F., 134, 142, 145
Eddy, Mary Ellen Slover (Mrs. Adolphus F. Eddy), 158, 163, 168, 172
Edgar, John, 12
Elkhorn Tavern, Battle of, 41
Ellis, Philander W., 144
Ellis, William, 16
Erbe, William, 132
Erysipelas, 120, 123
Evansville (AR), 42–44
execution: in Dandridge TN, 17, 27–28

falling stars (Leonid meteor shower), 11, 179 n.18
Fane, John, 7
farming practices, xxiii, 5–6, 9–10, 14, 132–33, 179 n.13; and corn, 14, 17, 70; in California, 122, 125
Farmington (CA), 151
Farragut, Adm. David, 66
Fayetteville (AR), 51
fire-eaters, 59
Fitzgerald, Aaron, 98

Fitzgerald, Archibald, 98, 103
Fitzgerald, D. W., 151
Fitzgerald, Frank, 141
Fitzgerald, Nathaniel D., 135–37
Fitzgerald, Walter D., 135
flat boats, construction of, 20
Foreman, David McNair, 57, 183 n.7
Foreman, Johnson, 48
Foreman, Thomas, 48
Forrest, Nathan Bedford, xxviii
Fort Alexander, 115, 192 n.10
Fort Concho, 113
Fort Cummings, 115
Fort Gibson, 66
Fort Griffin (TX), 112
Fort Smith (AR), 61, 64, 68, 73, 80
Fort Stockton, 114
Fort Yumah, 118
Franklin County (AR), 79
Freeman, W. M., 106
freemasonry. *See* Masons
French, John, 110
French, Sherril, 110
French Broad River (TN) xxi, 9, 11, 15, 153
Fresno County (CA), 164
Frog Bayou (AR), 77
Frye, Burrell J.(son-in-law), 164
Frye, Elizabeth Jane Slover Riggs Hicks (daughter), 164
Frye, Jennie, 150
Frying Pan (Tennessee River), 33
Fuquay, F. B., 110

Gila Trail, xxviii
Gilpatrick, Rufus (Kirkpatrick), 65
Glass, H. S., 146, 160
Golden Circle, Knights of the, xxvi
Gordon, John, 110, 113
Grace, John, 96
Grand Prairie (AR), 80
Granger Movement, xxx, 124

Grants Pass (OR), xxxi; Courier office at, 134
Green, James K., 48
Greenbacks, 88, 94, 111
Greens Bluff (Tennessee River), 34
Greer, J. W., 70, 78–79
Greer, James (son of J. W. Greer), 68, 78–79
Grimsley, Virgil, 165
grist mill-house, 3–5, 179 n.9
Guernsey, Amasa Allen, 126–28
Gunter's Landing (AL; Tennessee River), 21, 33

Hackney, Pauline (niece), 156
Halleck, Henry W., 72
Harbin, Jackson, 139
harvesting wheat, 13–16
Hays, Shaddon, 15
Henderson, William, 8
Henrahan, W. S., 123
Henry, Albert, 151
Henry, James R., 16, 151
Herman, Binger, 141
Hicks, Elbert S., 169, 171
Hicks, Stephen, 164
Hill, John, 9
Hindman, Thomas C., 72, 74
Hodges, Samuel, 141
Holder, T. W., 110, 150
Holland, Lizzie, 86
Holman, Russel, 49
homestead, Sam's Valley (OR), 135–36; challenged, 138, 141–42
Hunter, William, 110

immigration routes. *See under specific rivers; states*
Indian Territory, xix, xxii; Bayou Manard, 56; Chickasaw Indians, 62; Chocktaw Indians, 62; Creek Nation, 103; Park Hill, xxii, 48, 58, 69; Tahlequah, xxii, 56, 58, 59, 64, 65, 66–67. *See also* Cherokee Nation
infare (wedding) dinner, 12, 19
Ingram, Elizabeth, 30, 36, 37
Ingram, Harriet (Mrs. James A. Slover), xxi, 30; death of, 81
Ingram, Isaac (brother-in-law), 36
Ingram, James C. (brother-in-law), 36, 73
irrigation, xxix

Jenks, Carrie, 170–71
Jenks, George E., 170–71
Jones, Augustus D., 109
Jones, Carl T., 147
Jones, Evan, xxiv, xxv, xxvi, xxvii, 49–50
Jones, George E. 137
Jones, John B., xxiv, xxv, xxvi, xxvii, 49–50
Jones, Lou (sister-in-law), 150
Jones' Mill (Brush Creek AR), 42
Jones, Sarah (mother-in-law), 110, 150

Keetoowah Society (Pins), xxiv, xxvi, xxvii, 62, 71
Kern County (CA), 120, 165
Kimball brothers: Frank A., 170; Warren C., Levi W., George L., and Charles H., 119
Kirk, Hampton, 36
Knight, Moses, 31
Knights of the Golden Circle, xxvi
Knox, G. W., 36
Ku Klux Klan, xxviii

LaMarsna, Minnie (granddaughter), 151, 164–65, 170
Land, Joseph, 47
land law, xxix
Landmark Baptists, 177 n.55

INDEX 209

Langford, Elizabeth Slover (sister), 152, 156
Langford, James, 156–57
Langston, Jesse, 29
Langston, Samuel, 19
Langston, William, 19
Lanning, Tobias, 24
Lattie Schoolhouse (AR), 42
Lee's Creek (AR), 73
Linvill, Jeff, 141
Little River County (AR), 105, 106, 107, 108
Little Rock (AR), 36, 75, 80
Lodi (CA), 126
Long Savanna Creek, 29
Lookout Mountain (Tennessee River), 33

Madison County (AR), 36
Manion, A. D., 134
Martin, Hugh, 9
Masons, xxx, 101, 109
McClerry, Payne, 30
McCulloch, Benjamin, 63
McGrary, Thomas, 106
McIntosh, James McQueen, 63
Mesilla (NM), 115
Methodist circuit riders, 50
Methodist Episcopal Church, 18, 41. *See also* religious denominations
Mexican War. *See* battalion muster
Milquatay Valley (CA), 119
missionaries: finances of, 47, 49, 53, 54; and Indians, 53, 57–58; Methodist Episcopalian, 56; Moravian, xxii; northern Baptist, 60; Southern Baptist, 47, 55, 58, 70. *See also* religious denominations
Missionary Chapel Baptist Church, 41
Montgomery County (AR), 96
Moore, Nathan, 110
Morrison, Riley, 142–43

Mossy Creek, 26, 27, 153
Mount Comfort (AR), 40, 182 n.1
Muddy Creek (TN), xxii, 3, 5
Mulvany, William, 15
Murphy, Isaac, 105, 107
Murry, Abraham, 150
Muscle Shoals (Tennessee River), 33–34, 180 n.3.5
Muskingum River, 2
Mutual Aid Society, (Los Angeles), 124

New Echota, Treaty of, xxii
New Hope Church (Sam's Valley OR), 135, 137, 159; and building campaign, 143, 147
New Mexico: Los Cruces, 115; Mesilla, 115; Separ, 144
no fence law. *See under* California

Oak Hills, Battle of, 62
Odel, Maggie, 26, 28–29
Orr, John, 92–93
Owens, Jesse H., 62
Ozark (AR), 79

Pacific Baptist, 143
Pankey, Thomas, 139, 140, 142, 143, 148
Parker, Iva, 144
Park Hill. *See under* Indian Territory
Patriot Party. *See* Cherokee Nation: Ross Party
Pauley, James, 110
Pea Ridge, Battle of, xxiv
Pennebaker, G. F., 130, 132, 133
Pennebaker, William G., 150, 170
Perry, Martin, 141
Pike, (Gen.) Albert, 62
Pike's Arithmetic, 16
Pin Indians. *See* Keetoowah Society
plantation system, xxii
plow, 6

Prairie Ridge, Battle of, 72–73
Price, Sterling, 63
Proceedings of the Southern Baptist Convention, xvi

Rainwater, B., 154
Rainwater, Elie, 13
Rainwater, Katherine Slover (sister), 13, 154
Randals, James, 23
Randals, Richard, 23
reconstruction, xxviii
Redding (CA), 133
Red Rivers (AR), 95
Reed, Isaac, 55
religious denominations: Campbellite, 135; Congregational, xxii; Cumberland Presbyterian, 40; Methodist Episcopal South, 18, 41, 56, 123, 156; Moravian, xxii; Mormon (Church of Jesus Christ of Latter-Day Saints), 50; Presbyterian, 58; Roman Catholic, 101; United Brethren, 135. *See also* Baptists; Southern Baptists
Richards, Daniel, 160
Richmond (AR), 106, 107
Ridge, John, xxiii, xxvi
Ridge, Major, xxiii, xxvi, 174 n.18
Ridge Party. *See* Cherokee Nation: Treaty Party
Riggs, Hugh M., 130
Rio Grande River, 114–15
Robbam's Prairie (AR), 41
Rocky Comfort (AR), 104, 105
Rodgers, Josephine M., 97, 98, 104
Rogue River (OR), 137
Rogue River Valley (OR), xxxi
Ross, John, xxii, xxiii, 48, 58, 65, 67
Ross, Lewis, 67
Ross, Mrs. John, 58, 175 n.23

Ross (Patriot) Party, xxii–xxiii, xxiv, 174 n.18 n.19
Row, Lafayette, 141
Royal Manufacturing Co., 168
Russel, Jesse, 56
Russellville (AR), 86, 100
Ryan, Patrick, 134

Sacramento, 158
Saint Charles Hotel (New Orleans), 102, 104
Sam's Valley homestead, 135–36
San Diego, 119; Hotel del Coronado, 170
San Diego County (CA), 119; National City, 170
Sandy Ridge, 8, 153
San Francisco, xxxii, 163, 172; earthquake, xvi, xxxii; Sunset District, 163, 168
San Joaquin County (CA), 126
Sanger (CA), 164
Savage Hotel (Jacksonville OR), 134
sawmill (steam), 34
schools: described, 7–8, 10, 12, 16, 38, 40, 45–46; Lattie Schoolhouse (AR), 41, 43
Scruggs, Murrow, 32
Selph, William, 140
Sevier County (AR), 16, 27, 97, 104, 107
Shaddon, Hays, 15
Shelby, Joseph O., 98
Shovel Creek Springs (CA), 132
Siskiyou County (CA), 132
Sizemore, Lindsey, 140
skedaddling, xix, xxvii, 71, 95
Skillet Handle (Tennessee River), 33
slaveholders, baptism of, 49
slavery, xxii, xxiv, xxv, 49, 50, 59, 184 n.10, 185 n.5; Emancipation Proclamation, 59

Slover, Abraham (grandfather), xxii, 1, 3, 5, 13, 154; death of, 13
Slover, Mrs. Abraham (grandmother), death of, 5
Slover, Alonzo, 160
Slover, Elizabeth Jane (sister), 49
Slover, Elizabeth Jane (daughter), 123, 164
Slover, Fannie (sister), 144
Slover, Fannie Isadora (daughter), 122, 134
Slover, George H.(son), 134
Slover, George W. (brother), 11, 23, 29, 97
Slover, Harriet Ingram (first wife), 33, 68; death of, 81
Slover, I. B. (nephew), 154
Slover, Isaac (of Effingham County IL), 13
Slover, Isaac Wiley (brother), 5, 13
Slover, James Anderson, xix, 134,
Slover, James Anderson, Jr., 144
Slover, James Anderson, Jr.(son), xix, 118, 144
Slover, John (brother), 23, 97
Slover, John (father), 5, 29
Slover, John Ephraim (son), 117
Slover, John Thomas (nephew), 155
Slover, Josephine Rodgers (second wife), death of, 145
Slover, Katherine (sister), 13
Slover, Mary Ellen (sister), 7
Slover, Oliver Henry (son of nephew), 157
Slover, Rachel Malvinie, death of, 61
Slover, Rachel Taffe (mother), 3, 179 n.8; death of, xxi, 30
Slover, Raleigh, 13
Slover, Russel Holman (son), 114, 172
Slover, Thomas H. (brother), 13
Slover, Thomas Jacob Conway (son), 44

Southern Baptist Board of Missions, 66, 99
Southern Baptist Convention, xxii, 58, 100; Domestic and Indian Mission Board, 100, 102
Southern Baptists, xxxi
Stand Watie Regiment, 61, 70
Steele, Frederick, 83
Stockton (CA), 152
Story Cotton Company, 161
subscription schools, xx, 38, 45
Sultana (CA), 165
Sumner, M. T., 102
Swan, Mrs. Robert, 155
Spence, Dill, 170
Suck (Tennessee River), 32–33

Tahlequah. See Indian Territory
Taylor, John, 110
Taylor, Thomas, 53
tenant farmers, xxi
Tennessee, xix, xx
Thomas, John, 110
Thornton, Elisa, 5
Tipton, C. C., 19, 26
Tipton, Martha, 26
tornado, 42
Trail of Tears, xxii. See also Cherokee Nation
Treaty Party, xxiv
Tucson (AZ), 116
Tulare City (CA), 126
Tulare County (CA), xxix, 123, 125
Tule River (CA), 120, 121

Underdown's Ferry, 29
Underwood, Thomas, 19
Union Army, xix, 63, 65–69, 72, 78; and Union supporters, 69
U.S. Land Office: in Roseburg OR, 136, 137, 141–42, 147, 148, 161; in Fayetteville AR, 51

U.S. Land Office Commissioner, 141, 147

Van Buren (AR), 71, 73
Vandorn, Earl, 72
Vanhorn, T. B., 42
Visalia (CA), 120, 121

Walnut Bayou, 106
Walnut Grove (AR), 39
Washington County (AR), 36–37
water transportation. *See under specific rivers*
Waters, Thomas, 84
Watie, Stand, xxvi, 65, 70, 185 n.13. *See also* Stand Watie Regiment
wedding, 11
Wilkinson, Jake, 153

Wilkinson, Thomas, 54–55
Wilson, Archibald, 101
Wilson Creek, Battle of (Battle of Oak Hills), 62
Wilson, Rebecca, 101
Wilson, Thornton,
Wood, Adaline, 23
Wood, Melsena M., 11
Woodbridge (CA), 126
Woodville (CA), 122, 170
Worcester, Samuel Austin, 50
Wright, Amos, 110
Wright, John, 110
Wright, Thomas, 110
Wyat, Thomas, 142
Wyatte Park (MO) Baptist Church, 156

Yell County (AR), 83